God's Spies

"Elisabeth Braw has impressively traced the lives of those sisters and brothers in the GDR who acted not just in the name of God, but also in the interest of the East German secret police, the Stasi. Braw brings things to light that astonish even the most hard-boiled of experts."

HELMUT MÜLLER-ENBERGS, Professor of History, University of Southern Denmark

"Elisabeth Braw has rendered a service – she thinks like a scholar, writes like a journalist, and tells a story like a novelist. Her work is relevant for anyone interested in Germany, communism, freedom and 'unfreedom', and how we complex and contradictory human beings tick."

JEFFREY GEDMIN, editor-in-chief, *The American Interest* and former president, *Radio Free Europe/Radio Liberty*

"It is a testament to the power of religion that the East German Communist government expended so much energy monitoring thousands upon thousands of East German (mostly Lutheran) Christians, infiltrating the highest levels of the church. *God's Spies* reads like a spy thriller because that is what it is – except that it is not fiction. It is as sad as it is inspiring. This account is as instructive to post-Communist society as a warning against state-sponsored compromise to religious liberty as it is to faith communities to protect their independence and their commitment to the gospel."

FR. ROBERT A. SIRICO, President, *The Acton Institute for the Study of Religion and Liberty (USA)*

GOD'S SPIES

The Stasi's Cold War Espionage
Campaign Inside the Church

Elisabeth Braw

LION

For Lars Braw (1920-2019)

Published by
Lion Hudson Limited
Wilkinson House, Jordan Hill Business Park
Banbury Road, Oxford OX2 8DR, England
www.lionhudson.com

Paperback ISBN 978 0 7459 8008 9

Hardback ISBN 978 07459 8010 2

e-ISBN 9780 7459 8009 6

First edition 2019

Acknowledgments
Much of the quoted material in this book comes from interviews conducted by the author. Those interviewed include: Michael Beintker, the late Ingmar Brohed, Erwin Damson, Christoph Demke, Rainer Eppelmann, Gerhard Gabriel, Christoph Kähler, Jürgen Kapiske, Wolf Krötke, Helmut Matthies, Konrad Raiser, Richard Schröder, Curt Stauss, Friedemann Stengel, and Joachim Wiegand.

Many other quotes come from Stasi files which are held by *Der Bundesbeauftragte für die Stasi-Unterlagen* (the Federal Commissioner for the State Security Service of the former German Democratic Republic). The BStU website (https://www.bstu.de/en/) states: "The Federal Commissioner (BStU) supports research and media (press, radio and film). It also supports civic education agencies in their political and historical reappraisal of the activities of the State Security Service, the power mechanisms in both the former GDR and Soviet zone of occupation and National Socialist past." Following a request by the author, the Agency released the files of several Stasi informants for the purpose of this book.

CONTENTS

Preface		7
Introduction		12
Prologue		20
Dramatis personae		22
1	Establishing the Stasi	28
2	Pastor agents	47
3	A growing threat: seminaries	66
4	The fine art of recruiting	71
5	East Germans, escaping	92
6	Agents' vanities	114
7	Cunning infiltration	128
8	An exotic foreign assignment	141
9	Target: international organizations	152
10	Intercepting Bible smugglers	156
11	A literary underground railroad	177
12	Agents and their rewards	187
13	Spying and doing one's part for East Germany	196
14	An indispensable Bible smuggler (and Stasi spy)	213
15	Losing motivation	239
16	A crucial foreign mission	250
17	Churches spreading opposition	266
18	East Germany on its knees	278
19	The Berlin Wall collapses	285
20	Destroying the evidence	290
21	Anxiously waiting pastor spies	296
22	God's spies: what was the point?	310
Index		321

PREFACE

G rowing up in a small village in southern Sweden, the son of a shoemaker and a schoolteacher, young Lars Braw couldn't wait to get out and see the world. Before he was old enough to do so, he paid a daily visit to the grocery store, where he read the front pages of the newspapers. It was an exciting world there, far away from his little village, and as soon as he was old enough to leave home, he embarked on a career in journalism that would eventually take him to five continents – to interviews with Mother Teresa, Robert Mugabe, and Haile Selassie, the then-emperor of Ethiopia. Around the time of those interviews, I was born, Lars's first grandchild.

When I was growing up, Grandpa tried to make sure that I, too, developed an interest in world events. During my frequent visits with my grandparents, Grandpa always instructed me to join him in listening to the BBC World Service on his short-wave radio. I hated it because my English wasn't good enough.

Together with my grandmother Kaj, herself a journalist, Grandpa also set out to show me the world. First, they took me to Hamburg and Lübeck, which left me indifferent. Then came West and East Berlin, reached by means of an East German train. I was captivated – by the Eastern side. What a strange country, I thought, what with all its guards, its grey cityscapes, its all-permeating smell of coal. So geographically close to my home country of Sweden, separated only by the tiny Baltic Sea, yet completely different.

On 9 November 1989, the Berlin Wall fell. Less than a year later, the two Germanies were reunited. Meanwhile, brave citizens in other countries behind the Iron Curtain were staging their own velvet revolutions. The Soviet empire, imposed after World War II, crumbled. East Germany, the German Democratic Republic, had lasted for only forty years – a tiny interlude in world history.

But thirty years since the fall of the Berlin Wall, East Germany continues to fascinate. There have been academic books, novels, non-fiction books, songs, and conferences. Steven Spielberg has made a movie. East Germany's pedestrian crossing signal, the *Ampelmännchen*, is now Berlin's *de facto* mascot.

The Stasi – the Ministry for State Security – has been the subject of much of that attention; to many, the all-pervasive, all-knowing security police has even become synonymous with East Germany. Surprisingly, however, one of its cleverest and most successful activities has received little attention outside Germany. That activity is the Stasi's church espionage. Karl Marx vs Jesus Christ, you might call it.

For the final eleven years of the Stasi's existence, Joachim Wiegand led its church department. To this day, he remains a committed socialist. Without knowing him, most people would probably think him despicable for having spent a career in the Stasi, most of it spying on Christians.

Without Joachim Wiegand, this book would not have been written. He and I represent completely different world views and, of course, backgrounds. He has never before given an interview for a book. But I was lucky: Wiegand decided to speak to me. Not once, not twice, but several times. We spent countless hours discussing what many would call his and his staff's dirty deeds. Most of the Stasi's top officers are dead, and virtually all of the survivors have, like Wiegand, refused to speak publicly or write down their memories. Despite being so fascinated by the Stasi, the world knows very little of how the Stasi's officers operated, how they thought, what motivated them. Historians can, of course, read Stasi files and speak to victims – but without the Stasi officers' insights, a crucial piece is missing. I owe Joachim Wiegand immense gratitude for having decided to speak with me.

Jürgen Kapiske likewise had no obligation to speak to me. Like all other Stasi pastor spies, he has been uniformly vilified. Like a small number of other former pastor spies, he has also been defrocked. Speaking with me, as he did over many hours, in no way helps him. On the contrary, it opens wounds that have barely begun to heal. Whatever one thinks of Kapiske's actions, I owe him gratitude.

Wolf Krötke was one of the Stasi Church Department's victims. Despite wanting nothing to do with the Stasi, he has had to live with its shadows all his life – simply as a result of being a committed Christian and pastor. Krötke could be forgiven for not wanting to waste any more time on the Stasi. Instead, he has helped me with this book every step of the way, telling me about his own experiences, connecting me with others, explaining how East German churches operated. Pastor Curt Stauss, too, generously shared his time and contacts with me and helped me understand who was who in the world of East German Christianity.

Nevin Brown, Jeffrey Smith, Sebastian Braw-Smith, and Heidi Schubert-Erkrath read the manuscript at various stages of completion. Professor Helmut Müller-Enbergs at the University of Southern Denmark, a leading authority on the Stasi, read the final draft – as did Revd Dr Rune Imberg, a Swedish theologian. Rüdiger Sielaff at the office of the Federal Commissioner for the Stasi Records was an early interlocutor and went to great lengths to assist me in understanding Stasi records. Friederich Rother, also at the Federal Commissioner for the Records of the State Security Service of the former German Democratic Republic, responded to my seemingly never-ending file requests with great patience. Carola Schreckenberger and Andreas Kaufmann put me up on my many visits to Berlin without ever asking when my research might finally be complete. Daniela Braw-Smith regularly reminded me to write. My agent, Roger Freet, has been my indefatigable and cheerful companion since I first conceived of the idea for this book. Lyn Roberts and Jon Oliver at Lion Hudson and Mary Davis have expertly guided it through production. My heartfelt thanks to all of you. Any errors, of course, remain mine alone.

In addition to Wiegand, Kapiske, Krötke and Stauss, many other participants in East Germany church espionage drama spoke with me in personal interviews. In addition, I have used Stasi files that document actions and conversations. As conversations contained in the files are by definition somewhat truncated, I have gently reconstructed them. I have attempted to contact every organization and living person mentioned in the book. In some cases, organizations and individuals declined interviews; in several cases I was unsuccessful trying to locate them.

Espionage is by definition a murky business. Unless the information is contradicted by other written sources, I have used documentation from Stasi files. Likewise, I have used information provided to me by the participants, whether perpetrators or victims. In all cases, I have looked for verified information contradicting their accounts. I have found none. Did other East German parents in Vienna ostracize Jürgen Kapiske and his family? They may not have done so on purpose – but that's what the Kapiskes felt. Did Gerd Bambowsky's wild ride with Helmut Matthies happen exactly as Matthies remembers it? It may be been different, but there are no other witnesses. I have recounted what the participants have told me.

German church terminology is a matter worthy of many lengthy conversations. In translating German terms, I have chosen to use the most common English term even though ecclesiastical dictionaries in some cases propose a more precise translation. Before handing out files to researchers, the BStU (Federal Commissioner for the records of the State Security Service of the former German Democratic Republic) experts redact the names of people mentioned in the files, though the names of some high-profile individuals remain. When reading Stasi files, I have been able to establish the identities of some of the redacted names; with each redacted name, I have noted whether I have managed to establish the person's identity. In some cases, in order to simplify the reading, I have used a generic name; I have noted those cases as well.

Like "normal" espionage, the Stasi's church espionage was exhilarating, mysterious, and repulsive alike. But without Lars Braw (who passed away in February 2019), I would never have thought of writing a book about it – because I would not have experienced that most peculiar country named the German Democratic Republic. Thank you, Grandpa.

INTRODUCTION

Though it existed for just less than four decades (1950–90), the Stasi gained global celebrity status of a kind that few, if any, secret police agencies ever achieve. Indeed, if asked about East Germany today, the one thing most people will be familiar with is the Stasi. While the Stasi – an abbreviation for *Ministerium für Staatssicherheit* (the Ministry for State Security) – was distinctly less brutal than many of its sister Warsaw Pact secret police agencies, it perfected the art of snooping. By the time the Berlin Wall came down, the Stasi's formidable file collection featured 1.7 million informants. Half of the German Democratic Republic's population had been spied on. Sometimes the espionage consisted of little more than a record of the person's name, but often it recorded his or her life in detail. So pervasive was the Stasi's reach that citizens knew not to voice their opinions without first making sure that no strangers were listening.

The German Democratic Republic (GDR) – known abroad mostly as East Germany – prided itself on its official atheism, and its regime showed considerable skill at turning its citizens away from religion.[1] Schools educated young East Germans to become faithful communists. But because churches constituted East Germany's only semi-free space, Lutheran parishes' activities – which included decidedly secular ones such as peace groups, environmental groups, and human rights groups – attracted large numbers of East Germans who were unhappy with the regime. Indeed, many slightly rebellious young men and women who may not otherwise

---

1   Martin Luther, the great reformer of Christianity, was born in Eisleben in the heartland of what was later to become the German Democratic Republic.

have considered an ecclesiastical career became pastors because it was the only way of living somewhat outside the grips of the government.

The Stasi had a way of dealing with such non-conformist behaviour: an ecclesiastical department, known as Department XX/4, recruited agents who spied on their fellow Christians and congregations, on global church institutions, and on one another. These agents were known as *Inoffizielle Mitarbeiter* or IMs. Department XX/4 was not just a way of keeping religiously inspired East Germans under control – far from it. Christianity was communism's greatest foe because it represented a competing worldview. As such, it was also a direct threat to the regime in East Berlin because it possessed a global network ranging from grassroots to international institutions. East German Christians, the Stasi knew, were plugged into a world that allowed them to get new ideas and to maintain contacts around the world.

Not surprisingly, communist agencies successfully infiltrated international Christian networks. Indeed, over the years, the World Council of Churches (WCC) – the United Nations of Christianity – became riddled with assorted pastor agents from the Warsaw Pact. Not least through their pastor delegates, communist intelligence agencies managed to turn the body into a reliable critic of the United States.

Like any good espionage novel, the story of the Stasi's pastor spies involves betrayal, career advancement, even sex. Department XX/4 infiltrated Christianity at every level, from parishes and dioceses to international institutions such as the WCC. While some of the agents were rank-and-file pastors, others were bishops or ordained professors of theology. At least one of the Stasi's pastor spies infiltrated the Christian networks smuggling Bibles and other literature to the Soviet Union. The recipients were promptly arrested. Western Europeans, in turn, realized only too late that some of their East German brethren had dubious motivations. In Sweden, countless pastors and theologians were shocked to discover, in 2012, that an East

German pastor of Austrian origin who had turned up in their country in the sixties was, in fact, a Stasi agent.

To its credit, East Germany did not resort to the Soviet Union's brutal punishment of Christians, though some 110,000 East Germans served prison sentences for political offences. It operated no penal camps populated by political prisoners. Nonetheless, Department XX/4 – which I will refer to as the Church Bureau – discreetly made its presence felt, and that was enough to ensure a surprisingly compliant church.

Yet, successful though it was, the Church Bureau failed in its ultimate task of helping to ensure the survival of the German Democratic Republic. Despite their massive snooping efforts, both the spies and their handlers failed to detect any larger patterns in the events they so painstakingly reported and analysed. So it was that, in 1989, the extent of East Germans' discontent, bubbling under the surface in church-hosted events, caught the government by surprise.

"It was all futile," Department XX/4's ultimate commander, Colonel Joachim Wiegand, sighed years later. That is not true. Without his department's efforts, the church would have been a much stronger power in East Germany. Yet the efforts were not enough to keep the communist experiment that was the German Democratic Republic alive.

In November 1980, East Germany's Lutheran Christians gathered in Halle for their national synod. Only a year earlier, the Soviet Union had invaded Afghanistan. In Poland, a trade union soon to be known as Solidarity was organizing unprecedented worker strikes. East Germany's leaders were alarmed. The Lutheran church must not get any ideas. In Halle, the Stasi sprang into action aided by its pastor spies. The pastor spies' first task, as communicated by Stasi headquarters: make sure the delegates "stay away from provocations, which are reflected in attacks on the government and the [ruling socialist] party." A rapid reaction group consisting of two undercover Stasi officers in church positions and seven pastor spies set about their duties, bugging conversations, monitoring foreign guests, and transmitting the information to

Stasi headquarters in Berlin around the clock. The Stasi's team, for its part, sent instructions back as to which church officials should be made to acquiesce to government edicts. I will take readers back to efficient pastor spy operations such as this one, where men of the cloth functioned more as intelligence agents than disciples of Jesus Christ.

The Stasi's church espionage took place within East Germany's four decades of existence. As East Germany collapsed, the pastors, bishops, and theology professors who had served as its agents could sleep well in the knowledge that they would never be found out: the Stasi had promised them anonymity. How mistaken they were. In the mad rush after the collapse of the Berlin Wall, the Stasi's officers didn't have time to destroy or even tear up all their files, many of which are still intact.

Ordinary agents spy on the enemy; when their assignment is over they retreat to a safe home base. They are, after all, contracted by a government. Their daring work is rewarded with salaries and medals. The pastor spies received medals, too, but the medals are useless now. And unlike ordinary spies, when their cover was blown the pastor spies had no other country to which to return.

Aleksander Radler, the East German pastor with an Austrian passport, was a constant presence in my childhood, as my father – a theologian at the University of Lund and a well-known conservative pastor in the Church of Sweden – was one of the many Swedes that Radler befriended. Aleksander sometimes brought visiting pastors from East Germany to see my father and other Swedish clergymen. The Swedes had no idea that if their East German guests expressed any criticism of their regime, Aleksander could decide to report it to the Stasi. On average, at any given time, some 180,000 people were informants for the Stasi.[2]

Though only a small percentage of them worked for Department XX/4,

---

2   Jens Gieseke, *Mielke-Konzern: Die Geschichte der Stasi 1945-1990*, Stuttgart/ Munich: Deutsche Verlags-Anstalt, 2001, p. 113. About 30,000 were, at any given time, logistical helpers who, for example, let the Stasi use their homes as safe houses for meetings with agents.

many of those who did were extremely diligent. Even West Germans, on whom the Stasi could exert no pressure, spied for Department XX/4: in 1987, it had eleven West German agents. And despite their own atheism, Department XX/4's officers ran their agents extraordinarily well. The department formed a mighty cell within the enormous Ministry for State Security.

Rather ironically, churches' peace prayers led to the protests that brought East Germany down. Like "traditional" spies, the Stasi's pastors spied for a variety of reasons. Some saw Stasi collaboration as a way of fast-tracking their careers; some spied for material gain; others out of revenge; and some did it out of genuine loyalty towards the regime.

Eagerly passing along every snippet of information they came across, they generated enormous quantities of updates of varying calibre. One might be tempted to describe the fall of the Berlin Wall as the victory of faith over snooping – except that, as soon as the Wall fell, the Lutheran Church lost its crucial function as an opposition forum. A mass exodus of members followed. Today, only 4 per cent of residents in the former East Germany regularly attend church services, compared to 15 per cent in the early 1950s, the aggressive early days of Marxist rule.[3]

German media has covered the cases of individual pastor spies, and Swedish news outlets have reported on Aleksander Radler, whose full Stasi career became clear when German officials finished reconstructing the first 1,000 or so pages of his Stasi file several years ago. Germany's Lutheran Church has published reports on its informants, academics have researched some of them. But so far, no non-fiction book has tried to capture the full story of the Stasi's pastor spies.

The diligent staff at Germany's Stasi archive, the Federal Commissioner

---

3   Elisabeth Braw, "In Martin Luther's Church the Pastor Asks: Where Have All the Protestants Gone?", *Newsweek Magazine*, 24 February 2014, http://www.newsweek.com/2014/02/28/martin-luthers-church-pastor-asks-where-have-all-protestants-gone-245572.html.

for the Records of the State Security Service of the former German Democratic Republic, has painstakingly pieced together hundreds of thousands of the shreds hastily thrown into boxes by retreating Stasi officers as East Germany disintegrated – and there are more sacks left. The result of their hard work is a remarkable collection of letters, messages, Stasi notes and evaluations, conversation protocols, and expense receipts that reveal an enormous pastor spy operation, one based on cunning exploitation of human weaknesses.[4] Indeed, Stasi officers often took on a type of "Father Confessor" role with their pastor agents. And because the Stasi was extremely organized in its record-keeping, its recovered files form a treasure-trove for researchers.

The pastor spies' many victims play a crucial role in this Cold War drama. Wolf Krötke, who as a young man was sent to jail after a fellow theology student informed the Stasi about a critical poem Krötke had written, emerged from prison unbowed. As a result of his continued opposition to communism, Krötke had to teach at small church-run seminaries rather than the government's prestigious universities. Department XX/4, meanwhile, kept an eye on him. Rainer Eppelmann, a proletarian bricklayer-turned-firebrand pastor in Berlin, was the subject of a rare Stasi assassination plot. Department XX/4 left indelible marks on his life, too, causing him to alternate between anger and resignation over what fellow Christians did to him. In a symbolic act, East Germany's first and last democratically elected prime minister, Lothar de Maizière, appointed Eppelmann minister of defence, with the task of dismantling East Germany's formidable armed forces. Curt Stauss, a pacifist who as a teenager had turned down a Stasi recruitment pitch, once returned home to find someone had leafed through his diary; another time, bugs had been installed in his house. Pastor Stauss

---

4   The Stasi files are held by the Bundesbeauftragter für die Stasi-Unterlagen (the Federal Commissioner for the Stasi Records of the State Security Service of the former GDR). Most people simply call it the Gauck Agency, a reference to its first director, Joachim Gauck.

now works as his diocese's counsellor for Stasi victims, spending his days listening to people traumatized by Department XX/4's officers and agents.

So what was the point of it all? "Those who would give up essential Liberty, to purchase a little temporary Safety, deserve neither Liberty nor Safety," Benjamin Franklin famously said.[5] Throughout the twentieth century, authoritarian governments purchased temporary safety by giving up their citizens' liberty. The German Democratic Republic was not the most cruel purchaser of safety, but thanks to the Stasi it was certainly among the most conscientious. And its Church Department in the homeland of Protestant Christianity – and the birthplace of Martin Luther – was a hugely clever attempt at defeating the enemy from within.

But, in the end, the Stasi's ambitious effort came to naught. The church not only survived the infiltration but triggered East Germany's 1989 peaceful revolution. More than a quarter-century later, Joachim Wiegand is still trying to make sense of his country's collapse. His agents and officers had monitored every church decision (and often influenced decisions too), kept track of contacts between East German Christians and their brethren abroad, and shadowed dissident pastors at home.

Why, then, did church-based protests manage to topple the German Democratic Republic? Few believed in the system whose safety they were purchasing. Intelligence agencies prefer agents who spy for material rewards over those who are ideologically motivated because the former are more flexible and less cumbersome. Department XX/4, too, featured many agents who spied for material reasons. But the cigars, stipends, and restaurant meals provided by Colonel Wiegand and his team were hardly a match for the goods any citizen in Western Europe could easily purchase for himself. And when Department XX/4 could not meet its agents' lofty

---

5   "Ben Franklin's Famous 'Liberty, Safety' Quote", NPR, 2 March 2015, https://www.npr.org/2015/03/02/390245038/ben-franklins-famous-liberty-safety-quote-lost-its-context-in-21st-century?t=1557553586775 (accessed 19 May 2019).

expectations, many agents simply delivered lesser-quality work. And across the Stasi, agents who had been pressured into service often attempted to cleanse their conscience by delivering inferior or useless information.

Indeed, while many pastor spies may have been prolific, by and large they were not particularly effective. If the selfishly motivated agents understood the larger meaning of what they were reporting, most of them didn't bother explaining it to their masters.

Put in American terms, Department XX/4 was good at the work the CIA's Clandestine Service does – that is, assembling the intelligence. Disastrously, it lacked skills at the CIA's Directorate of Intelligence, where the enormous quantities of information of vastly different quality collected by spies are turned into a meaningful picture.

In infiltrating East Germany's church-based opposition and partially emasculating its churches, Department XX/4 arguably helped prolong the German Democratic Republic's life. By how long? Two years? Ten years? We can only speculate. And in propping up East Germany's unpopular regime, Department XX/4 helped shape the Cold War. This, then, is the story of God's Spies.

PROLOGUE

L ate in the evening of 4 January 1978, Department XX/4 Lieutenants Winkler and Bartnitzek drove to an autobahn rest area about an hour south-west of Berlin. They staked out their positions. At 10.55 p.m., they saw a minivan with Dutch licence plates approach. One of their pastor agents, IM Gerd, had alerted the officers to the van's scheduled stop. He had arranged with Dutch Bible smuggler contacts that he would meet the minivan at the rest stop at 11 p.m.

Department XX/4 wanted information about the van. If it could identify the members of the Dutch team using it, Stasi Division XIII – in charge of surveillance – would begin watching the vehicle and its passengers.

As the van arrived ("Ford-Transit, colour grey, licence number [redacted] Netherlands (NL)", Bartnitzek noted), one of its passengers got out and walked onto the pedestrian bridge with its clear view of the parking area.[6] He seemed to be surveying the rest stop to make sure they were not being watched. Then another passenger also stepped out of the car and scanned the parked vehicles. Winkler and Bartnitzek kept watching the Bible smugglers.

But where was the pastor agent? Had the smugglers been stood up? Seconds passed, then minutes. And then – at 11.05 p.m., IM Gerd's van entered the rest area. Unbeknownst to each other, the two teams waiting

---

6   All Stasi files are kept by the Gauck Agency which is "responsible for the safekeeping, utilization and accessibility of all records of the Ministry for State Security" (https://www.bstu.de/en/).The names of persons other than the IM and certain high-profile individuals, as well as identifying information about them such as home addresses and licence plate numbers, are redacted by the Gauck Agency before the IM's file is released.

for him breathed sighs of relief. IM Gerd – known to the Bible smugglers under his real name, Gerd Bambowsky – chatted briefly with the smugglers. Then he got back into his van, they got into theirs and both vehicles drove off together. Winkler and Bartnitzek followed as the two vans headed back onto the dark autobahn.

Department XX/4 swiftly learned more about the Dutch group. The efficient officers at Division XIII had registered the names of the van's passengers as it passed the border crossing from West to East Germany, and Winkler and Bartnitzek had confirmed that it was the same van. Winkler and Bartnitzek now knew that one of the passengers was a Dutchman, two were Americans, and one was a Finn. They knew their names and passport numbers. "Verification and search measures of the individuals and the vehicles were initiated," Bartnitzek noted in his report. The Bible smugglers would be monitored.

DRAMATIS PERSONAE

STASI AGENTS – INOFFIZIELLE MITARBEITER (IM)

Gerd Bambowsky (code name IM Gerd) East German Lutheran pastor

Ingo Braecklein Lutheran Bishop of the Diocese of Thuringa

Paul Dissemond Roman Catholic priest, permanent secretary of the East German Catholic Bishops' conference

Heinrich Fink East German Lutheran pastor and theology professor, appointed rector of Humboldt University

Hans-Georg Fritzsche (code name IM Fritz), professor of theology at Humboldt University

Horst Gienke Lutheran bishop of Greifswald

Detlef Hammer (code name IM Detlev, later IM Günther), joined as a student at Halle University; later a church lawyer at Church Province of Saxony; promoted to *Offizier im besonderen Einsatz*, Officer on Special Duty (OibE Günther); later President of the Church Province of Saxony

Knuth Hansen boyfriend of Bambowsky/IM Gerd, Mennonite pastor

Jürgen Kapiske (code name IM Walter), East German Lutheran pastor, later editor of church newspapers

Siegfried Krügel (code name IM Lorac), East German Lutheran pastor and theologian

Günter Krusche Professor at the Sprachenkonvikt, member of the World Council of Churches' central committee, assistant bishop in Berlin [not to be confused with Bishop Werner Krusche]

Ernst-Eugen Meckel High-ranking East German Lutheran pastor

Hanfried Müller (code name IM Hans Meier), professor of systematic theology, Humboldt University, married to Rosemarie Müller-Streisand

Siegfried Plath (code name IM Hiller), East German Lutheran pastor

Aleksander Radler (code name IM Thomas), recruited as a young theology student at Humboldt University, later an Austrian–East German Lutheran pastor and lecturer at University of Lund, Sweden; later a visiting professor at Jena, and professor at both Naumburg seminary and Halle

Wolfgang Schnur Lawyer who later co-founded a new political party, *Demokratischer Aufbruch*

Manfred Stolpe (code name IM Sekretär), top lay official at Diocese of Berlin-Brandenbug, later Social Democratic Party politician

Frank Stolt (code name IM Hermann Schneider), recruited as a teenager, later East German Lutheran pastor

Knud Wollenberger (code name IM Donald) opposition activist, married to Vera Wollenberger (now Lengsfeld)

STASI OFFICERS

Major Hans Baethge Head of the Church Bureau's Catholic Church unit

Lieutenant Gerdhardt Bartnitzek Handler for IM Gerd

Lieutenant Erich Blümel Handler for IM Lorac

Lieutenant Blüth Handler for IM Lorac

Lieutenant Böhm Handler for IM Thomas

Willi Butter First Director of Stasi Department XX/4 (1955–57)

Lieutenant Jürgen Diepold Stasi officer

Lieutenant Heindke Handler for IM Lorac

Major Heinig Handler for IM Thomas

Lieutenant Heinritz Handler for IM Gerd

Lieutenant Ditmar Heydel Handler for IM Walter, also for IM Thomas

Lieutenant Hübner Stasi officer

Lieutenant General Paul Kienberg Head of Stasi Division XX

Lieutenant Kunth Handler for M Lorac

Sergeant Falk Kuntze Stasi officer in Halle

Erich Mielke Minister of State Security (1957–89)

Lieutenant General Rudi Mittig Deputy Minister of State Security

Master Sergeant Ollik (code name Hiller), Stasi officer

Major Otto Handler for IM Gerd

Major Radziey Handler for IM Thomas

Major Klaus Rossberg Director of Stasi Department XX/4's Lutheran Church department

Hans-Dieter Schlippes HVA officer who had previously served undercover in West Germany, handler for Jürgen Kapiske

Major Schramm Handler for IM Gerd

Wolfgang Schwanitz Appointed head of newly formed Agency for National Security (AfNS) (1989–90) following dissolution of the MfS

Lieutenant-Colonel Franz Sgraja Case handler for IM Lorac and IM Gerd, later Director of Stasi Department XX/4 (1957–79)

Marion Staude (code names Anke Brandt and Elke Köhler), undercover Stasi officer

Colonel Joachim Wiegand Director of Stasi Department XX/4 (1979–89)

Lieutenant Winkler Case handler for IM Gerd

General Markus Wolf Director of East Germany's foreign intelligence agency, the HVA

Ernst Wollweber Minister of State Security (1953–57)

Wilhelm Zaisser Minister of State Security (1950–53)

POLITICIANS

Yuri Andropov Leader of KGB, later Soviet leader (1982–84)

Willy Brandt Foreign Minister, West Germany (1966–69)

Leonid Brezhnev Soviet leader (1964–82)

Jimmy Carter US president (1977–81)

Hans-Dietrich Genscher West German foreign minister (1974–92)

Mikhail Gorbachev Soviet leader (1985–91)

Gustav Heinemann President of West Germany (1969–74)

Erich Honecker Communist leader of East Germany (1971–89)

Gyula Horn Hungary's foreign minister (1989–90)

Kurt Georg Kiesinger Early member of Nazi Party (1933–45), served in Adolf Hitler's foreign ministry, leader of Christian Democratic Union, West Germany (1967–71), Chancellor of Germany (1966-1969)

Egon Krenz East German Politburo member

Heinrich Lübke President of West Germany (1959–69)

Angela Merkel Daughter of left-leaning pastor; later Chancellor of Germany

Alois Mock Austria's foreign minister (1987–95)

Hans Modrow Reformist Socialist Unity Party official, last communist leader of East Germany (1989–90)

Ronald Reagan US president (1981–89)

Günther Schabowski East German government spokesman who announced the opening of the Berlin Wall

DISSENTERS AND OTHERS

Milan Balabán Czechoslovak Lutheran pastor and Old Testament scholar, signatory of Charter 77

Michael Beintker Theologian, Halle University; later Dean of the University of Halle theology department, befriended by Aleksander Radler

Oskar Brüsewitz East German pastor

Erwin Damson Member of staff at *Licht im Osten*, in charge of book-smuggling

Christoph Demke East German Lutheran pastor, later Bishop of the Church Province of Sxony

Katrin Eigenfeld East German Christian youth worker, jailed for anti-government subversion (sister of Gerhard Gabriel)

Rainer Eppelmann East German Lutheran pastor, later co-founder of the political party *Demokratischer Aufbruch* and then Minister of Defence

Heino Falcke East German assistant bishop who, along with others, demanded access to his Stasi file

Henning Frunder Physics student in Jena

Gerhard Gabriel East German student at Halle University, later Lutheran pastor, friend of Detlef Hammer (brother of Katrin Eigenfeld)

Joachim Gauck East German Lutheran pastor, first director of the BstU (also known as the Gauck Agency), later President of Germany (2012–17)

Václav Havel Czech playwright, signatory of Charter 77, later President

Christoph Kähler East German Lutheran pastor, friend of Aleksander Radler's, later co-founder of the political party *Demokratischer Aufbruch*

Wolf Krötke Theology student, later Lutheran pastor and professor at the Sprachenkonvikt

Bishop Werner Krusche Bishop of Saxony, chairman of the Lutheran Church in East Germany, vocal opponent of the government

Dietmar Linke Pastor in Neuenhagen, well-known regime critic

Milan Machovec Czechoslovak Marxist philosopher, fired by the government for his non-conformist views, signatory of Charter 77

Kurt Masur East German conductor, spoke to the Leipzig mass demonstration on 9 October 1989

Helmut Matthies West German Lutheran pastor, editor of the conservative Christian weekly *IDEA Spektrum*

Heinrich Rathke Lutheran pastor, later Bishop in Schwerin

Andrey Sakharov Soviet nuclear scientist turned dissident, Nobel Peace Prize Laureate

Richard Schröder Pastor in Blankenfelde, professor at the

Sprachenkonvikt, later a Social Democratic politician

Ernst Sommerlath Professor of theology in Leipzig; uncle of Silvia Sommerlath (later Queen Silvia of Sweden)

Friedemann Stengel Pastor, professor of church history, leader of research project into Stasi pastor/theologian collaborators

Curt Stauss Lutheran pastor and diocesan counsellor for Stasi victims

Gleb Yakunin Soviet Russian-Orthodox priest

CHAPTER 1

ESTABLISHING THE STASI

April 1952. The German Democratic Republic – East Germany – was barely three years old. A strapping young man took the train to East Berlin from his home town of Oschatz near East Germany's border with Czechoslovakia. In East Berlin, he changed to a local train that took him to Potsdam, a city outside East Berlin famous for its Versailles-inspired Sanssouci Palace – an enduring legacy of the eighteenth-century king Frederick the Great. In 1952, Sanssouci still resembled Versailles, what with its cheery rococo buildings and stunning terraced gardens. But arriving in Potsdam, the young man didn't head towards the Sanssouci or any of the city's nineteen other palaces.

The young man's name was Joachim Wiegand. Even though this was his first visit to the city of Frederick the Great, he most certainly didn't have relaxation in mind. Instead, he steered his steps towards the Eiche-Golm neighbourhood and its recently erected concrete buildings.

He walked past several military-like installations guarded by young men like him. With East Germany still lacking armed forces, the paramilitary

Barracked People's Police had taken over the barracks used by Nazi Germany's Wehrmacht only a few years previously.[7] But even though the barracks were populated by young men of about the same age as Wiegand, they were not his destination. Neither were the Soviet garrisons. The Red Army was officially East Germany's liberator and protector, but its soldiers were not allowed to fraternize with locals. If Wiegand had decided to stop at the gates of the Red Army's 34th Artillery Division for a chat with his contemporaries, he would have been asked to leave, or worse.

More nefarious Soviet activities were also taking place in Potsdam. In Leistikow Street, a half-hour walk from the Sanssouci, Soviet military counter-intelligence had appropriated a vicarage and turned it into a jail where it held suspected spies. The vicarage's windows and doors had been sealed by bricks, with only tiny openings for the inmates to see the daylight. Though passers-by such as Wiegand couldn't see them, around three dozen Germans and Russians were being held in the vicarage, which now housed thirty-six cells. They were often beaten too. Until the mid-fifties, between 900 and 1,200 mostly innocent people would be imprisoned here.

Soon, Wiegand had arrived at 28 Karl-Liebknecht-Strasse, another former Wehrmacht site.[8] The lanky twenty-year-old with the thick dark hair and winning smile presented himself to an official. Raised by a single mother, Wiegand had been forced to start working at a young age, assisting at a farm near his home town. Until now, the idea of further education had never entered his mind. But soon he found himself in a classroom with other young men. Like Wiegand, they came from working-class backgrounds; most of them had been working as farmhands, bricklayers, welders. They

---

7   The Barracked People's Police or *Kasernierte Volkspolizei*. The Wehrmacht was the armed forces of Nazi Germany.
8   Karl Liebknecht Street. The German Democratic Republic renamed many streets, giving them names of famous socialists. Karl Liebknecht, who co-founded the early socialist movement, the Spartacist League, was killed by members of a right-wing paramilitary group in 1919.

were to have incalculable consequences for their country. Wiegand's new school was the *Schule des Ministeriums für Staatssicherheit*, the School of the Ministry for State Security. The teachers and students already called it the MfS School, using the Ministry for State Security's acronym. Joachim Wiegand had dedicated his life to the MfS – or the Stasi, as most people call it.

The MfS School was the Stasi's new cadre factory. Founded in 1951, the MfS School would "give cadres political knowledge and convey to them the teachings of Marx, Engels, Lenin and Stalin as instructions for action" – as Wilhelm Zaisser, East Germany's first Minister of State Security, had declared upon opening the school, adding that it would also teach the students operative work. Like their communist comrades around the world, the German Democratic Republic's communists loved the word "cadre", an originally Latin word that Western dictionaries define as "a small group of people specially trained for a particular purpose or profession". If you were deemed to be a promising communist, you were selected as a cadre.

Zaisser was himself a veteran communist warrior. Born in 1893, he had initially worked as a teacher in Germany before becoming a communist official, serving the Communist Party in China, Czechoslovakia, and the Soviet Union. The Moscow communists had then dispatched him to the Spanish Civil War, where right-wing Nationalists were fighting left-wing Republicans. Despite his lack of previous combat experience, Zaisser excelled at the task and rose to lead the Republicans' international brigades.[9] His nom de plume: General Gomez.

Now Zaisser had returned to Germany – or rather, he had returned to the part of the country that was now East Germany. Under his direction, the MfS had devised a curriculum that mixed intelligence classes, weapons

---

9   "Wilhelm Zaisser 1893–1958", *Haus der Geschichte der Bundesrepublik Deutschland*, https://www.hdg.de/lemo/biografie/wilhelm-zaisser.html (accessed 3 May 2019).

training, and sports with *Polit-Unterricht*, a course in communist ideology. "After each thought of Lenin that we discuss, the teacher asks us: 'What did Stalin say about it?' We quickly react and soon add Stalin's opinion without being prompted," one student described such lessons.[10] The students were , of course, also taught about the operations of Western intelligence agencies.

When returning home during school breaks, Wiegand told his friends in Oschatz and Meissen (the nearest larger town) nothing of the education he was receiving. In fact, doing so would have been a terrible idea. Officially, the MfS School didn't exist, and MfS officials habitually referred to it as the Eiche School. Even at this early stage, the school had the logistics in place: there was an auditorium and seminar rooms, and barracks where the students slept. Students were assigned to guard duty on a rotating schedule. In order to maintain secrecy, the MfS School didn't let its students leave the compound during the school week. Every now and then the students played football, and an occasional collective excursion to the cinema was an eagerly awaited luxury. Perhaps predictably, one of Wiegand's classmates got lonely. To his delight, a young woman began appearing at the school gates. They struck up a conversation, then a friendship. The young man fell in love. But his superiors were watching: the young woman was a French intelligence agent, the other students were told. The Stasi cadet was given a sentence. Was the woman really a French spy? Whatever the truth, Wiegand and his classmates got the message: they must be on their guard.

Until 1989, some 10,000 students – 99 per cent of them men – would attend the MfS School and go on to stable careers with the omnipresent Stasi. But, as they sat at their rudimentary school desks in the Karl-Liebknecht-Strasse, the MfS School students in Wiegand's class had little idea that they would make history as perhaps the most meticulously organized secret police agency in history.

I have come to visit Wiegand at his home in Berlin and ask him about

---

10   Gieseke, *Mielke-Konzern*, p. 55.

those early days. Like his fellow students, Wiegand hadn't applied for the school or even considered a Stasi career. "Earlier that year, an official had approached me and asked if I wanted to work for peace and against fascism", he explains. "Of course I wanted to protect peace. Who's against peace? And I had experienced this horrible war."

It had been a horrible war indeed. Petrified residents of Oschatz had waited in horror when Allied bomber planes flattened nearby Dresden in February 1945 as commanded by Britain's "Bomber Harris", Air Marshal Arthur Travers Harris. Red Army forces advancing from the East had subjected civilians to more callousness still, brutally raping tens of thousands of teenage girls and women, even elderly ones. When Red Army soldiers entered Meissen after capturing it on 6 June 1945, they looted it.

Wiegand's friendly recruiter had explained that he was from the Ministry for State Security and offered Wiegand a job. The official had also promised him a salary of 700 East German marks per month, a huge increase from the 30 marks he had been making as farmhand. After confidentially consulting with his grandfather, the young man had signed on the dotted line: not only did he want to work for peace; the salary would also help him support his widowed, impoverished mother.

Settling into his new student life, Wiegand had eagerly soaked up the knowledge conveyed by his teachers, though in many subjects the teachers were barely more knowledgeable than their students. The MfS School, in fact, lacked precedent in Germany. Wiegand's teachers were communists of the old kind, mostly working-class men who had amassed considerable experience as communist underground activists fighting the Nazis. The school's director, Colonel Erwin Koletzki, had served several jail sentences in Nazi Germany for communist activity and possessed a wealth of subversive experience which, at least partly, made up for is lack of formal education. Some of the other teachers had attended communist schools in the Soviet Union, but most were learning about secret police work along with their students.

As the years went by, the MfS School would grow more ambitious. In 1965, it became a university, rebranded rather grandly as the Potsdam College of Jurisprudence.[11] The university promptly began offering not just degrees but doctoral programmes as well. By the time it was closed on 31 March 1990, the Potsdam College of Jurisprudence had bestowed doctoral degrees on 476 Stasi officers, who had written a total of 174 doctoral dissertations covering every conceivable aspect of intelligence work, always with an appropriately communist angle. Some dissertations had enormous value for the Stasi, but in other cases the slender volumes amount to nothing more than academic masquerading by officers unworthy of a PhD. As the fateful year of 1989 drew to a close, the Potsdam College of Jurisprudence's last doctoral candidate received his PhD. Like all other degrees awarded by the university, it was soon declared void.

But such academic affairs were far off in the future when Joachim Wiegand and his fellow young proletarians became only the second class to attend the MfS School's nine-month officer course. The course was intended to be longer, but there was a shortage of teachers. Yet even this perfunctory education made Wiegand and his fellow rookie officers better trained than most of men with whom they were soon to serve at Stasi offices around the country. Like the teachers at the MfS School, most of East Germany's communists had little formal education, having only learned a trade and perhaps attended a communist party school in the Soviet Union. Older Stasi officers had acquired skills in the dark arts of secret police work from their Soviet comrades-cum-occupiers.

Upon graduation from the MfS School, Wiegand was assigned by the MfS to its regional headquarters in Rostock, a northern port city. Sleepy and remote though Rostock may appear, the MfS station there conducted crucial work. Located only 100 kilometres as the crow flies from the West German city of Lübeck, and 181 kilometres from the larger port city of Hamburg, Rostock

---

11   *Juristische Hochschule Potsdam.*

was the perfect vantage point from which to observe Western European intelligence agencies' activities in West Germany.

I have come to visit Wiegand again. In communist times, the Lichtenberg train station near his home was a major rail hub. With only the U-Bahn and a few local trains stopping here now, it has a ghostlike atmosphere. Each platform features a square announcer booth which, in East German days, also featured an official calling out arriving and departing trains and exhorting passengers to board without delay. Today, most of the announcer booths are empty; there isn't much to announce anyway.

Exiting this transportation relic, I head out onto a street that features a couple of takeaway places. In hipper parts of Berlin, there's bustling commerce with trendy eateries, vegan supermarkets, law offices – but not here. After a short walk, I reach the Frankfurter Allee, an imposing thoroughfare lined by high-rises from East German times.

Soon I've reached Wiegand's street, a bombastic architectural project featuring row upon row of identical multistorey buildings accompanied by modest car parks. In East Germany, owning a car was a luxury. Other cities have tried to smarten up such streets and neighbourhoods by renovating the buildings and painting them in cheerful mixes of bright colours but here, in Wiegand's street, the buildings look just like they did in the 1970s, though these days the car parks feature more BMWs than East German Trabants.

Just off the Frankfurter Allee, the Ministry for State Security, operating from twenty-nine buildings, ran its efficient machine. The mission of its 91,000-member staff: keeping the country's regime in place. That meant, for example, preventing East Germany's 16 million citizens from openly criticising the regime. Today, the main building houses a Stasi museum, with long-standing Minister of State Security Erich Mielke's office a particularly popular attraction.

Having entered Wiegand's flat, I'm further immersed in the German Democratic Republic. In fact, it's as though the GDR never ceased to exist.

The home, where Wiegand lives with his wife, Gerda, has two bedrooms and a living room that is furnished in the quintessential East German style. A dark wall-to-wall cabinet-television and bookcase dominates the room, with demure carpeting and a small dining table taking supporting roles. The colonel, fit and friendly, greets me at the door, as does Gerda, who immediately offers me coffee and cake. Wiegand takes my coat. As was customary in East Germany, I take off my shoes and put on a pair of slippers reserved for guests, and Wiegand and I sit down in the living room.

Apart from government ministers and leaders of the ruling Socialist Unity Party of Germany – the SED – East German officials didn't live in opulence, and this apartment has been the Wiegands' home for over four decades. Gerda brings us the coffee and cake, then excuses herself and diplomatically leaves to run errands. She's a supportive spouse, a woman who's seen the Stasi at its apex, with her husband playing a crucial part. She's seen it dissolved, ridiculed. Mere association with it is still enough to ruin a person's career and reputation. Many of Wiegand's agents, men and women he shared meals with, whose families he knew, still deny ever having met him. Is he disappointed? No, he insists in his native Saxony dialect coloured by many years in Berlin. "Everyone who was in touch with us, whether a pastor or a driver, has to protect themselves." That's a lot of people, and that's why I'm here.

Wiegand, an atheist proletarian with no experience in church matters, would go on to run arguably the most successful church espionage operation in modern history. Though he presided over a rather modest team of only some 120 officers, the Stasi's Church Department was peerless in getting bishops, pastors, deacons and church volunteers to inform ceaselessly on one another and Christians abroad, and in enlisting them without resorting to violence.[12]

---

12   Thomas Auerbach, Matthias Braun, Bernd Eisenfeld, Gesine von Prittwitz, Clemens Vollnhals, *Hauptabteilung XX: Staatsapparat, Blockparteien, Kirchen, Kultur, 'politischer Untergrund* [MfS-Handbuch] (Hg BStU, Berlin, 2008), http://www.nbn-resolving.org/urn:nbn:de:0292-97839421301343, p. 100.

The colonel and I sit in his living room, the freezing winter draught kept at bay by the central heating. Central heating was the main attraction of these multistorey apartment buildings. As soon as the buildings went up in the fifties and sixties, East Germans queued for an apartment in them. This was the modern, convenient life. And living in an old house meant using coal for heating, while the new apartment buildings featured not just heat but hot water as well. Who would want to drag coal from the cellar to the oven every day? With construction materials a rare luxury, renovating an old house was, at any rate, extraordinarily difficult. But when Germany's reunification swiftly brought the market economy to the East, anybody with a bit of ambition bought a house and renovated it. Only those who couldn't afford a house stayed in the grey apartment blocks. So did the believers, who remain convinced that socialism could have prevailed if executed correctly. Many former East German officials shed their socialist beliefs the moment having them became inconvenient. They seamlessly converted to capitalism, founded companies, bought houses. But Wiegand remains a believer.

In 1953, at his new job with the Stasi's counter-intelligence unit in Rostock, Wiegand had been assigned to the group focusing on West Germany's intelligence agency, the *Bundesnachrichtendienst* (the BND) and its counter-intelligence agency, the *Bundesverfassungsschutz*. Other teams focused on the French, British, and American intelligence agencies as well as the US consulate in Hamburg. Convinced that the enemy was operating in East Germany's smaller cities as well as in Berlin, the Ministry for State Security had built up impressive counter-espionage teams around the country.

"My first task was to build an observation group," Wiegand tells me. "In this group we had three people, all Lübeck residents. Thanks to our IM, we knew that an East German train engineer who drove intrazone trains had been recruited by the BND and had travelled to Hamburg to meet with them."[13] Instead of arresting the train driver, the Stasi's Rostock officers trailed him to Hamburg, where they put the BND's regional office under surveillance. "That helped us identify several of the BND's East German agents," Wiegand explains.

Counter-intelligence in a region bordering enemy territory had hardly a bad start for a newly minted Stasi agent. It was the most interesting time of his life, Wiegand tells me. In espionage, an inconspicuous person such as the driver of a long-distance train can be much more useful than somebody more closely affiliated with government or politics, simply because nobody is paying any attention to him. The scheme was to bear fruit.

While Wiegand was trying to catch West German agents from his perch in Rostock, the Stasi's new Church Bureau – then called Department V/IV – was beginning to take shape.[14] It belonged to the Stasi's likewise newly created Division V, in charge of preventing subversion. "The reactionary leaders of the Lutheran and the Catholic Church... are engaged in enemy activities with the goal of undermining the measures decided on by the government," new Stasi chief Ernst Wollweber – a former sailor who had made a career sabotaging the fascist countries' ships in the 1930s – thundered as he announced the creation of Division V. "It has been proven in many cases, especially recently, that intelligence agencies are using the churches and sects for their criminal activity against the GDR, the USSR, and the countries of people's democracies."

The Church Bureau officers – in 1955, numbering a meagre seventeen men – would have to foil enemy intelligence agencies' nefarious doings towards East Germany by spying on the church.[15] But infiltrating religious denominations by means of a cadre of young men lacking any religious background posed a considerable challenge. Agents were "young and

---

13   Intrazone trains travelled between East and West Germany. An *Inoffizieller Mitarbeiter,* or IM, was an unofficial collaborator (agent).

14   Auerbach et al, *Hauptabteilung XX,* p. 92.

15   Auerbach et al, *Hauptabteilung XX,* p. 90.

inexperienced and are afraid of conversations with clergymen", grumbled Willi Butter in 1956, one year after being appointed the Church Bureau's first director.[16]

Butter, himself a former metal worker, had some sympathy with his staff: like the Stasi's other departments, the Church Bureau employed an impressive assortment of carpenters, welders, cabinet makers, agricultural workers, plumbers, and factory workers. There was an undeniable logic behind it. In this self-proclaimed nation of workers and peasants, workers and peasants should have access to all jobs, including the best ones. But as a welder with only perfunctory theological knowledge, what do you talk about when you first meet with a pastor you'd like to recruit? And once you've managed to engage in conversation, how do you proceed from generalities to the business of betraying secrets? Finding himself overwhelmed by the task of infiltrating the church, in 1957, Butter resigned.[17]

That apparently did the trick. At any rate, later that year the Bureau's new head Franz Sgraja reported that "we've firmly established ourselves in the church leadership, except in Greifswald and Rostock".[18] His department, he noted, had already managed to recruit several high-ranking church officials as informants. By 1960, the Church Bureau had 122 informants – mostly pastors or other church employees secretly acting as the Bureau's agents.[19]

In Rostock counter-intelligence, meanwhile, things were progressing smoothly. "In the years around 1959 to 1966, each year we arrested around ten to twelve agents who were working for the West Germans", recalls Wiegand. "One year it was even fifteen. It was a normal thing. They were arrested and questioned, and in most cases quickly admitted what they'd been up to." He tells me how the MfS – former MfS officers and other East German officials always use the agency's official name, never Stasi –

---

16   Auerbach et al, *Hauptabteilung XX*, p. 92.
17   Auerbach et al, *Hauptabteilung XX*, p. 91.
18   Auerbach et al, *Hauptabteilung XX*, p. 93.
19   Auerbach et al, *Hauptabteilung XX*, p. 93.

intercepted coded letters sent in invisible ink and shadowed dead letter boxes.[20] He mentions the local artist who worked for West Germany's intelligence agency, the BND, watching barracks in the Rostock region. The artist would record how many people and vehicles entered and exited, what types of vehicles the soldiers used. Wiegand and his colleagues arrested the man but kept his arrest secret, hoping that they would be able to make him a double-agent who would spy for the East Germans as well as the BND. "I went to him in jail and said, 'Will you work with us? We'll continue together,'" Wiegand tells me. "He said yes. I told him he could be certain to be bought out by the West." Then the artist could start spying for the Stasi. West Germany habitually bought East German prisoners, paying the East German government a tidy sum for their release. Between 1963 and 1990, West Germany would pay the East German government no less than 3.44 billion Deutschmark – $2.12 billion at the 1980 exchange rate – for the release of 31,755 prisoners.[21]

Duly bought out by the West Germans, the artist resumed contact with Wiegand and proceeded to identify several cover addresses where two of Wiegand's agents – inconspicuous retirees – began intercepting the letters. This way Wiegand learned where the BND operated in Hamburg, northern Germany's largest city.

Citizens of autocratic countries take for granted that the secret police infiltrates courts, youth organizations, and political parties. And in the Soviet Union, the KGB had plenty of priest spies in the country's Orthodox Church. According to the agency's last deputy chairman, Anatoli Oleynikov, only 15 to 20 per cent of Russian Orthodox priests approached

---

20   Dead letter boxes are a technique used by intelligence officers and agents to exchange information without meeting in person. The dead letter box can, for example, be a particular rock or a brick in a wall.

21   "Eine Diktatur in Zahlen", *Stern*, 26 October 2009, http://www.stern.de/politik/deutschland/mauerfall/statistik-des-schreckens-eine-diktatur-in-zahlen-3448144.html (accessed 3 May 2019).

by the KGB refused collaboration.[22] Dissident priest Father Dmitri Dudko, for his part, described the situation thus: "One hundred per cent of the [Russian Orthodox] clergy were forced to cooperate to some extent with the KGB and pass on some sort of information – otherwise they would have been deprived of the possibility to work in a parish."[23] But East German Lutherans? Had not many Lutheran pastors, fighting alongside communists, bravely opposed Adolf Hitler? Had some of them, such as Dietrich Bonhoeffer, not paid for their rectitude with their own lives?

At Stasi headquarters, the bosses had been grappling with how to handle East Germany's foremost global icon, Martin Luther. For Christians from around the world, not least from the United States, the home of the Reformation has a special place, and that was true during the days of the German Democratic Republic as well. It was after a visit to Luther's home region in 1934 that a Baptist preacher from Georgia named Michael King Sr decided to change his first name and that of his son Michael Jr to Martin Luther.[24] Such reverence of Luther continued during the days of the German Democratic Republic. Besides, for a country conscious of a cultural heritage that included Johann Sebastian Bach, Johann Wolfgang von Goethe and Friedrich Schiller, sending pastors to penal colonies was not a viable option. But how else to minimize the voice of the Lutheran Church and the 80 per cent of the population who initially belonged to it – and the voice of smaller denominations such as the Catholic Church and Jehovah's Witnesses?

According to Klaus Rossberg, a Stasi officer who would later serve as Wiegand's deputy, East Germany's leaders were initially at a loss about

---

22   Christopher Andrew and Vasili Mitrokhin, *The Mitrokhin Archive* (London: Penguin Books, 2000), p. 639.
23   Andrew and Mitrokhin, p. 639.
24   The Martin Luther King, Jr. Research and Education Institute, "Commemorating the 50th Anniversary of King's Berlin Trip", Stanford University, 6 October 2014, https://kinginstitute.stanford.edu/news/commemorating-50th-anniversary-kings-berlin-trip (accessed 21 May 2019).

how to fight the alien body in their midst. Should the regime "completely annihilate this power factor massively supported by the West, as attempted in the Soviet Union, or neutralize it through clever policies"? they asked themselves.[25] At first, Erich Mielke – appointed Stasi chief in 1957, succeeding the ailing Wollweber – leaned towards the brutal approach he had observed during his exile in the Soviet Union. Pastors and bishops who didn't toe the line were threatened with prison sentences and sometimes jailed.

One day in 1957, two well-meaning clerics from the city of Magdeburg travelled to West Berlin to bring back money belonging to East Germany's Lutheran Church. Even though there was nothing illegal about the manoeuvre, transporting the money turned out to be a very bad idea: Mielke's men swooped in, arrested the pastors and interrogated their colleagues. One of them died of a heart attack while being questioned. The following year, a brave pastor in the town of Zeitz was arrested for speaking up on behalf of farmers whose properties were being collectivized. And in Leipzig, during a boring lecture, a first-year theology student named Wolf Krötke scribbled a line to himself about the silliness of the government. After the lecture, he absentmindedly left his notepad behind. Another theology student turned it in to the police. Krötke had to serve a one-year jail sentence.

By 1960, the Stasi – now boasting a workforce of around 20,000 – was becoming rather skilled at keeping political order in the country. A position with the Stasi meant secure employment with plenty of career opportunities. Those who landed in the Church Bureau did their best to immerse themselves in church circles and ecclesiastical terminology, learning obscure words like *Oberkirchenrat* – a senior clergy rank – and *Una Sancta* Movement. The SED's top church official, Willi Barth, a veteran anti-fascist who had been hunted by the Gestapo during World War II

---

25   Klaus Rossberg and Peter Richter, *Das Kreuz mit dem Kreuz* (edition ost: Berlin, 1996) p. 25.

and ended up incarcerated in Canada, even held a recurring three-week theology course for new Church Bureau officers.[26]

But there was a problem: East Germans kept leaving the country, most of them simply crossing over to West Berlin never to return. By the summer of 1961, East Germany had lost a staggering 3 million citizens. The country was haemorrhaging doctors and other skilled workers. On top of that, some 50,000 East Germans worked in West Berlin, earning not just much higher wages but bringing home their income in West German Deutschmarks, which were worth four times as much as the East German mark.[27] The East German government decided that the situation couldn't continue: what sort of message would it send by allowing countless East Germans to leave for the West?

By the spring of 1961, rumours were circulating that the government was about to build a wall across Berlin. In June, the rumours had gone so far that East German leader Walter Ulbricht felt compelled to deny them. "Nobody has the intention of erecting a wall!" he proclaimed on 15 June.[28] But on 13 August, Berliners awoke to see that a wall was being built.

We will return to the Berlin Wall throughout this book, but one of the effects was that the Stasi had to get even better at monitoring its citizens, especially the booming activity of escapes to West Berlin. In 1964, the Stasi again reorganized it ranks. The new Division XX was given an astonishing task: spying on the totality of East Germany's civic and political life, including would-be escapees and their helpers. With its nine subdivisions, Division XX was given responsibility for government agencies, the healthcare system, the courts, social democrats, "subversive propaganda", mass organizations,

---

26 The SED is the *Sozialistische Einheitspartei Deutschlands*, Socialist Unity Party of Germany. Auerbach et al, *Hauptabteilung XX*, p. 92.

27 "Niemand hat die Absicht, eine Mauer zu errichten!", Die Bundesregierung, https://www.bundesregierung.de/Content/DE/StatischeSeiten/Breg/Deutsche_Einheit/ mauerbau/ulbricht-berliner-mauer.html (accessed 3 May 2019).

28 "Niemand hat die Absicht", *Die Bundesregierung*, eine Mauer zu errichten! (accessed 3 May 2019).

political parties (except the SED), universities, all sports clubs, people helping East Germans flee, escapees critical of the SED, culture, mass communications, colleges and tertiary educational institutions other than universities, and political subversion. The new Department XX/4 – which I will keep referring to as the Church Bureau – would tackle the church: Lutherans, Catholics, and smaller denominations.

Even the hard-line Erich Mielke had by now realized that it would be counterproductive to prosecute every theology student who voiced dissent or jail pastors who, say, listened to Western radio stations. Thanks to its pastor agents, the Stasi was, in fact, already well aware of some pastors' habit of secretly listening to enemy broadcasts. "The [redacted] family only listens to BBC London," reported pastor agent IM Lorac about a fellow pastor in 1963. "The clergy generally prefers the foreign capitalist radio stations, both to improve their foreign language skills but also out of arrogance." But pastors arrested for listening to Voice of America or the BBC World Service would have resulted in an international outcry. The East Germans would have to be smarter than the Soviets.

In Rostock, Joachim Wiegand was by now a successful spy-catcher. Six years into the job, he had been appointed head of the regional office's counter-intelligence unit. On the home front, however, there was trouble. Wiegand was happily married to Gerda, a bookkeeper whom he had met at the cinema in Rostock, and they were proud parents of a young son. But they had long sensed that there was something wrong with their boy's eyesight. Now the doctor had told them their son had cataracts. With primary school approaching, the doctor informed Joachim and Gerda that their son would not be able to attend a regular school. Joachim and Gerda would have to send him to a special boarding school. The Wiegands were heartbroken: how could they send their only child to an institution? In desperation they began looking for alternatives. East Berlin, they soon learned, had a day school for visually impaired children. That was the only option, the Wiegands decided. Joachim would have to ask for a transfer.

But in the MfS, officers were not supposed to ask for new posts; higher-ups bestowed positions. And for a counter-intelligence officer to ask for a transfer to headquarters? It would seem highly suspicious. Because counter-intelligence officers often run double agents, they have contacts on the enemy side and may even have been recruited by the enemy themselves. Worse yet, one of Wiegand's agents, a sailor in Hamburg, had turned out to be a BND agent. Wiegand now seemed suspect: perhaps he had been turned by the BND? It would have been best to lie low. But Wiegand decided to ask for a transfer anyway. How could he possibly send his son away?

At first, nothing happened. But one of the officers at headquarters had previously worked in the Rostock office. Wiegand made his case to him, and in 1966 he finally received an answer: yes, we will be able to transfer you. There was just one catch. Wiegand would have to accept a one-rank demotion – and a position in Department XX/4. "The church!" Wiegand laughs as he recalls his transfer. "The church was fine." Spying on the Lord's flock seemed like a dead-end career move.

But the church posed an enormous task for the Ministry for State Security. Facing the officially atheist German Democratic Republic was not just the fact that it was the home country of Martin Luther and thus a Christian Mecca of sorts. Christians are, by definition, part of a global network; they have autonomous international contacts of their own. Making matters worse, even though Germany was divided, churches on both sides kept in close contact and even had joint decision-making bodies. Though Wiegand initially considered the Church Bureau a backwater, in reality it had an enormously complex task. "The church structures have existed for centuries!" Wiegand points out. "That's extremely hard to tackle." Every church steeple seemed like a reminder that the communist regime was facing the mighty West, even the Lord Almighty. "In all sovereign countries the church's borders are identical with the country's borders;

only the Federal Republic [West Germany] and its churches opposed such independence. They did their part for the Cold War," Klaus Rossberg writes in his memoirs.[29]

By the time Wiegand arrived at the two-year-old Department XX/4, his superiors had decided that the best way of weakening the Lutherans was to infiltrate their ranks.[30] The task awaiting 34 year old Wiegand when he reported for duty at the Normannenstrasse was thus to recruit men of the cloth (and the occasional woman) as informants. He learned ecclesiastical titles and hierarchies, who decides what, how a sermon is put together, and how clergy of different ranks interact with one another.

"I had no clue about the church," Wiegand tells me. He wears glasses that are slightly outdated now, but back then he didn't need any, and with his tall build and thick dark hair, he still cuts a dashing figure, just as he had done as a student in Potsdam. "My contact with the church basically consisted of my mother, who was a poor peasant, giving the pastor sausage. Yes, I had been confirmed, but I knew nothing about the church or religion," he explains. In his living room, I notice plenty of theological books with titles such as *Theologisches Lexikon* (Theological Lexicon), *Grundwissen für Christen* (Basic Knowledge for Christians), *Kirche im Krieg* (The Church in War), and *Grosse Christen unseres Jahrhunderts* (Great Christians of our Century). There's a book called *Die Päpste* (The Popes) and one about the CIA.

In 1966, after a period of immersion into the world of God, Wiegand made his first contact with a pastor. He introduced himself and the two men engaged in a pleasant conversation. Then the cleric told Wiegand: "You're a perfectly reasonable man, but since you're from the MfS I can't stay in touch. If you hadn't told me that you're from the MfS we might have been able to work together." Most pastors would, of course, quickly

---

29   Rossberg and Richter, *Das Kreuz mit dem Kreuz*, p. 34.
30   Auerbach et al, *Hauptabteilung XX*, p. 98.

surmise that a government official wanting to make their acquaintance was actually from the Stasi. But if the pastor wasn't told the official's real affiliation, he could feign ignorance. Thus enlightened, Wiegand ordered IDs from various government ministries and suggested to colleagues that they should too.

When dealing with prospects and recruits, Wiegand would from now on always identify himself as, say, an official from the education ministry. Advertising under a false flag, the MfS called it. And Wiegand decided to be even softer with his churchmen than his colleagues were, not to put them on the defensive before or after recruiting them. "My approach was that we should leave church activities alone but tackle the church's abuse of politics," he explains with no hint of irony. "Let them pray, let them sing, but they shouldn't do politics against the GDR. If they want to rant about West German warmongers, that's fine." It was a strategy that would reward countless pastors with university places for their children, trips to the West, good cigars, fine cognac, and flowers for their wives.

"That's the evil Stasi man," Wiegand says, smiling and pointing to a framed photo on the wall in the entrance hallway as I get ready to leave. The picture shows a happy Wiegand, wearing a Santa Claus hat, with two of his great-grandchildren on his lap: the doting grandfather. His grandchildren and great-grandchildren call him Opa Joe, Grandpa Joe. He certainly doesn't seem like an evil man, more like a man committed to communism and willing to use people's weaknesses to advance its cause. But his buddy-with-presents strategy would sabotage the church in the homeland of the Reformation.

CHAPTER 2

PASTOR AGENTS

"**P**astor [*name redacted*] has recommended a young man who would like to study theology at the seminary," said Dr Siegfried Krügel. "I don't want to accept a student who will be troublesome. Can you help?" It was 1962. Krügel, who had just joined the faculty at the Lutherans' Theological College in Leipzig, was not talking to a fellow theologian but to a Stasi officer. They two men were sitting in Conspiratorial Apartment Balkon in the Hans-von-Bülow-Strasse. Conspiratorial Apartment is the German term for safe houses; each Stasi safe house had a name.

The prospective student was, by all accounts, unsuitable to join the clergy: although he had trained as a deacon in his native West Germany, he had abandoned that path because he didn't agree with Lutheran teachings. Until recently, he had instead wanted to pursue a career in the East German armed forces.

Krügel knew that the prospective student was a terrible candidate for the clergy. But Krügel was a new IM and he knew that it was important to distinguish oneself early on. Without telling his case officer what he knew, he asked the officer for advice. After examining the Stasi's file on the young man, the officer – not surprisingly – concluded that the young man would not be a good pastor. In one move, Krügel had managed to establish his credentials as a reliable ally – and had damaged the reputation of the fellow pastor who had recommended the young man.

Not that Department XX/4 had any doubts about Krügel's commitment. Despite only recently having become an IM, Krügel – codename IM Lorac – had already reported that a pastor Dresden had delivered a sermon where he used the Old Testament to made veiled references to the German Democratic Republic. Krügel had attended the service and written down the offending passages. "The people of Israel were really suffering. It was divided into zones that were ruled by enemies. Only the capital remained relatively free," the preacher, Pastor Georg-Friedrich Schmutzler, had said.

The Stasi was well aware of Schmutzler's dissident leanings: he had already served a prison sentence for conducting an evangelization week. But the Stasi still needed to keep a close eye on him. "IM Lorac judges Schmutzler's sermon to be against socialist morals," wrote Lieutenant Erich Blümel. IM Lorac had also delivered information about his students' and fellow faculty members' views on "US aggression" – unfortunately most of the students considered the Cuban missile crisis a "US victory over Russia", he reported – and other theologians' deficiencies. On the positive side, a fellow pastor had recently labelled US incineration of surplus grains a crime. "It's time that the US finally learns from the socialist system," he had told Krügel.

Krügel had considerable deficiencies himself. Students and fellow faculty considered him stiff and uptight, and he wasn't even a good academic. That was why, despite his strong pro-government credentials, no university had hired him; it would have damaged their reputation. Instead, he was working at the Theological College in Leipzig, a more practice-oriented institution.

The resentful lecturer was, however, completely committed to the Stasi.

In fact, the Agency presented his best chance of gaining career advantages and various perks. Those perks had already included tickets to the St John Passion and the St Matthew Passion, Johann Sebastian Bach's masterpieces. Despite their undeniably Christian content, both oratorios were performed around the country every year: the government knew that along with Martin Luther, Bach was East Germany's top PR asset.

The anticipated career advantages made IM Lorac an extremely eager agent. But had the Stasi's officers in these early days of church infiltration done their homework a bit more thoroughly, they would have discovered that Krügel's pastor colleagues didn't much like him. Conversely, it annoyed IM Lorac that colleagues kept getting away with potshots at the government. Krügel told a handler about a morning prayer meeting where his wife had commented to a pastor on the beautiful weather. "Yes, much too nice weather for May 8," the pastor had responded. On 8 May 1945 – VE-Day – Nazi Germany had surrendered. Mrs Krügel, her husband informed Blümel, had then upbraided the pastor about his lacking sensibility regarding 8 May as well as 1 May, the International Workers' Day. "I didn't participate in the conversation," Krügel told the officer during a three-hour meeting in Conspiratorial Apartment Balkon. "I'm just telling you to show how obstinate these people are." The travel secretary of the women's mission society, he further informed the officer, was "psychologically unstable, which is connected to the fact that she lacks a man".

More importantly, as IM Lorac explained to another Stasi officer, fellow clergymen were not afraid of applying for and being denied the travel permits East Germans needed to visit the West. In July 1963, a pastor had told his colleagues he had been denied a travel permit to attend the Lutheran World Federation's upcoming world conference in Helsinki. Since the conference took place only every five to seven years, the pastor was understandably upset. "But he was consoled by the fact that in church circles people are saying that whoever has character was turned down" for a travel permit,

IM Lorac reported. For the Lutheran Church, however, the travel permits were now posing a problem. Pastors from one diocese had been granted permits, and pastors forced to remain behind were now concerned that the ones allowed to travel would pretend to be the sole representatives of East Germany. For the Helsinki Conference, they had come up with a clever solution: Bishop Hanns Lilje, the German Lutheran Church's top bishop, would walk up to the East German delegates in Helsinki and ask: "How come that you got to go while the pastors from Saxony did not? Are you quislings?"[31]

This was tricky. If the East German government allowed only politically reliable pastors to travel abroad, international church representatives would start avoiding East German delegates altogether, correctly reasoning that they were too close to the government. But allowing dissident-leaning pastors to travel would give them better access to international church networks. Some pastors, in turn, considered the government's refusal to issue them travel permits a badge of honour, while others argued that if they pushed hard enough, the government would relent. IM Lorac informed Stasi officer Alexander that the interior ministry had asked a colleague of his for a meeting. "He's hoping he'll get the travel permit for India," IM Lorac explained to the officer. "If he gets it, he'll sit on his high horse and spread the theory that you have to speak harshly to the government; weaklings achieve nothing." The Church Bureau would have to act. Alexander noted in his file that he had "immediately contacted Berlin and demanded that the travel permit be denied (without, of course, mentioning the context)".

While the Church Bureau pondered how to tackle the wider issue of travel permits, Neues Deutschland used its standard strategy: complete denial. Though Luther himself hailed from now East Germany (having been born in the town of Eisleben and lived in Eisenach, Erfurt, Magdeburg and

---

31   Vidkun Quisling was a Norwegian politician who acted as Norway's leader during German occupation. Today his name is used as a synonym for traitor.

Wittenberg), Neues Deutschland didn't even mention the global conference bearing his name. And even though a wide range of news outlets covered the conference's final day, Neues Deutschland instead led with a story about an East German canoeing victory in Austria.[32]

Intelligence agencies follow a great many rules, but when it comes to how to handle agents, rules barely matter. That's because a successful agent relationship depends on the officer understanding the agent's personality, his quirks and desires. Brute force accomplishes little. When IM Lorac met with his case officer he was nearly always upbeat and talkative. In fact, he seemed to crave the meetings where he would, for once, have someone's undivided attention. He usually spent more than three hours – mostly starting at 9 a.m. – with Alexander or another handler in Conspiratorial Apartment Balkon, having arrived laden with documents he thought might interest them: church bodies' meeting protocols, letters to and from the College, the College's files on its students, notes from meetings, confidential memos from the bishop. If the document was a student's final thesis, he would helpfully provide the officers with instructions such as "pay particular attention to page 43".

The students and faculty at the Theological College were not dumb: they realized that the Stasi was trying to infiltrate the school and probably already had ears and eyes there. But who were its agents? One February day in 1964, the faculty members met to discuss a student's report that the Stasi had tried to recruit him. At the meeting, it was discovered that another student, too, had been approached by the Stasi. Would it dawn on the professors that Siegfried Krügel was often missing for several hours on certain weekday mornings? But miraculously, the conversation moved on. The professors concluded that it was only natural that the Stasi would try to

---

32   "Archiv der Ausgaben von 1946–1990", *Neues Deutschland*, 12 August 1963, https://www.nd-archiv.de/artikel/1449898.sensationeller-triumph-der-ddr-kanuten-in-osterreich.html (accessed 3 May 2019).

recruit agents in their midst and gave no further attention to the matter of who might have put forward the students' names. Besides, they knew that suspecting Stasi involvement everywhere would only drive them crazy. IM Lorac could continue his undercover work.

One morning in Conspiratorial Apartment Balkon, the theologian reported that one of his students had asked for several days' leave, explaining that he belonged to an all-German working group in Berlin. Alexander considered the information important. An all-German working group, which through its sheer existence questioned the validity of the German Democratic Republic, needed to be watched.

Krügel had more information: another student had called him a "half-Christian" because Krügel had voted in the last election. In that election, nearly every East German voter had – as predicted – approved the government-proposed distribution of seats in the Volkskammer, the parliament. As in previous elections, where an overwhelming majority of voters also participated and voted in favour of the Volkskammer proposal, the SED won the most seats, with several other official parties each receiving a set number of seats. But around the country, brave seminarians and other opposition-minded citizens had stayed away from the polls. IM Lorac told Alexander that two of his students hadn't voted. One of them had even told the armed forces as much during his mandatory conscription assessment. Rather perversely, IM Lorac wanted the Stasi to provide him with more dirt on his students. "Would you be able to tell me who has voted?" he asked. "I don't want to draw attention to myself by asking around, but it's important to me to know who voted."

The lecturer kept delivering distinctly gossipy news. At a party, students had been smoking "West cigarettes"; another student was having sex with his landlady. One student had just become a father – but wasn't yet married to his girlfriend. If he wanted to work as a pastor, they'd have to get married quickly. At the beginning of one academic year, IM Lorac reports that, among the new students, there were "again many with previous convictions" – that is, Christians who had been convicted for politically motivated actions such as refusing to perform military service.

And he used his Stasi reports to undermine fellow clergy, regardless of their political leanings. He judged one pastor's sermon to be "excellent with many good points. Almost progressive," while denouncing another colleague for "not voting in the elections on principle". IM Lorac enthusiastically carried out specific assignments, too, for example "putting under operational control" – observing – his students and fellow faculty on the anniversary of the German Democratic Republic.

Meanwhile, a female theology professor colleague was feeling lonely in Leipzig and wanted to move to another city. "She would like to do something else within the church but strangely they won't let her go," IM Lorac informed Alexander. "Not strange to us," the officer cryptically noted in his files. "She pushes herself very hard," IM Lorac added. "That's not just menopause but clerical fanaticism. She sees herself as the unofficial student chaplain here."

IM Lorac did, however, deliver some useful intelligence as well, for example reporting that three students at the prestigious Thomas Oberschule ("two are pastors' sons") were planning to flee the country. This was part of the agent's thank you to the Church Bureau for helping him secure a place for one of his sons at the prestigious school, which was affiliated with the city's famous St Thomas Church. "[Lorac] is certain that this will help us get information about the church's influence at the – for us important – Thomas Oberschule," Alexander noted after IM Lorac had lobbied him for a place at the school.

Occasionally, the agent delivered something other than negative evaluations of pastors and students. At one of his regular meetings with Alexander, he surprised the officer by suggesting that East Germany should dispatch missionaries around the world. "Capitalism has 30,000 missionaries," he explained. "We should change missionary work by sending missionaries as socialist countries' unofficial collaborators." That would have been quite a coup for the home country of Martin Luther: taking the world by surprise by flooding the world with missionaries competing with the traditional missionaries from the West, with the East German missionaries spreading not just the gospel of Jesus Christ but the gospel of communism as well. Department XX/4, however, didn't act on IM Lorac's suggestion.

One day, Krügel told Alexander about a minor dilemma. An article by Krügel had been published in a West German academic journal. But how to get the fee, DM35? "Tell them to send the money to one of your relatives in West Germany and not to send you anything because it would be seized anyway," Alexander advised. The officer represented the East German government, but he was not naïve about its methods. And, being a good officer, he encouraged his agent to think of him as a friend.

But more importantly, IM Lorac was counting on the Church Bureau to further his career. One day in 1964, he told Blümel that he would like a new job. Indeed, he felt that the Stasi had promised him such assistance. But presenting a demand, he realized, would be too obvious. "I would really like to work in the area of ethics," he told the officer instead. "That way I could quietly help unmask the representatives of the political clericalism. I've got such good knowledge of the personalities in the church that I could easily do this kind of work, and I would also like it more than what I'm doing now."

Blümel was too shrewd to dismiss the proposition to IM Lorac's – Krügel's – face. Much as Krügel would have enjoyed a more challenging position, a move would have made make little sense from an intelligence-gathering perspective. Blümel gave an evasive answer, promising the theologian the Stasi's full support while praising his important work for East German society. To keep Krügel happy, Blümel mentioned the possibility

PASTOR AGENTS

of a position in West Germany, knowing that, like many East Germans, Krügel secretly yearned to live like the West Germans even while openly criticizing it. The agent got excited. He was, in fact, planning to apply for a university position in West Germany, he informed Blümel, reciting the contacts that he was certain would help him.

Meanwhile, Neues Deutschland kept the population informed about East Germany's progress. On 15 September 1964, it reported that anti-fascist resistance fighters from the Soviet Union, Czechoslovakia, Great Britain and Denmark had visited East German soldiers on border patrol duty at the Brandenburg Gate in Berlin. "The guests informed themselves about the GDR's protection measures", Neues Deutschland reported, adding a comment by one of the Soviet guests: "I'm happy to get to know the soldiers of the new Germany who are guarding the peace here."[33] The newspaper didn't add that the peace-guarding soldiers were armed and would shoot any East German trying to escape. By the time the Wall fell in 1989, East German soldiers had killed at least 140 such people.

On 15 September, the Theological College welcomed the year's new intake of students. Ever alert, IM Lorac immediately informed Blümel that "again there are a number of previously convicted people" and provided their names. Students' crimes mostly consisted of simply having refused to perform military service, but it was in IM Lorac's interest to appear to the Stasi as a bastion of sanity inside the Theological College. The Church Bureau, for its part, provided him with helpful advice. Try to get rail-fare reductions for the students, Blümel recommended. Another seminary had already managed to get reductions for its students, and such a step would strengthen Krügel's position at the college, Blümel advised.

More than three hours had passed in Conspiratorial Apartment Balkon on 15 September, one of countless such meetings. As Joachim Wiegand

---

33   "Archiv der Ausgaben von 1946–1990", *Neues Deutschland*, 15 September 1964, http://www.nd-archiv.de/ausgabe/1964-09-15 (accessed 1 May 2019).

explained to me many years later, you can't rush a pastor. Agent-handler sessions were also a rare opportunity for IMs to unburden themselves. Their handlers knew their espionage secret – but also the full extent of their professional and personal lives. And the agents knew that while it may not be a good idea to share their professional frustrations and desire with colleagues, they could trust their case officer. And Blümel and his colleagues could help. Uneducated in Scripture exegesis though they might be, they acted as Father-Confessors-cum-mentors.

Now, with lunchtime fast approaching, it was time for Blümel to go through IM Lorac's next assignments. With the anniversary of the GDR approaching on 7 October, Blümel asked IM Lorac to monitor his students and fellow lecturers: were they showing excitement or – more likely – opposition or disdain? "Take [three names redacted] under operational surveillance," Blümel instructed. IM Lorac was also to provide Blümel with the addresses of the seminar's "troublesome additions" (the students convicted of political crimes) and report to the Bureau from a pastor gathering. Spying on his students and fellow pastors didn't trouble the ambitious Dr Krügel: he "behaved in a relaxed manner and arrived well-prepared," Blümel noted. In the safe house, the officer usually served coffee and cake, which the agent readily consumed; sometimes there were cigars too. By now IM Lorac even knew the protocol for emergency meetings when urgent news had to be communicated. At a specified time, the agent and Blümel were both to appear at the central hospital, exchange their information, and leave.

But as Joachim Wiegand had by now discovered in East Berlin, the Church Bureau's operations were not particularly sophisticated, and no information was too menial for its files. In Naumburg "[name redacted] is supposed to succeed [name redacted], who had an affair with a young colleague and has become untenable," Blümel, for example, noted after a meeting with Siegfried Krügel. Several months later, Krügel informed

Blümel that a fellow pastor has brought "materials" from West Germany that mustn't be found by the authorities, and that the pastor had made comments such as, "after all, we live in a prison here in the GDR". Another pastor, IM Lorac reported, had defended apartheid. Blümel took the information down. Was there a point in collecting every single comment? Most officers wrote them down anyway – even the slightest piece of information might be useful one day.

There was another reason for the Stasi's extraordinarily industrious reporting and file-keeping. Wiegand explains: "You were promoted based on how many meetings you had with IMs and how much material you produced. In order to make a good impression, you had to provide as many reports as possible, so officers had a whole lot of meetings and filed a whole lot of reports that were not very useful."

In other words, Church Bureau officers and other Stasi officers collected enormous amounts of pointless information because their own professional advancement depended on it. Since the Stasi lacked other quantifiable methods of evaluating its officers, volume had to do. That included the number and length of reports as well as the number of meetings with agents – which is why Wiegand annoyed his superiors with his long meetings with pastors. Long meetings did, indeed, seem to make little sense. But as Wiegand and other officers discovered, trying to conduct intelligence work by means of brief conversations was counter-productive. "You come to visit them, you stay for dinner," he tells me, referring to the pastors. "You can't rush a clergyman."

In August 1965, having attended a meeting for pastors in the northern region of Mecklenburg, IM Lorac pointed out to Blümel what was obvious to everyone moving in church circles: many pastors wore Western clothes. However, what had possibly eluded the Church Bureau was that – as IM Lorac informed Blümel – pastors often received their clothes from West German sister parishes. And, IM Lorac added, West German parishes sent East German pastors washing machines and refrigerators as well. Clandestine capitalist washing machines: this was yet more proof that the church was East Germany's Achilles heel.

As the Stasi was well aware, Lutherans on both sides of the German border maintained extraordinarily close links on both the personal and the institutional level. East Germany's eight church regions – which I will refer to as dioceses – had partner dioceses in West Germany. In fact, officially, the East German Lutheran Church was still a member of the all-German Lutheran Church now based in West Germany. Further down the chain, countless parishes also had sister parishes on the other side of the border. Both the West German parishes and individual members regularly sent gifts to their East German friends. The Church Bureau had seen East German clergy in Western clothing before.

For good measure, IM Lorac added this assessment: "The pastors are better off thanks to the gifts from the other side and are in a position of strong dependence on the Bonn military church." (The Bonn military church: he was referring to the Lutheran Church in West Germany.)

Four months later, the Leipzig Christmas market was bustling with people. But despite the festive atmosphere and the abundance of mulled wine, Stollen Christmas bread, and gifts for sale at the stalls, IM Lorac was worried.[34] At his weekly meeting with Blümel, he enjoyed the usual coffee and cigars. But there was something on his mind this December day. Krügel was having trouble at work. Colleagues, he had discerned, considered him a prickly man unwilling to compromise. But as he told Blümel, he couldn't compromise because that would harm the Stasi. The connection between compromising and harming the Stasi wasn't entirely clear to Blümel; in fact, it was nonsense. Nevertheless, the officer listened patiently. "Try to take [name redacted] into your confidence," he counselled. IM Lorac agreed that it was a good idea. "I wouldn't have poured my heart out to you if I didn't

---

34   Stollen is traditional German Christmas bread.

know that you would have sympathy for my problems," he said. "Apart from you there's no one I can talk to."

Only two months previously, IM Lorac had had a similarly calculated heart-to-heart with Blümel. He told the officer of a colleague who had phoned him saying: "Brother, would you like to become my successor?" The fellow theologian, Krügel continued, had told him that he would propose Krügel as his successor rather than another theologian, "who hasn't achieved anything", as Krügel related to Brümel. If the officer found the story hard to believe, he didn't show it. He knew why IM Lorac was sharing this promising news with him: the agent wanted the Stasi to help him get the professorship.

That motivation was shared by many other of the Church Bureau's growing line-up of pastor agents. They didn't have to be blackmailed into working for the Stasi. On the contrary, they received attention and sympathy from men who knew almost everything about them – and assistance with practical matters.

Regular spies fight foreign governments: it's a fight between equals. What makes authoritarian states' domestic spying so dirty is that it involves agents reporting on defenceless citizens who have committed no crime other than harbouring views different from those of the regime. Even more troubling is the fact that authoritarian regimes manage to recruit and retain such Machiavellians. As his Stasi career progressed, IM Lorac used his perch at the Theological College in Leipzig to denounce a steady stream of students to the Stasi. One student, for example, who "wore an existentialist beard" had been rejected by the prestigious Humboldt University in East Berlin and had, in the past, uttered "the provocative demand that the order to shoot [escaping East Germans] at the border be lifted".[35]

Many domestic spies have a red line, though: they don't use their

---

35   An "existentialist beard" was an untidy beard worn by some East German men to signal their focus on matters more profound than attire.

children for espionage. IM Lorac had no such qualms. On the contrary: one of his sons, a pupil at the Thomas-Oberschule, was unwittingly a highly useful accomplice. The prominent high school counted among its pupils the older choir boys at the city's famous St Thomas's Church, where Bach had once been choirmaster. Though he had no idea that he was indirectly working for the Stasi, Krügel's son dutifully collected any information his father requested and answered his father's questions about other boys. Asked about one of his classmates, whom the Stasi suspected of rebellious leanings, the boy told his father that the boy had "recently said that he doesn't understand why the [Soviet bloc] states always stress that they have the largest army. That way, he said, they just incite other countries to arm themselves even more."

Pupils at the Thomas-Oberschule were unruly and often weren't given homework, IM Lorac informed Blümel. But he told the officer that there was good news: at a recent meeting with parents, the school had demanded of them a promise not to let their children watch West German television. A couple of weeks later the industrious agent, courtesy of the younger Krügel, provided Blümel with further information about the behaviour of one of the Thomas-Oberschule pupils. Recently, when the class was studying the benefits of collective farms as practised in East Germany, the boy had argued that collective farms don't work. "Look at Poland [a fellow socialist country]; it's all individual farms. Socialism in agriculture is nonsense," the boy had said, according to Krügel's son. "How can he afford to say such things?" Krügel had asked his son, who had informed him that the boy's father was an Austrian citizen.

A boy who dared to challenge the East German system, and who could do so with the relative protection of an Austrian father: that was dangerous. IM Lorac promised to keep Blümel updated on the boy. The Church Bureau, in turn, informed the city authorities. It didn't occur to IM Lorac to treat a teenager's opinions as just that; instead, everything around him provided fodder for his Stasi career. There were men with ponytails (suspect); male students who received female visitors overnight (even more worrisome). Blümel tried to steer his agent towards more useful intelligence-gathering – for example, instructing him to find out which people were expected at certain church events. That could help the Church Bureau establish how particular networks operated.

Meanwhile, opposition to the regime was growing in church circles. While East Germans had no choice but to accept that they were now locked up in their country, many internationally connected East German Christians refused to cooperate with the system imposed on them. IM Lorac kept his ear to the ground among fellow clergy. "Nobody asked me, and nobody asked the population either," a pastor – whom we shall call Günther Albrecht – declared at a Theological College faculty meeting in 1966. The faculty members were discussing their country's political system. Pastor Albrecht continued: "It was done under the protection of the Soviet occupation power and was not the result of the people's will." And as far as the elections were concerned, Pastor Albrecht said, "What we have are no elections."

In the four national elections to date, over 98 per cent of eligible East Germans had voted, every time giving nearly unanimous support to the "unity list" – led by the SED. Such astounding results were possible because, in reality, voting was often not secret: in many cases, no booths were available. "We just want secret ballots as our election laws stipulate," Pastor Albrecht argued at the meeting. Adherence to the election laws and the universal principle of the secret ballot: Pastor Albrecht was just asking for practices that East Germany officially abided by.

Even church music was becoming a headache. Much like their colleagues in many Western countries, an increasing number of pastors and church musicians had taken to replacing the traditional hymns and choir pieces with jazz. East German Lutherans were not the only Christians discovering jazz: all over the Western world, clerics and church musicians were incorporating contemporary music into church services. But as far as the Stasi was concerned, jazz was undesirable because it was not only American but also dangerously subversive. "A 'modern' youth church service has been announced in the Bethany Church," IM Lorac reported on one occasion. "It has been agreed with the government that a band (jazz) is approved for church services, but the band can only be used for church purposes."

At another meeting, IM Lorac told a handler that he had identified two clerics who opposed jazz in church. "But they don't voice their opinion publicly because they don't want to get a reputation of being against modern and new things," he explained. Nevertheless, the two clergymen were deemed to have informant potential as the Church Bureau took up the fight against jazz in church. The handler, Lieutenant Blüth, instructed IM Lorac to talk to one of the pastors to better determine the latter's views on "the introduction of modern music in church" and to strengthen the other pastor "in his position vis-à-vis jazz". Unbeknownst to the two pastors, their love of Lutheran chorales and Johann Sebastian Bach had earned them support from the Stasi.

Another meeting in Conspiratorial Apartment Balkon; another person's reputation in shreds. What did a conspiratorial apartment look like? I ask Joachim Wiegand. It could be set up in different ways, he explains. Sometimes it was an apartment owned by the Stasi and used only as a meeting place, but very often it was a room in an ordinary home, "a grandmother who rented out a room to us," as Wiegand describes it. Such Stasi hosts were listed as "*Inoffizielle Mitarbeiter*" with the additional letter K – IMK – indicating that their role was the provision of logistical assistance. With safe houses owned by the Stasi, officers and agents had to be particularly careful. Neighbours could – and did – often identify such apartments because nobody seemed to live in them, but every grandmother receives visitors. IMKs provided excellent cover for officer–agent meetings.

In the summer of 1967, the Stasi had decided that IM Lorac was being seen at Conspiratorial Apartment Balkon too frequently. The officers decided to move meetings with the agent to a different safe house in Leipzig, an apartment located in a larger apartment block where it was harder for neighbours to figure out which apartment a stranger might be visiting. But when IM Lorac arrived for his first meeting at Conspiratorial Apartment Sonneneck, he was not met by his friend Lieutenant Blümel, whom he knew under the cover name Bürgel. Instead he was greeted by a Lieutenant Kunth. "Comrade Bürgel is unable to continue meeting with you," Kunth informed him. "The road from him to the MfS is too long and doesn't correspond to the practices of security," the officer cryptically added.

IM Lorac (Krügel) was at a loss. What was happening? Where was his handler? "We don't have any concerns about Comrade Bürgel, but we have to provide for his security and follow the existing guidelines," Kunth explained. It dawned on IM Lorac that Blümel had been demoted or removed altogether. But Kunth provided no further details. From now on, Kunth said, the meetings would take place here at Conspiratorial Apartment Sonneneck. Kunth (who had introduced himself using a cover name) instructed IM Lorac to memorize the apartment's location and closely examine the name list at the front door in case he knew any of the residents. In that case, it would clearly not be safe to meet here. But IM Lorac knew nobody in the building. And he knew he had to make a good impression on this new handler. He told Kunth that he was comfortable meeting at Conspiratorial Apartment Sonneneck and that, by the way, he didn't mind switching handlers. "The most important thing is, I need a clear picture," he explained. "I need to know who I can speak openly with."

An agent who spies out of conviction may baulk at being reassigned to a different handler and refuse to continue. But since walking away from the assignment is not an option for an agent who wants to keep his perks, IM Lorac kept up his energetic delivery schedule. He delivered the Theological

College's file on a student who had just been arrested trying to flee to the West via Hungary. After being arrested by the Hungarian authorities, the student had been handed over to the East Germans and would, of course, now be prosecuted. That put IM Lorac in a bind. The prosecutors were bound to contact the College about the student, and the College staff would inevitably discover that the student's file was missing – Krügel had removed it. They would now know for certain that there was at least one IM in their midst. Could the Church Bureau ask the prosecutors to wait until the file has been returned? IM Lorac asked Kunth. The officer said he would talk to the prosecutors.

Kunth, however, had a hunch that Krügel's colleagues might still suspect what he was up too. In September 1967, with Krügel planning another trip to West Germany, Kunth instilled in him the risk of being identified as a Stasi agent and the behaviour he was to adopt if faced with this accusation. Always be prepared, always react correspondingly, the officer advised. "React correspondingly" meant deny the accusation and turn it around.

Soon the would-be-escapee at the Theological College went on trial. Krügel was in the court room, as were friends of the accused, who had turned up to show their support. Though Krügel was hoping to land a job in West Germany, he had no time for the blue-sky-thinking students who were risking their lives attempting to get there. Relating the student's defence of his failed escape, IM Lorac reported to the Church Bureau: "Initially [the student] behaved very awkwardly and spoke about personal freedom, freedom of speech, freedom of movement, things he said he's missing here and that Western countries have." Freedom of expression: the court was not impressed. It sentenced the student to one year in prison followed by two years' probation.

In East Berlin, a newly recruited agent – Aleksander Radler – was already making his mark, infiltrating the murky world of escape networks. And in Siegfried Krügel's Leipzig, far from the border with West Germany, the student Müller was far from the only one dreaming of freedom. Often the dreams didn't extend to freedom of speech or freedom of movement; East Germans just wanted the liberty to make their own daily decisions. Such desires had a habit of being expressed at church events. The Church Bureau dispatched IM Lorac on a routine assignment, to monitor a church youth event. It was well-attended; some 250 teenagers had turned up. A pastor got up to speak. "It's very nice that you like to come to the church's events, because it's voluntary," he told the teenagers. "And that at a time when you mostly have to do what you don't want to do. But it's also nice, for once, to do what you want to do." Were West Germans to listen in, they would consider the pastor's speech unremarkable. But to the Stasi, they were poison. "It's nice to be able to do what you want to do": such words might inspire East Germany's youth to form human rights groups, to flee the country or to start organizing public protests. IM Lorac reported: "As he [the pastor] received strong applause, he became frightened and realized what he had said."

CHAPTER 3

A GROWING THREAT: SEMINARIES

By the late sixties, Joachim Wiegand was firmly convinced that persecuting Christians held no prospect of success. Indeed, he was certain that punishment and discrimination merely encouraged Christians and their many international friends to try to defeat communism. Fortunately for Wiegand, the MfS top brass had drawn a similar conclusion and begun shifting the Agency's focus from jailing opponents to nipping criticism in the bud. That meant expansion of its surveillance – more officers and more informants.

"If somebody wants to pray and go to church, let him pray; and the GDR built new churches," he tells me. "My strategy was not to attack the church but to try to win their people over." In short, Wiegand wanted to charm clerics into working for him. There would be fewer heavy-handed threats, less blackmail, but more flattery and bribery.

A growing worry for the Stasi was the Lutherans' expanding pastor-training programme. Before the Berlin Wall was built, many West German pastors who couldn't get a job in West Germany, or who simply wanted to do a good deed, relocated to East Germany for several years. Horst Kasner – the father of three children including Angela, today known around the world as Angela Merkel – was one of the pastors who had taken this step. But when the Wall was built, the pastors faced enormous difficulties returning to West Germany. Understandably, the supply of West German pastors willing to make the move without the chance to return almost completely dried up.

To alleviate the resulting pastor shortage, East Germany's Lutherans opened several new seminaries. By 1969, the seminaries were training several hundred students, including young men and women who hadn't originally considered ordained ministry but had opted for pastor training because the church was one of very few spaces that provided some degree of freedom. Many other seminarians had been barred from attending regular universities after refusing to join the FDJ, refusing to perform military service or otherwise showing lacking commitment to the German Democratic Republic.[36] And unlike universities, the seminaries offered plenty of academic freedom. That, too, made them attractive even to students who would have been able to attend university.

"The idea was, if you don't show loyalty to the government, the government won't show loyalty to you," Wolf Krötke tells me. After being released from prison for the offence of having written a poem critical of the regime, Krötke had managed to gain his theology degree at a university, but he was pretty sure that he would never be allowed to teach at one.

---

36   The FDJ (*Freie Deutsche Jugend*, Free German Youth) was a socialist youth organization. It was the only youth organization recognized by the East German government; membership was a must for teenagers who didn't want to ruin their career prospects. Angela Merkel was a functionary in her local FDJ group. "DDR-Vergangenheit holt Merkel ein", NTV, 13 May 2013, https://www.n-tv.de/politik/Nichts-verheimlicht-nicht-alles-erzaehlt-article10631536.html (accessed 21 May 2019).

And the more universities enforced a strict curriculum, the more attractive the seminaries were becoming. "With the word freedom you can quickly win the youth over," IM Lorac told Lieutenant Kunth. "That can't end well." One of the agent's sons was by now also training to become a pastor and theologian in Leipzig, the Karl Marx University, an institution ordinarily in line with the regime. But even at the Karl Marx University, there were some opposition-minded students, the Church Bureau had learned. Kunth asked IM Lorac to assess the current third year-class via his son.

Wiegand was already well aware of the seminaries' subversive nature. "Many people who had capsized in some shape or form ended up in the Lutheran Church," he tells me. "These were people who, for example, were not allowed to study medicine or not allowed to attend university. They were broken individuals. They usually ended up in the church's educational system, but they couldn't deal with their hate and their rage." As result, he explains, they fought against their own country "out of personal conviction, writing pamphlets and so forth. These schools were the companions of the opposition here in the GDR. The church was pleased when it got such people, especially since they were not stupid."

When I ask for examples, he mentions Vera Lengsfeld, who was to become one of East Germany's most vocal dissidents. "Her father was one of us," he says. "Because she had problems at home, she ended up in the opposition movement. Such disruptions in the personality development brought people to the church."[37]

Until 1969, when she was seventeen years old, Vera had been unaware that Franz Lengsfeld was an MfS officer. Then she happened upon his work ID. Her budding opposition gathered steam. Eventually, she enrolled at the Sprachenkonvikt, a church-run seminary in East Berlin.

---

37   During East German times, Lengsfeld was known under her married name, Wollenberger.

Another of these "capsized existences" was Rainer Eppelmann, a carpenter's son from East Berlin. Finding himself cut off from his West Berlin high school after the Wall was built, Eppelmann at first had to find a new high school in East Berlin. That had proved challenging for a teenager who had not only refused to join the FDJ but had also attended school in West Berlin. The East German authorities had instead assigned Eppelmann a job as a thatcher's aide; he later trained as a bricklayer.

"The idea was that we had to prove ourselves since we were traitors," Eppelmann tells me, referring to himself and other teenagers attending school in West Berlin. Eppelmann and I are meeting at the Federal Foundation for the Study of Communist Dictatorship in East Germany, a government-funded agency that promotes public awareness of East Germany's authoritarian system.[38] Though he bears a stunning resemblance to Vladimir Lenin, he remains adamantly opposed to the communist rule the Russian revolutionary leader preached.

But blue-collar work had failed to make young Eppelmann an obedient citizen. By 1966, aged twenty-three, he was a committed foe of the regime. Like many other Christians, Eppelmann had refused to carry weapons during his military service, opting instead to be a construction soldier. But he had also refused to swear the mandatory conscript oath to the East German government. As a result, the authorities had jailed him for eight months.

After being released from prison, Eppelmann had to decide what to do. "I had to ask myself, what will you do in this enclosed country?" he tells me. "And what do you do not just to earn a living but also in the hope of being content and, occasionally, even happy? The only thing I could think of was being a pastor." He enrolled at the Paulinum, a Lutheran seminary in East Berlin.

Seeing the independent seminaries attract a motley crew of bright men

---

38   *Bundesstiftung zur Aufarbeitung der SED-Diktatur.*

and women, clerics in the Stasi's fold were trying to help. At the Humboldt University, theology professor Hans-George Fritzsche – IM Fritz – had already provided the Church Bureau with advice on how to harm the Sprachenkonvikt. And the dean of the Humboldt's theology department, Professor Hans Hinrich Jenssen, had written to the government's top official for church affairs proposing measures to stop the seminaries' "boundless expansion".[39]

39   Wolf Krötke, "*Das Profil des Berliner Sprachenkonvikts für die selbständige Theologenausbildung in der DDR*", http://www.theologischeskonvikt.de/fileadmin/ekbo/ mandant/theologischeskonvikt.de/netblast/My_files/Kr_otke-Profil_des_Berliner_ Sprachenkonvikts.pdf (accessed 3 May 2019).

CHAPTER 4

THE FINE ART OF RECRUITING

"How do you recruit an informant?" I ask Wiegand. Meticulous research is crucial, he explains: "Where does he live? What sort of work does he do? What sort of connections does he have? Does he have a family? What are his interests, opinions, preferences? How is his marriage going? What sort of things would he like to have or achieve? Then you look for a reason to have an initial conversation with him." Though you get much of this information from existing agents, they don't know whom you're planning to recruit – and they definitely don't know when the prospective recruit crosses the line and becomes an agent.

What were his interests, opinions, how is his marriage going? Ah, a gold mine. Perhaps a pastor didn't much like his colleagues or his bishop; perhaps he felt he was being passed over in favour of those less qualified than him? The Stasi knew about it and, as the number of informants grew, it became easier recruit new ones. But before PCs and Excel sheets, how did the officers keep track of whom they were tracking through their agents and everyone was connected to others? There was a method for that too.

For each person in its system – that is, anyone it was tracking, anyone associated with that person, and all its agents and potential recruits – the Stasi maintained a large sheet, called a WKW, *Wer Kennt Wen* (who knows whom).

Once a Church Bureau officer had decided to approach a prospective agent, he scheduled a discreet meeting with the pastor; in a restaurant, perhaps, or in the pastor's office. They chatted about generalities, perhaps a bit about the need to help East Germany survive and thrive, about the pastor's work situation, his family, his marriage. And then? "You go and see the person, chat for a couple of hours in order to establish contact or deepen your friendship with him," Wiegand tells me. "If you establish a good relationship, things go beyond general conversations. You give the person small gifts, ask how their family is doing, if the son wants to attend university you arrange a place for him." That was a key moment. Stasi officers could help. "Someone in my position has the privilege of making things happen," Wiegand says. "Sometimes it violated laws and regulations, for example the school regulation and the university regulation, but if it benefits the cause? You do what you have to do. There's an element of 'you give me, I give you.'"

"I began our conversation by saying that we would like to speak to progressive theologians and inform ourselves about a few things," logged Church Bureau Lieutenant Hübner in 1956 after his first meeting with Hans-Georg Fritzsche, then a thirty-year-old theologian at East Berlin's famous Humboldt University. The Humboldt was founded by the nineteenth-century Prussian educational reformer, Wilhelm von Humboldt and, by the twentieth century, the university had established itself as one of the world's leading seats of learning. To teach at the Humboldt was to have reached the highest echelons of German academia.

Fritzsche was not hostile to his unexpected visitor, but was a rather conservative theologian. Hübner had planned ahead. "In response to his question as to why I had come to him and not to somebody else, I said that he had been described to us as trustworthy and somebody who has a progressive attitude towards our democratic development," he noted.

This was flattery, and it worked. Hübner had made the short journey from the Normannenstrasse to the Humboldt's theology department, precisely because the Stasi needed informants in West-leaning, conservative church circles. Fritzsche fit the bill perfectly. People like him, who had an affinity for Western Europe and even America, had friends or colleagues there, or had perhaps even visited themselves, offered just the connections the Stasi wanted. If recruited, they would inform on their friends, acquaintances, and colleagues and might even act as agent provocateurs in their circles. And they could easily be swayed by Western consumer goods. Fritzsche had no inkling that his arch-enemy on the theology faculty, the staunch communist Hanfried Müller, was already a Stasi agent.[40]

Several years later, Master Sergeant Ollik drove to a rural church near the northern port city of Stralsund, hoping to chat to the pastor, Siegfried Plath. Plath was conducting a confirmation class when Ollik arrived, but the officer politely introduced himself anyway, giving his name as Hiller. The pastor invited the officer to wait in his office, adjacent to the classroom. The confirmation class over, Plath joined the officer. The pair chatted about current issues in local politics.

"His personal room is not identifiable as that of a clergyman", noted Ollik in Plath's new file. "Only a small wooden cross serves as a reminder of the church." As for his personal qualities, Ollik observed that "speaking with him, one wouldn't know that one is speaking with a clergyman", adding that Plath made an intelligent impression that was further supported by his diction. "He said that he could have stayed in Sweden [where he had been living] but as a German he wants to serve his people and contribute to improvement", noted Ollik. Plath had a progressive approach and "the

---

40   Müller, IM Hans Meier, had been recruited in 1954.

overall impression is good", he summarized. Under the rubric "further observations" he added that Pastor Plath "is probably a heavy smoker, as he accepted every offered cigarette without hesitation". Such things were useful ammunition in recruitment pitches.

Although the conversation was cordial, Plath couldn't linger: he had another meeting. "I deeply regretted to have come at such an inconvenient time as I would have liked to speak with him about other problems", noted Ollik. "P. responded that perhaps another day would be more suitable, as one could continue the conversation then." Evaluating the pastor's attitude, Ollik concluded: "In his whole behaviour he is polite and friendly, but not in an exaggerated manner." Plath volunteering to remain in contact was an excellent sign. "Maintain contact", Ollik suggested in his report.

As Plath rose through the ranks of the church, he would become one of the Stasi's most trusted informants. His file contains numerous receipts for cigars, gifts from his handlers. Plath's cover name: IM Hiller. He must really have liked his handler.

Ollik had conducted meticulous research before meeting with Plath, identifying him as "positive" and "open-minded" (positive and open-minded towards the regime, that is). In time, all Church Bureau officers learned to evaluate potential targets rigorously before approaching them.

Wiegand recalls another early meeting: "Right at the beginning [of my time at Department XX/4] I had an initial conversation with a pastor, and he said, 'If you hadn't showed me your MfS ID I would have been able to talk, but now I can't. Now I have to tell my bishop.'" For future meetings, the officer presented an ID from the foreign ministry or the ministry of church affairs. "I'd say, for example, 'you have contacts with Geneva [the seat of the World Council of Churches], and you're going to Geneva for such and such conference. Perhaps we could have a chat?'" he explains. "Then we'd talk and after a while he'd realize that I worked for the MfS. But since I didn't say that I was from the MfS, he didn't have to feel guilty for talking to me, and I got what I needed. A number of pastors would say, 'I can imagine where you're from, but don't tell me.' That way they didn't have to report the contact to their superiors."

It was "don't ask, don't tell", East German-style. Honest pastors, of course, still reported the conversation, whether or not the officer showed a Stasi ID and, if the bishop was an upright man and not a Stasi informant himself, he backed the pastor up. But, as the Ministry's voluminous files show, many pastors eagerly took the bait. The trick even proved useful in West Germany, where Department XX/4 managed to recruit pastor spies despite not being able to exert any pressure whatsoever. In 1987, the Church Bureau had eleven West German agents on its rolls.[41]

"But surely potential recruits must quickly have recognized where you really worked?" I ask Wiegand. "Of course," he says. The colonel possesses a sharp mind and astonishing memory and has the erect bearing of a military man. To the pastors it must have been immediately obvious where he worked. But he has a polite and outgoing manner. The many men (and some women) who chose to talk to him, even become his agents, knew well what they were doing – and did it anyway.

But it wouldn't be intelligence work if it weren't a bit dirty. "I'll be honest and say that we sometimes applied a bit of pressure," Wiegand adds. He doesn't specify the pressure but there were, of course, the pastors who had been caught visiting red-light districts and were thus vulnerable. And the ones who wanted something – like assistance with a better career – from the government. In his memoirs, Klaus Rossberg provides more details: "We kept expanding the circle of our IMs and contact persons in all areas and convinced hesitant ones both with our arguments by confronting them with compromising materials, for example moral lapses or having helped themselves to church funds."[42]

---

41   Auerbach et al, *Hauptabteilung XX*, p. 100.
42   Rossberg and Richter, *Das Kreuz mit dem Kreuz*, p. 35.

Like the CIA, the Church Bureau also operated front publications promoting certain policies and groups and discrediting others. Wiegand mentions the journal *Christliche Verantwortung* (Christian Responsibility). Founded in 1965, *Christian Responsibility* was ostensibly published by Jehovah's Witnesses for Jehovah's Witnesses, but behind it was Department XX/4. Even more than the Lutherans, East Germany's Jehovah's Witnesses caused a constant headache for the government, with their strong links to the United States and their refusal to perform military service. We created *Christliche Verantwortung* with former Jehovah's Witnesses," Wiegand tells me. "We gave them office space, money and so on to work against the Jehovah's Witnesses."

In Moscow, the KGB was even more concerned about the Jehovah's Witnesses. Adherents were given lengthy sentences in prisons and penal camps. One of its leaders, whom the KGB had code-named PAVEL, was suspected by the authorities of "drawing new members into the sect, conducting illegal gatherings, inducing young believers to refuse to serve in the army, holding and disseminating religious literature".[43] The KGB subjected PAVEL to a vicious defamation campaign where even his children signed a newspaper article denouncing him.[44] Yet most Witnesses in the Soviet Union stoically stuck to their faith.

Today, such measures would be called disinformation or information warfare. The MfS used the term "subversive measure". "It's not a nice word, but when you work for The Firm, you have to do it," Wiegand says. Like intelligence officers around the world, MfS employees referred – and still refer – to their agency as The Firm.

As far as the colonel is concerned, he had a job to do, and he intended to do it well. If the weaknesses of others facilitated that, it didn't bother

---

43   Christopher Andrew and Vasili Mitrokhin, *The Mitrokhin Archive* (London: Penguin Books, 2000), p. 660.

44   Andrew and Mitrokhin, *The Mitrokhin Archive,* p. 660.

him or his colleagues. Some pastors could have given their recruiter the cold shoulder, and many did, obeying the church's rule of always telling the Stasi officer that they'd report his visit to their bishop. "Please don't take it personally, but I want absolutely nothing to do with the institution you represent," a brave pastor named Heinrich Rathke told Rossberg and his colleague Harry Otto when they explained the nature of their visit.[45]

It's getting dark outside, but here in Wiegand's living room it's toasty. He pulls out several issues of a scholarly journal edited by a group of pastors and theologians close to the government (and some of them close to the Stasi too). The group included Horst Kasner. Pastor Kasner "was pro-GDR, a peace pastor," Wiegand says. The periodicals have been sent to his home address, years after East Germany's collapse. Wiegand's friends have remained loyal to him.

Like detectives Thomson and Thompson in the Tintin comic books, the Stasi's task was to know everything. After abandoning the strategy of primarily jailing disobedient Christians, the Church Bureau focused on recruiting better IMs. By 1971, it still only had 144 IMs regularly providing reports, but they were increasingly high-ranking and now included two Lutheran bishops who could influence church decision-making as well.[46] Indeed, the Church Bureau operated on two tracks: gathering information on church operations, and influencing them.[47] However, early on, Erich Mielke – Minister of State Security – had decided that regular pastors were of more use to the Stasi than bishops or other high-ranking clergy. Many bishops were too closely connected to their bishop colleagues in West Germany, he decreed, and their "reactionary activities are contrasted by the majority of the faithful, who are in favour of peace".[48] Supporting peace meant supporting East Germany.

---

45   Rossberg and Richter, *Das Kreuz mit dem Kreuz*, p. 81.

46   Auerbach, *Hauptabteilung XX*, p. 96.

47   See for example Rossberg and Richter, *Das Kreuz mit dem Kreuz*, p. 45.

48   Rossberg and Richter, *Das Kreuz mit dem Kreuz*, p. 30.

Major Rossberg describes how he and other Church Bureau officers would constantly travel around the country to monitor activities, and "everywhere were 'our' church people with a certain influence".[49] They also cultivated more IMs in opposition-leaning groups operating under church auspices. When Vera Lengsfeld married fellow opposition activist Knud Wollenberger in 1980, she had no way of knowing that he would spend years reporting on her to the Stasi.

Another Stasi task was, of course, to communicate its findings upwards. The country's leaders needed to be informed about the mood of the people, or otherwise the intelligence-gathering would be pointless. As the Church Bureau's director during the turbulent eighties, Wiegand regularly provided highlights of his department's findings to officials including Werner Jarowinsky, the SED official in charge of church matters. "We delivered information to the party leadership about forty to fifty times per year," he explains. "It wasn't only information about the church. It was also an opportunity to highlight things that the politicians were doing wrong and that had come to our attention."

"What sort of things?" I ask. "If people are protesting because they're against something, we can't fix that by arresting them," he explains. "It requires a political solution." But the socialist rulers weren't keen to listen to the grass roots' voices, even if the information was relayed by the Stasi. "They rarely accepted our suggestions," Wiegand sighs. Rossberg remembers the situation similarly: "Wiegand often returned in despair from his talks with Jarowinsky, who had again understood nothing and taken the wrong decisions. Wiegand, in particular, presented our suggestions for reforms of society time and again, which required plenty of courage given the increasingly obstinate leadership."[50]

Wiegand and I have been talking for several hours. Gerda has returned from her errands and is still making herself busy around the apartment. At no point does she check in to see what we're discussing. More than four decades

---

49   Rossberg and Richter, *Das Kreuz mit dem Kreuz*, p. 35.
50   Rossberg and Richter, *Das Kreuz mit dem Kreuz*, p. 47.

as the wife of a Stasi officer have instilled in her a habit of discretion.

Our conversation turns to Wolfgang Schnur, a lawyer who for decades represented opposition-leaning pastors and other dissidents – and who, thanks to his privileged access to church decision-making, provided the Stasi with extraordinary insights. Schnur was a star agent. "You should really take a look at his file," says Wiegand, who otherwise displays the detached attitude of a professional intelligence officer when it comes to agents' findings. "It will open your eyes." By 1987, Schnur's reports filled a whole cabinet in Wiegand's office. Because Schnur is dead, Wiegand considers himself released from his vow of secrecy towards the Church Bureau's agents. If the agent is still alive, he refuses to discuss any details I don't already know. In some cases – when the agent's family can be significantly harmed by revelations, I surmise – he declines to provide details about deceased collaborators as well.

Though Schnur was prolific, at the government agency in charge of the Stasi's files, one cabinet is a tiny percentage. The information provided by 620,000 IMs between 1950 and 1989 fill 111 kilometres of files in the agency archives (the Federal Commissioner for the Records of the State Security Service of the former German Democratic Republic). Most people simply call it the Gauck Agency, after its first director, Pastor Joachim Gauck.

The Church Bureau's officers were clearly productive. In the late sixties, the Bureau had fifty-three officers; by 1971, there were still only seventy-eight of them.[51] By 1988, the Bureau had forty-four full-time staff in East Berlin and six to nine staff in each of its eight regional offices around the country.[52] In addition, the department had ten undercover officers who worked in church institutions, and six officer students.[53] Thirty of the staff were "useful colleagues", as Wiegand explains. Fourteen of the officers led the Bureau's departments: two in charge of the free-church section, for example; two in

51   Auerbach et al, *Hauptabteilung XX*, p. 95.
52   Auerbach et al, *Hauptabteilung XX*, p. 100.
53   Auerbach et al, *Hauptabteilung XX*, p. 99.

charge of the Catholic department and two in charge of the Lutherans.

Two directors for each type of faith: a nicely symmetrical set-up, just as it had been two decades previously. But, in truth, it would have been better to have a smaller Catholic unit and more staff in the Lutheran section. East Germany had many more Lutherans than Catholics, and the Lutherans were far more politically active. Their pastors often used the pulpit for veiled criticism of the government. Many of their teenagers attended confirmation classes in addition to participating in the government's *de facto* mandatory secular confirmation, the *Jugendweihe*. Some, including the then Angela Kasner, even refused to do the *Jugendweihe* and opted for Christian confirmation only. And because the church was somewhat protected from government interference, people opposed to the regime for all kinds of reasons were drawn to it, not only as seminarians and pastors, but as congregation members as well. In the seventies and eighties, Lutheran churches would host groups concerned with the environment, human rights, or the global arms race.

And while many Catholic priests and laypeople in East Germany and elsewhere beyond the Iron Curtain were passionately opposed to their communist regimes, they saw their faith as largely a liturgical and diaconal one. By contrast, many Lutheran pastors argued that they had a wider role, one reaching outside the church building, and acted as community organizers as well. Luther had, after all, taught that there were two kingdoms – the kingdom of God and the secular kingdom – and that Christians should be engaged with both.[54] To some East German pastors and Lutheran laypeople, that even meant that they should openly oppose the regime.

Rather logically, then, it was the Lutherans that took up most of the Church Bureau's attention. When it came to agent recruitment, the Bureau's officers turned their attention to a particular clergyman for a variety of reasons: he could influence the right people, had connections abroad and

---

54   Robert Kolb, Irene Dingel and Lubomír Batka, *The Oxford Handbook of Martin Luther's Theology* (Oxford: Oxford University Press, 2014), p. 207.

showed potential to rise through the church ranks.

And if the clergyman was a desirable recruit but unlikely to respond to officers' pitch about aiding the GDR and world peace, the officer applied a bit of pressure. "In some cases, we'd have evidence of goods being smuggled so we'd tell the person, 'we know you're smuggling such and such goods, and please feel free to go home, but let's keep in touch'", explains Wiegand matter-of-factly, as if such talks are the most natural thing in the world. Ah, the light touch again. "We'd research their personal connections," Wiegand adds. "People had loads of connections to the Federal Republic [West Germany]. You can't simply cut a country into two. If you do your research and know what you want, you'll find things to talk about [with potential agents]."

Even more useful, from the Normannenstrasse's perspective, were family connections in West Germany. Sometimes, West Germans – spoiled as they were by democracy and freedom – make silly mistakes that the Stasi could leverage. Wiegand explains: "We could say, 'Your [West German] uncle who works for the police in Hamburg – I'd like to chat with him.' In this particular case, the uncle had travelled to the GDR without permission from his employer. As a result, this man and his uncle were more inclined to speak with us. Contacts didn't happen just like that; you had to do your homework."

Department XX/4 kept tabs on clergymen's more significant shortcomings as well. If a pastor, a theology professor, or a bishop had frequented the country's red-light districts, if he'd helped himself to money from the church's bank account, the Stasi knew about it.

Indeed, the Stasi was equipped with informants among cops and sex workers. The letters "HWG" in a prospective informant's file stood for *Person mit häufig wechselndem Geschlechtspartner*, a person with frequently changing sexual partners. Having a HWG annotation in one's Stasi file was disastrous. A clergyman with an HWG annotation in his file had no choice but to become an informant or otherwise face the humiliation of confessing to his bishop.

Many chose the former. One of them, a certain Oberkirchenrat Ernst-Eugen Meckel, became an industrious IM.[55] "Of course he was in a position of coercion, but he also felt – as he subsequently told us – that he could find a common language with us in matters of church politics," remembers Rossberg, who recruited the cleric.[56] Meckel went on to influence church decisions on his handlers' instructions, brought them internal church documents, and introduced them to West German church officials who might be open to recruitment. The two men sometimes dined together and took day trips in the Berlin region. It was a cordial relationship. Oberkirchenrat Meckel even helped a stunning undercover Stasi officer get a job at the Lutheran Church's Berlin headquarters. Her task: seducing clergymen.[57]

Klaus Rossberg remembers another cleric with the dreaded HWG annotation. This pastor reacted very differently: instead of agreeing to report for the Church Bureau, he immediately informed the officer that he would instead confess to his bishop.[58] His name was Horst Kasner. Had he really been caught in a HWG situation, or was an IM trying to set him up? I ask Wiegand, but he refuses to reveal any details that I don't already know.

In 1975, the East German Catholic Bishops' conference appointed Prälat (Monsignor) Paul Dissemond as its new permanent secretary. Like his predecessor, Dissemond was expected to maintain official contacts with the Ministry for State Security – there was no way around it. Joachim Meisner, the internationally prominent bishop of Erfurt who had completed his doctorate in Rome, made Dissemond swear that he had no secret contacts with the Stasi. Unfortunately for the bishop, Dissemond was already a Church Bureau agent.

---

55   *Oberkirchenrat* is a senior clergy rank.
56   Rossberg and Richter, *Das Kreuz mit dem Kreuz*, p. 81.
57   "Sex-Partys bei 'Micha'", *Spiegel Online*, 21 September 1992, http://www.spiegel. de/spiegel/print/d-9285961.html (accessed 3 May 2019).
58   Rossberg and Richter, *Das Kreuz mit dem Kreuz*, p. 81.

Dissemond kept up his Stasi work, for example informing the Church Bureau that Meisner "thinks he's the greatest".

Dissemond's undercover work was, however, an exception: the Catholic Church in East Germany was so non-threatening that it didn't require much subversion. "In general, the Catholic Church in the GDR was apolitical," Wiegand tells me. "They did religion, which was fine. They had apostolic administrations, since the Vatican didn't recognize the GDR, and they had close contacts with the Catholic Church in West Germany." But the Catholics steered clear of politics. "For example, when Catholic hospitals in the GDR needed equipment or medicine, they received it from West Germany, or when the Catholic university bookshop in Erfurt needed books, they got them from West Germany," Wiegand explains. "It had to be approved by us, but we said, 'be sensible', and approved it."

One day in the early eighties, Colonel Wiegand went to see Meisner. The bishop had continued his stellar career and was now Bishop of Berlin and chairman of the bishops' conference. Pope John Paul II had also made him a cardinal. Wiegand went to see the cardinal armed with information from two IMs in Meisner's office as well as from the East German customs agency. "I said, 'here in Berlin there's somebody who regularly goes to West Berlin and engages in currency manipulation.' It was in the order of 100,000 marks. I said, 'Either we put him in jail for five to six years or you give us 200,000 Westmark and minimize your attacks on the [East German] government.' 'Fine, we'll do that,' answered the bishop."[59] But this was a rare Stasi interaction with the Catholic Church.

Department XX/4 was not alone in fighting the rebellious Lutherans. The government branded Lutheran youth groups illegal organizations, making

---

59   Cardinal Meisner died in July 2017. I didn't have a chance to ask him about Wiegand's report. "Erzbistum Berlin trauert um Kardinal Meisner", Erzbistum Berlin, 5 July 2017, https://www.erzbistumberlin.de/medien/pressestelle/aktuelle-pressemeldungen/ pressemeldung/news-title/erzbistum-berlin-trauert-um-kardinal-meisnerein-requiem-13-juli-2017-1800-uhr-in-der-st-h/ (accessed 3 May 2019).

membership a criminal offence, and banned many Lutheran students – especially those who hadn't done the *Jugendweihe* – from attending university. But judging from the number of environmental and human rights groups hosted by parishes – and attracting an even wider audience – the efforts were clearly counterproductive.

Department XX/4 also ran what, in MfS parlance, was called an evaluation unit. Today, intelligence officers can access public information with the click of a mouse, but before the internet, tracking and analysing international news was a task for full-time experts. The Church Bureau's evaluation unit did exactly that. Five of Department XX/4 staff members located in the East Berlin suburb of Pankow were in charge of collecting and assessing religious news from radio, TV, and newspapers. They even listened to the Vatican's broadcasts. As always, the full-time staff were assisted by IMs, including two theology professors at Humboldt University.

On 16 October 1978, the Pankow analysts were watching TV coverage of the papal conclave in Rome. The cardinals had convened in the Sistine Chapel on 14 October. The first ballot had been unsuccessful. The second one too. Around the world, analysts, political leaders and the faithful were in suspense. Who would replace John Paul I, who had died after just thirty-three days? Like everyone else, the Pankow analysts were expecting the cardinals to elect another Italian. That had, after all, been the custom for the past four centuries. Then white smoke emerged from the roof of the Sistine Chapel: a new pope had been elected.

Soon a cardinal emerged on the balcony of St Peter's basilica and pronounced the electric words, "*Habemus Papam*". The crowd outside cheered wildly. But when the cardinal spoke the name of the new pope, there was confusion among the spectators: far from announcing an Italian pope, the cardinal pronounced a Polish name: Karol Wojtyła.

Was it good news for the Soviet bloc that one of its priests had been elected to the most powerful position in global Christianity? Or, on the contrary, would it highlight the persecution of Christians in communist countries? The following day, the Soviet ambassador to Warsaw forwarded to Moscow the Polish secret police's assessment of Wojtyła. He was a "virulent anti-communist", Ambassador Boris Aristov reported.[60] The Polish secret police, Służba Bezpieczeństwa, had been keeping Wojtyła under surveillance for years, and the KGB had a thick file on him too. But in the confusion following Wojtyła's unprecedented election, the Pankow team beat the Poles. Within two hours it had written a detailed memo on the Polish cardinal, which the Church Bureau dispatched to Erich Honecker (East Germany's leader). Wojtyła chose the name Jean Paul II.

Many years later, thanks to Dissemond, Wiegand and his colleagues knew in advance that Pope John Paul II had decided to appoint Cardinal Meisner archbishop of Cologne, the most powerful position in Germany's Roman Catholic Church.

Like other Western diplomats, Wayne Merry – posted to the United States embassy in East Berlin in the late seventies and early eighties – maintained relations with East German pastors and other Christians. He summarizes how one of them, an opposition-minded pastor named Curt Stauss, viewed Christianity: Stauss, Merry says, engaged in activities that were not what one might call church in the traditional sense. Wiegand provides a similar evaluation: "The Lutheran Church was a different matter, because it was much more political than the Catholic Church."

I take the high-speed train to Halle, the old university town some two hours south-west of Berlin where the composer George Frederic Handel was born almost four centuries ago. I've come to see Curt Stauss, who now lives here. A tall, soft-spoken man in his early sixties, Stauss is the quintessential Lutheran pastor: wearing a sweater and jeans, no clerical collar, and exuding an air of kindness, he could easily pass for a high school teacher or an environmental activist. On this day as on most days, Pastor

---

60   Andrew and Mitrokhin, *The Mitrokhin Archive*, p. 660.

Stauss is getting around Halle on his bike. In addition to parish work, he leads his diocese's outreach efforts to Stasi pastors' victims. Personally, though, Stauss frowns at the term "victim", preferring instead the term "those spied upon". It's unwieldy in English, but in German it's one handy word: *die Bespitzelten*. By calling yourself a victim, he explains, you make yourself a passive participant in your fate; you let the IMs who reported on you determine your life.

Stauss was the only child of a single mother who was a passionate pacifist and social democrat. As a teenager, he had decided that while he was not completely enamoured with what he knew about West Germany, there were many things in the German Democratic Republic that were plain wrong. Its heavily militarized society, for example, which included military drills in schools and paramilitary units in workplaces. Stauss even dared decline membership in the socialist children's organization, the Pioneers, and refused to participate in the *Jugendweihe*. As a result, he was barred from academic-track high school, instead having to train as a car mechanic. That meant he would not be able to follow his calling and study theology. "That's not as bad as it sounds," his mother consoled him. "In the GDR, there's no future for the church. You have to learn a profession."

In 1967, it was time for car mechanic Curt Stauss to perform mandatory military service. But when summoned for the armed forces' assessment, Stauss told the panel that he was a conscientious objector and would refuse to serve.

Soon after his interview with the assessment board, one of its members contacted him. "I found your arguments very interesting," the friendly man said. "Would you like to meet?" Stauss, excited by this unexpectedly positive reaction to the refusal he'd been certain would only bring him further trouble, happily agreed to meet in a local restaurant. He told the fatherly man about his strong support of world peace. Only gradually did it dawn on him that his friendly listener was a Stasi officer and that the man was making a recruitment overture. Smiling, the officer asked Stauss to phone him if he would like to follow up. No threats, just a handshake and a phone number. Stauss knew that assisting the Stasi would enable him to finish his high school degree and gain admission to university. But he was certain that he wanted nothing to do with it. He didn't call the friendly man.

In the end, Stauss did manage to become a pastor by attending one of the Lutherans' high schools followed by seminary training. And his opposition to the regime remained firm. As a result, he sometimes found that his diary and letters had been opened, his apartment searched and his phone bugged. Before turning the ignition key in his Trabant, car mechanic Stauss would always make sure the car had not been tinkered with.

Often, though, the officer's friendly words fell on fertile soil. Back in East Berlin several years previously, Hans-Georg Fritzsche griped about some of his colleagues in the theology department, then complained about how the department was divided into two camps, "the progressive ones and the ones who have to criticize and whine about everything". He told Stasi officer Hübner about three professors who were "just tolerated but don't have any academic expertise to speak of". As the two men chatted away, Hübner mentioned "foreign intelligence agencies' hostile activities" in East Germany, giving examples of how they worked. What a coincidence: Fritzsche had a student who fitted that pattern. When Hübner asked the professor if he would be willing to "support our work", Fritzsche agreed. While theorizing on the problem of evil, his academic specialty, Fritzsche became a diligent agent.

Several months after Fritzsche's recruitment, when a debate about NATO's use of chaplains was causing friction between East and West German Lutherans, Fritzsche briefed Hübner as to who stood where on the matter. He also mentioned that a certain bishop was going to retire. The likely successor, Fritsche told Hübner, had certain prejudices vis-à-vis the GDR but was better than the other candidate. Then, as they were dining in a local restaurant in East Berlin, Professor Fritzsche casually mentioned that there was another matter on his mind: a female relative had failed to win a place in medical school. Could the Stasi help? Hübner promised to try. A give and take, as Wiegand might call it.

Youthful sins? Within Department XX/4, there was the possibility of redemption not just for conscientious objectors like Curt Stauss – though he turned it down – but for other kinds of youngsters in trouble as well. "I, Frank Stolt, born on 24 October 1955 in Klosterheide, have through my actions in the past put myself in conflict with the GDR", wrote a young man on 3 January 1971, sitting in a Stasi office. He was barely seventeen years old. "I illegally acquired a West German passport." The teenager went on to detail how he came to possess West German, American, French, Danish, Austrian, Italian and Dutch currency. "I planned an illegal border crossing [to the West]", he wrote. "I deeply regret my actions. I am a citizen of the GDR and as such I have the duty to live and work in the German Democratic Republic according to its social norms." According to Stasi Lieutenant Stumpf in an accompanying document, Stolt had wanted to get a better life for himself than what he saw in East Germany. The teenager had enthusiastically watched spy movies and read every spy book he could get his hands on. Soon Stolt had begun seeing himself as one of the movie protagonists and started planning an escape to the West. One cannot but admire the industriousness of young Frank Stolt in his pursuit of the free world so near him, yet so far behind that impenetrable wall.

At home in East Berlin, to achieve his goal, Stolt had begun approaching any tourist speaking a language he identified as being Western European. After offering himself as their tour guide, he showed them around and they paid him in their currency. Even more creatively, he asked for their addresses and remained in touch: they would be useful contacts as he planned his escape to Western Europe.

Unfortunately, the all-seeing Stasi caught Stolt. But the young man was told that there was a way for him to redeem himself. "I agree with the road to redress suggested by the Ministry for State Security and commit myself to cooperation with the Ministry for State Security", wrote Stolt in his neat pupil's handwriting. "This is, I now understand, the most appropriate way of realizing my wish to become a spy." Taking on the father role that so many Stasi handlers played vis-à-vis their spies, Lieutenant Stumpf advised the intelligent but somewhat rebellious pupil that in order to be a successful informant, he needed to do well in school and finish his vocational training.

By 1974, Stolt – codename IM Hermann Schneider – had failed in vocational school. But not to worry, he told Stumpf: how about I become a preacher instead? That October, he enrolled at the Paulinum, the Lutheran seminary in Berlin that Rainer Eppelmann had also attended. "The IM considers his work in a church institution and his current studies at the preacher school Paulinum an MfS task", noted Stumpf some time later. "He assesses that this way he can work for the MfS even better than heretofore, as he has acquired the necessary foundation for it."

It was a highly accurate assessment. Stumpf noted that at the Paulinum the young man had come into his own, his intelligence had come to the fore, and he was making many new friends. On the negative side, Stolt tended towards dangerous spontaneity. "It is therefore particularly important to give the educational side particular attention," Stumpf advised.

Thanks to the officer's mentorship, Stolt soon joined the ranks of the clergy. As a youth pastor in East Berlin, he reported on the Lutheran Church's policy conferences – so-called synods – and made great efforts befriending foreign diplomats. While still a seminarian, Stolt had met Wayne Merry, the young US diplomat who had become friends with Curt Stauss. But Merry felt uneasy about Stolt and wondered why he was so eager to make his acquaintance.

Merry resolved to find out more before having any further conversations with Stolt. He asked Stauss if he knew anything about the young man. After several days, Stauss had some information: "Yes, he's a seminary student though not a very good one," he reported. Merry dropped the contact. Other diplomats, however, did talk to Stolt, who had arranged to be added to embassy invitation lists.

In Halle, Stauss and I walk to the university theology department of theology. These days, the department resides in a sleek, recently renovated building. With its absence of anything resembling church – not a single wall features a cross, though the flyers on the bulletin board do include one with an image of Jesus – it looks more like a Scandinavian office than a seminary. Here, on the second floor, Friedemann Stengel leads an extraordinarily depressing research project. The ordained pastor and professor of church history functions as a one-man repository of Stasi collaboration among his fellow pastors and theologians. Following the collapse of the GDR, the Lutheran Church carried out mostly cursory investigations into Stasi collaboration, suspending only a handful of clergymen. Universities were more diligent in purging their ranks of Stasi informants, a move not always welcomed by students, who often saw popular professors replaced by mediocre ones from the West.

When it comes to cataloguing the Stasi pastors and understanding the extent and damage of their activities, Stengel is a pioneer. The pastor's son is an energetic man with close-cropped hair and wire-rim glasses. He effortlessly catalogues any churchman's work for the Stasi and can explain in detail what the cleric told the Stasi about colleagues, and how he influenced church decisions on behalf of Erich Mielke's agency. Through his Stasi research, Stengel has developed a proficiency in the depths of human deception. Stengel keeps adding pastors to his inventory; one recent addition was a woman who enrolled as a theology student on the Stasi's instructions and was preparing for a Stasi-directed ecclesiastical career when the Berlin Wall fell.

"Why did churchmen agree to become informants?" I ask Stengel.

I knew these pastors who declined faced minor disadvantages; a missed career move, perhaps, or fewer trips to Western Europe. But as Christoph Demke, the opposition-minded bishop of the Church Province of Saxony, has pointed out to me, most pastors who refused the Stasi's advantages received no punishment at all. "Some wanted a professorship or other promotion; the tacticians and careerists, I call them," Stengel explains. "Others had practical reasons; I know of cases where someone signed up because he wanted wiring for his house. Some were naïve, thinking that they were doing the church a service by correcting Stasi misperceptions about it. Some were ideologues; they believed in communism. And some did it simply to damage others."

"That's the way people are," Wiegand tells me after recounting the informant careers of clergymen who spied for him because they wanted West German consumer products. "That's the way people are." In the medieval legend that inspired Christopher Marlowe, Johann Wolfgang von Goethe, and Thomas Mann, the successful but frustrated Faust sells his soul to the devil in exchange for unlimited knowledge and worldly pleasures.

CHAPTER 5

EAST GERMANS, ESCAPING

Wednesday 1 September, 1965, was a day like any other in East Berlin. "Soviet Union warns of nuclear fever in Bonn", reported *Neues Deutschland*, explaining that the official Soviet news agency TASS had criticized reported West German attempts to develop nuclear weapons.[61] It was a catchy headline for a far less alarming development: West Germany had recently applied for full membership of NATO, three of whose members – the United States, France, and Britain – had nuclear weapons.

East Berliners reading their *Neues Deutschland* over morning coffee also learned that the West German government had "once again" turned down final negotiations for a peace treaty, and that poor weather had forced East German farm workers to finish the harvest in a rush. They had, of course, completed the task with great success.

Even musicians from Bach's home city of Leipzig, on tour in Cyprus,

---

61   "Archiv der Ausgaben von 1946–1990: TASS.i Der Kriegspartei den Weg verlegen", *Neues Deutschland*, 1 September 1965, https://www.nd-archiv.de/artikel/1327289.tass-i-der-kriegspartei-den-weg-verlegen.html (accessed 3 May 2019).

had been targeted by the West's nefarious intrigues: "In a cloak-and-dagger act, Bonn traffickers tried to convince members of the Bach Orchestra of the Gewandhaus Orchestra to defect from the GDR there and then."[62]

In the German Democratic Republic, by contrast, *Neues Deutschland* chronicled continuous progress and optimism. The country had just celebrated the completion of the 300,000th Trabant, the much-ridiculed tiny car featuring a body made of plastic resin. "The small car, internationally respected for its performance, design and spaciousness, is an increasingly dominating image in our streets. It's also being exported to eighteen countries", *Neues Deutschland* proudly reported.[63]

After a long day at the Humboldt, 21-year-old Aleksander Radler quickly swung by his apartment before heading to the underground station. The global standoff couldn't be far off Radler's mind as he locked his door. He was, after all, one of very few East Berliners who could painlessly cross over to West Berlin and back again. Indeed, he travelled back and forth between East and West Berlin as though it were still one city. And, like most Berliners, Radler knew that the city was a potential powder keg. The US-led NATO and the Soviet-led Warsaw Pact were already clashing, not militarily but manifestly so through espionage. Radler was also well aware that his recently acquired Austrian passport made him particularly attractive to the Stasi. Few Westerners chose to live in the GDR.

This afternoon, following instructions by a Stasi officer named Jürgen Diepold, Radler made his way to a residential address in Frankfurt an der Oder, a city some eighty kilometres east of Berlin. Frankfurt an der Oder is, in fact, as far east as you can get in Germany, located as it is on the

---

62   "Archiv der Ausgaben von 1946–1990: Bonner Nachi-und-Nebel-Aktion in Nikosia", *Neues Deutschland*, 1 September 1965, https://www.nd-archiv.de/artikel/1327199. bonner-nachi-und-nebel-aktion-in-nikosia.html (accessed 3 May 2019).
63   "Archiv der Ausgaben von 1946–1990: "300,000 'Trabant' aus Zwickau", *Neues Deutschland*, 1 September 1965, https://www.nd-archiv.de/artikel/1327260.300-000-btrabant-aus-zwickau.html (accessed 3 May 2019).

border with Poland. Frankfurt an der Oder is also a divided city, its other half having become Polish after World War II.

After arriving in the city, Radler headed towards an unremarkable apartment building where the Stasi had a safe house. As he approached Conspiratorial Apartment Weser, he quickly scanned his surroundings. Had he been seen? As with the Stasi's other safe houses, there was nothing to indicate that the apartment was used for anything unusual, but East Germans were an observant lot. To his relief, Radler didn't see anyone.

He hurried up the stairs to the apartment. Lieutenant Diepold was expecting him and expertly put Radler at ease. "How are things going at university?" he inquired. "I'm really enjoying it," Radler responded. "I'd say I'm among the best students in my year."

Radler was not the modest type. Perhaps his immediate comfort around Diepold and his interest in the clandestine encounter had to do with his favourite professor, Hans-Georg Fritzsche, who had established the connection. Fritzsche was, of course, himself an IM.[64] On 24 August, Diepold had proposed Radler as prospective recruit and scheduled this initial meeting.

At the safe house in Frankfurt an der Oder, Diepold knew that an officer mustn't overwhelm a would-be agent at their first encounter. The cardinal rule of agent recruitment everywhere around the world is to make the prospective recruit feel comfortable, get him or her used to conversing with the officer. The officer – often using an undercover identity – discreetly sounds the potential recruit out, casually bringing up topics in order to probe his or her reaction. Depending on what the agency's initial research has unearthed, the officer may bring up the prospective recruit's personal frustrations or talk about his or her interest in being of use to the country.

---

64   Wolf Krötke, "Die Theologische Fakultät der Humboldt-Universität 1945–2010" in *Geschichte der Universität Unter den Linden 180–2010*, Akademie Verlag, pp. 47–90, http://wolf-kroetke.de/fileadmin/user_upload/pdfs/Geschichte.pdf (accessed 3 May 2019).

If the candidate is eager to leapfrog his or her competitors on the career ladder, the officer will weave career considerations into the conversation.

Diepold and Radler chatted about the Humboldt's theology department, which doubled as a divinity school. In a tradition dating back several centuries, Germany's Lutheran pastors are typically trained at universities' theology departments, taking the same courses as students aiming for a career as academics. Indeed, most professors of Lutheran theology are also ordained pastors, and that was the case in East Germany as well. "There are thirty students in my group," Radler told Diepold. "Almost all of them want to become pastors."

Diepold was pleased to hear Radler confirm what he already knew. He needed Radler to keep an eye on these potential troublemakers. Radler, too, was planning to become a pastor. "I believe in the resurrection of Jesus Christ, though I have some issues with the church's politics," he told Diepold. The church, he explained, was partly responsible for Germany's two disastrous world wars, and he didn't want anything like that to happen again. Diepold made a mental note of this fact: a good indication of Radler's willingness to help East Germany.

Radler needed little prodding to get talking. Though he was safely ensconced at the Humboldt theology department, on the personal front he was rather a lost soul. Despite possessing an obvious talent for making friends, he often seemed restless. He talked plenty but revealed little. The perceptive Lieutenant Diepold wasn't entirely surprised when Radler told him he had many actor friends: Radler possessed considerable acting skills himself. They might become useful.

If Radler seemed rootless, it is because he was. In fact, he mostly lacked a family. Radler's birth certificate listed his birth to a Helga Radler on 17 May 1944, in the city of Poznan. At the time of Radler's birth, Poznan was called Posen – which remains its German name – and located in Germany's farthest north-eastern corner. Inevitably, it was one of the first German cities captured by the advancing Soviet Red Army during the final months of World War II. By the time Baby Radler was eight months old, Adolf Hitler had declared Posen a "fortress city", to be fiercely defended. But the last-ditch effort was of no avail. On 23 January 1945, after one month of intense fighting that claimed the lives of some 5,000 German soldiers and some 6,000 Soviet ones, Germany's Wehrmacht withdrew. More than half of the medieval city's buildings had been reduced to rubble. As the Red Army took over the city, most of the city's ethnic Germans fled.

Helga Radler packed up her baby and a few belongings and joined the great procession of people heading west from the advancing Soviets. Mothers with children were a common sight in these months, as most German men had been drafted by the Wehrmacht. But Helga had no husband, and she had no baby named Aleksander. Radler's birth name was Wolfgang Clifford Radler.

Aleksander didn't need to fill Lieutenant Diepold in on his family's complicated history; the officer already knew. Young Radler also didn't need to tell Diepold that when he was a young child, Helga had deposited him in an orphanage and checked herself into a mental hospital. Aleksander sometimes mentioned his time at the orphanage to friends at university, though he never revealed his mother's stays at mental institutions. Instead, he told them that she was an Austrian communist who had survived incarceration at Theresienstadt, the Nazi concentration camp in Czechoslovakia.

When he started primary school, Wolfgang Clifford Radler was moved to another institution, the Rosa Thälmann orphanage in Weimar – named after a pioneering German communist. The Thälmann villa had previously belonged to a wealthy couple who had lost their adult sons during the war and committed suicide in desperation. It's a striking mansion situated in a park from which the orphans could walk to school. But Radler didn't quite fit in among the other children, who really had no parents. In his school record, his mother's name has been neatly entered, but the line for the father's name is marked with a cross. At school, the other children called him Cliff, he later told Diepold. The name, with its flair of the big world outside the sealed-off GDR, made the not-quite-orphan even more unusual.

Around age of sixteen, for reasons as mysterious as his English middle name, Wolfgang Clifford announced he would now be called Aleksander. Not Alexander as spelled in German but Aleksander, the Polish way. Around the same time, he left the Friedrich Schiller School in Weimar – an unusual step as he had not been expelled, nor was he academically deficient. He just vanished. His classmates and fellow orphans wondered what happened, but they were used to Wolfgang Clifford-turned-Aleksander's habit of avoiding intimate friendships.

If Diepold had wanted to surprise Radler at this first meeting, if he had wanted him to lose his composure, he could have asked him about his name change and his abrupt departure from Weimar. But Diepold's aim was to charm, not shock.

There was another odd thing about Radler: his Austrian passport. Though he was not Austrian, Latvian-born Helga had once lived in Vienna. That, Aleksander had learned, made him eligible to become a citizen of Austria. On 28 May 1965, Radler – using the first name Aleksander – had acquired Austrian citizenship at the country's consulate-general in West Berlin.

This Western link made Radler even more attractive to the Stasi. Although the MfS was always prospecting for informants, Radler was a rare find, especially now, with the Berlin Wall causing trouble. The government had not anticipated the constant flow of East Germans escaping from East to West Berlin in simple but ingenious ways. Some hid in trunks of West German cars, crossing from the city's eastern to its western sector; others paddled across the river – the Spree – in rubber boats. An informant had told the Stasi about a large tunnel dug by crafty West Berliners that had allowed no less than fifty-seven East Berliners to escape. Helpers in West Berlin had dug other tunnels as well. A flourishing trade in West German identity documents supported the escapes. Though one of the Stasi's units dealt exclusively with escapes, Erich Mielke had commanded all Stasi units, even the Church Bureau, to help.[65]

East Germany's leaders were predictably irate at losing citizens to the West, but the frequent escapes also gave the impression that the country's borders guards were incompetent. The escapes also highlighted an uncomfortable reality: many East Germans were desperate to leave the self-proclaimed socialist paradise. But even though the Stasi and the border force were painfully aware of the people-smuggling across the border, they were struggling to establish how, exactly, East Germans were doing it and how their West German helpers were organized.

Most of the escapees were young, many of them students. Large numbers of West Berlin students helped East German friends and acquaintances get across the border. In addition, some entrepreneurial West Berliners smuggled people for money. The Stasi needed a mole, a person with good contacts among would-be escapees and their West German helpers, who could easily travel back and forth across the border.

The year before recruiting Radler, Diepold had signed up another young man he considered a star prospect. Walther Kauer, a 28-year-old small-time criminal from Switzerland, had simply turned up in East Germany and requested political asylum. The Stasi decided to try him out. It was a serious mistake. On his very first assignment to West Berlin, Kauer happened upon a West German tabloid journalist whom he told – for a fee of DM100 – that East Germany was the largest concentration camp in history. The incident caused huge embarrassment, both for the Ministry for State Security and for Diepold personally.

---

65 Auerbach et al, *Hauptabteilung XX*, p. 30.

And now, Aleksander Radler in Conspiratorial Apartment Weser, declared himself willing to work for the Stasi because he considered it his obligation as a Christian to work for peace, as he put it. He then casually revealed that, in addition to actors, he knew plenty of "operationally interesting persons" (being opposition-minded East Germans). Diepold decided he had struck gold.

Radler and Diepold shook hands in farewell, pleased with the outcome of their conversation. They agreed to meet two weeks later, again in Conspiratorial Apartment Weser. Diepold headed back to his office and dictated his notes. In Radler's file he also noted the next steps: request Radler's file at the Humboldt; initiate a contract for him; look into the matter of Radler's passports and nationalities; ask Stasi colleagues for information on Radler's theatrical friends. 1 September 1965 had been a good day in the career of Jürgen Diepold. His intuition about the young man with a Western passport and many friends had proven correct. It didn't bother Diepold that Radler was rootless. On the contrary, the prospective agent's lack of a stable family life was an asset. Agents with such backgrounds often see in their handlers a substitute family.

Radler immediately signed the contract and chose a codename, IM Thomas. If IM Thomas felt troubled by this life-changing turn of events, he didn't show it. Soon he was meeting with Diepold almost every week, each time bringing new updates: which East German, West German and foreign students he had been spending time with, which new ones he had met, what their political convictions were, where they travelled, assessments of their looks ("very lively in conversation, attractive appearance"; "she uses make-up, but not too much"), even information on whom they were having sex with and whether they were promiscuous or gay. One young man wasn't very choosy about girls and had already persuaded several to have abortions, IM Thomas informed Diepold, providing as many names as he could. One former pastor-in-training with opposition leanings, who had managed to be smuggled to West Berlin, was now running what amounted to a gay brothel there, IM Thomas informed Diepold.

Nothing was too insignificant for IM Thomas, who was rapidly becoming an industrious snooper. He drew diagrams of restaurants where he had met with acquaintances and described the homes of suspected people-smugglers. He reported that the neighbour of a West Berlin friend was said to be working for US intelligence, and that US military vehicles were often parked nearby. With the Cold War raging in both parts of Berlin, this was useful information.

As instructed, Radler provided meticulous reports on staffing and procedures at West German border crossings. The Stasi was also interested in the guests and staff at particular restaurants. In one such restaurant, the *Jägerheim-Gaststätte*, IM Thomas observed that the female proprietor had fat legs. This piece of information, too, was logged in the Stasi's files. No wonder the Gauck Agency has 111 kilometres worth of files.

But Radler also scouted out locations from which one could observe East Berliners suspected of planning an escape; in the case of one would-be-escapee, Radler identified a playground as the ideal surveillance spot. On Diepold's instructions, he even asked friends he suspected of smuggling East German defectors in their car if he could ride with them to Hamburg. His mission: to find out if the friends seemed accustomed to driving across East Germany, as one has to do to reach Hamburg. Or would they instead seem wary at the thought? If so, he would know that their supposed trips to Hamburg were really people-smuggling operations.

Radler also delivered insights into his fellow theology students' opinions and news about successful defections. With many East German students already having defected to West Berlin, Radler had plenty of opportunities to gather intelligence among their friends. "I steered the conversation towards [redacted], who had been smuggled to West Berlin", he reported from one meeting. On another occasion he noted that "the car that [redacted] hid in was driven by a Moroccan". He heard that the smuggling fee had dropped to

DM6,000–8,000 – still a fortune for East Germans, who had to acquire the sum from West German relatives. IM Thomas even delivered news of several East Berliners who had recently reached freedom by crawling through the city's sewers.

In Leipzig, meanwhile, IM Lorac – Siegfried Krügel – had told his case officer that several of his students seemed to be up to something fishy, going to Bulgaria together and telling nobody about it. "Usually they joke when somebody plays hooky during term time," he reported. "But this time they're all quiet and give me evasive answers." Though preventing escapes from East Germany was really not Krügel's brief, after telling the Stasi he reported the students to the police, for good measure.

In Berlin, IM Thomas kept hearing people mention a man they called Mephisto, who supplied would-be escapees with West German passports. The word on the street, IM Thomas told Diepold, was that Mephisto acquired the passports from "the Gehlen secret service" – West Germany's foreign intelligence agency. He had also heard that American Quakers and Jehovah's Witnesses maintained close relations with some of the West German people-smugglers.

Though he took breaks from his Stasi assignments to study, Radler managed to further speed up his ambitious Stasi schedule. He was, by now, a social butterfly in East and West Berlin, completely unafraid to turn up at friends' and acquaintances' doorsteps and spend a jolly evening drinking wine with them while copiously making mental notes of every detail, including the cars parked outside. Once, he hitchhiked across West Germany, using friends to help him contact escapees. He then inconspicuously quizzed them about the details.

At the Humboldt's theology department, the students and faculty didn't see a lot of Radler. And while his fellow students liked to linger in long conversations in the university canteen, the young Austrian always seemed to be on his way elsewhere.

Sometimes, though, someone would show more interest in Radler's life. That made him uncomfortable. One day in November 1967, Radler turned up at the apartment of an old friend now living in Hamburg. To his surprise, several other people were already there. One of them, an American, was fascinated by how Radler was able to travel back and forth between East and West Berlin. "Well, I've got an Austrian passport," Radler enlightened him, explaining that in addition to the Western passport he had a visa that allowed him multiple entries to West Germany. "Can I take a look?" the American asked. He flipped through the pages. "Why was your visa processed in West Berlin when the embassy is in Bonn?" he intently queried. Radler could, of course, have pointed out that West Berlin made a lot more sense than far-away Bonn, but attention to his person could be dangerous. He cleverly steered the conversation towards the Vietnam War and the political situation in West Germany.

Only several days previously, Radler had had trouble on account of his magic passport again. That time – and it was not the first time – one of his friends had wanted to borrow the passport and, by extension, Radler's identity to leave East Germany. Many young East German would-be-defectors asked the same favour of West German acquaintances. It was just so much easier to leave East Germany using the passport of a West German lookalike than wading through a sewage tunnel. When the friend inquired about using his passport, Radler couldn't explain why it would be a very bad idea. Instead he explained that he never let people use his passport.

After finishing his conversation with the American at the party in Hamburg, Radler fell into conversation with a Dutchman. "I was in East Germany several years ago. Someone's got to do it," the Dutchman volunteered. "What do you mean by 'it'?" Radler inquired. "Intelligence missions," the Dutchman responded. Now Radler was paying close attention. "I'm a lieutenant in the CIA," the Dutchman told him. "But once you're burst, there isn't much you can do." An undercover officer is "burst" when caught on enemy territory. That's what had apparently happened to the Dutchman, who had been operating in East Germany using a West German passport. Acting on a tip-off from one of the Dutchman's contacts, East German authorities had arrested him. It had taken the authorities six weeks to establish his identity, the Dutchman told Radler. After some more time, he had been exchanged for East German spies caught in West Germany. The Dutchman volunteered all this information to a stranger at a party. Was it for real? Was he pulling Radler's leg? The story seemed too exotic, but better inform Diepold just in case.

IM Thomas had also picked up more intelligence news in Berlin. The Israeli intelligence service was operating a smuggling ring in Germany, he informed Diepold. The ring's contact person was a "Polish Zionist" employed in the Bonn bureau of a British tabloid.

West Germany's capital of Bonn, located near the French border, was (and remains) far from Berlin. But in the world of churches that was Department XX/4's domain, national borders mattered little. East Germany's foreign intelligence agency, *Hauptverwaltung A* (Main Directorate A or HVA), commanded by the legendary General Markus Wolf, was feared by every Western spy. But the Stasi's domestically-focused agents, too, could pitch in with foreign intelligence. Division XX forwarded Radler's news about the Dutchman and about how East German escapees were mixing with CIA agents to the HVA. Diepold soon learned the Dutchman's cover name. Apparently there was a grain of truth to what the mysterious partygoer had told IM Thomas.

IM Thomas also delivered intelligence Diepold hadn't requested. Often the intelligence was distinctly mundane, but at this early stage, IM Thomas's main task was simply to infiltrate people-smuggling networks. He delivered reports about East German friends asking him to post letters to potential smuggling collaborators in the West and made observations of the recipients and their homes.

Diepold recorded everything, ticking off the appropriate boxes on the Stasi's official forms used after agent meetings. The forms had boxes indicating a verbal or written report; whether the information had been "verified", "not verified", or "not verified but deemed credible". As Joachim Wiegand had learned, IMs liked to inflate their reports, so officers had to constantly double-check. On the form, the officer also indicated whether the information was part of an operative process – in other words, Stasi surveillance of a person – and whether it would be used to support future operations. He then added the information to the file kept on every person and vehicle the Stasi was watching. This efficient cataloguing system allowed officers to cross-check intelligence with information in their files.

This time, Diepold made a special note of IM Thomas's report that East Germans who had been smuggled had had their smuggler fees reimbursed by the West German government. "Add to the offence index as an enemy method", Diepold's supervisor decided.

In December 1966, Joachim Wiegand was acquainting himself with church terminology. Christianity was on other East Germans' minds too. It was Advent season, even in the socialist East Germany. At Christmas markets around the country, merchants were selling aromatic mulled wine and gingerbread cookies. The government's slightly liberalized economic policies, introduced in 1961 after its pure Stalinist planned economy had floundered, meant that shoppers could even buy presents from private Christmas market merchants. And though choirs were mostly singing secular seasonal songs, people remembered what the season was about. The birth of Jesus, however, would only be celebrated in a low-key fashion in churches and Sunday schools.

Aleksander Radler had no time for Christmas shopping. One evening, he again went to visit a friend who had successfully defected to West Berlin. Radler had brought with him photos from a mutual East German friend. Over a cup of tea, the two young men chatted about the major political events unfolding in West Germany. "Are you and others who don't belong to the SED disappointed with the grand coalition?" Radler's friend asked. Many West German Social Democrats were feeling deeply betrayed that their Social Democratic Party, led by former anti-Nazi activist Willy Brandt, had joined a grand coalition with the Christian Democrats earlier that year. Brandt had sold out to "Nazi-Kiesinger", they argued, referring to Christian Democratic leader Kurt Georg Kiesinger. Kiesinger had not only been an early member of the Nazi Party but had also served in Adolf Hitler's foreign ministry.

Radler's friend, Rudi Schultze, was not concerned about Kiesinger.[66] Instead, he was worried that Foreign Minister Brandt would try to make friends with East Germany. "We're not opposed to ministerial talks between the FRG and the Zone," he told Radler, referring to West Germany and East Germany, respectively. "But this construct [East Germany] must absolutely not be recognized [as a state]. In a state where people disappear daily without a noise, and where people bleed to death at the Wall, people's fundamental right is being violated."

Later, Schultze's wife joined the conversation. She had baby equipment that she wanted Radler to deliver to friends in East Berlin who had just had a baby. These friends were desperate to escape too, but with an infant it was difficult. Radler and the Schultzes brainstormed about their friends' options: once the newborn was a bit less fragile, it would be easy for a West German to smuggle it to West Berlin. The parents could then follow separately. But if the parents were unwilling to be separated from their baby, the family could escape together via Czechoslovakia or Hungary. The drawback was that the family would then face a very stiff smuggling fee.

It was around midnight when Radler took the train back to East Berlin. Radler's girlfriend, Monika, delivered the baby equipment to the family.[67]

---

66   Not his real name.
67   Monika is not her real name. The girlfriend's name is redacted in Radler's Stasi file.

Sometime after that, the young father stopped by to talk to Radler. "I don't know anybody who could give me DM6,000," he sighed, referring to the smuggler fee. Tough luck. "He's somebody who would love to go to the West as soon as possible," Radler reported to Diepold. "But he doesn't take the initiative to push it forward. Instead he's waiting for people to organize everything for him and even give him the money." This time, at least, it looked like East Germany would be spared the humiliation of another escape.

IM Thomas's dealings with the Schultzes and their friends showed Diepold that he had perfected the art of infiltrating smuggling networks. Participants on both sides of the border now trusted him to carry messages and goods between them, and they listened to his opinions on escape options. They saw in him a Good Samaritan who used his Western passport for the benefit of less fortunate friends and acquaintances. Their enthusiasm over this unexpected help made them push aside any concerns about exactly why Radler voluntarily kept returning to East Germany when the rest of them were so desperate to leave.

In the spring of 1967, Radler moved to Jena, the old university city some three hours south-west of Berlin where the playwright and poet Friedrich Schiller once taught. His plan was to continue his theology studies there – and, of course, his work for the Stasi. IM Thomas "will report to us about people who make contact with him on account of his citizenship," Diepold noted in his file.

Christoph Kähler was one of the many students befriended by the gregarious Austrian. "He was an exotic character," Kähler tells me. "He had an Austrian passport and lots of women around him." But Kähler felt uneasy about Radler. What made Kähler apprehensive was the fact that Radler seemed to be paying scant attention to his studies. "I wonder if he's connected to the Stasi," Kähler thought to himself. But he mentioned his reservations to no one. It would have been wrong to spread rumours.

Radler, IM Thomas, was already reporting on world politics as interpreted by the students in Jena. At 7.45 a.m. local time on 5 June 1967, the Israeli Air Force launched a massive attack against the Egyptian Air Force. Though they had previously mobilized against Israel, the Egyptians were caught by surprise, and their allies Jordan and Syria could do little to help. By lunchtime, the superior Israelis – flying at low altitude so as not to be detected by radar – had decimated their three enemies' air forces. Most of the Arab planes hadn't even managed to leave the tarmac.

Israel was, in fact, so superior that it only needed six days to defeat its three neighbours. On 11 June, having lost the West Bank, Gaza Strip, Golan Heights, and the Sinai Peninsula up to the Suez Canal, the Arab countries conceded defeat. Thanks to shrewd military planning, Israel had more than doubled its size while losing only some 700 soldiers. Its enemies had suffered some 18,000 casualties. International media immediately dubbed the super-short conflict the Six-Day War.

On the morning of Israel's surprise attack, IM Lorac – Siegfried Krügel – was travelling to East Berlin with several colleagues. They too heard the shocking news. "All three were in favour of Israel and the aggression," he reported to the Church Bureau. One of them called the Israelis "the Prussians of the Orient". Unusually, IM Lorac had delivered useful intelligence. The Stasi was well aware that Israel had supporters among East German Christians, even as East Germany and its brother socialist states supported Israel's Arab enemies. As a result, the Church Bureau needed to identify East German Christians who sympathized with Israel and monitor them.

Meanwhile, in Jena, students were animatedly discussing the strange war that had lasted for less than a week. Warsaw Pact governments had, unsurprisingly, sharply condemned the Israeli attack, and that meant that ordinary East Germans citizens had to condemn it too. A protest letter had been placed in the university canteen for the students to sign. IM Thomas memorized the list. "Almost no theology students have signed it," he reported to Lieutenant Diepold.

Worse still, some theology students and their professors were speaking dismissively of the Arabs. IM Thomas quoted one of them to Diepold: "Arab states systemically hound Israel in order to annihilate it, and as a result Israel has to fight for its existence." Other Jena theologians were arguing that it was wrong for East Germany to oppose Israel, saying that Israelis had suffered through difficult times. Some were even saying that East Germany had expressed solidarity with the Arab states because the USSR had done so, and because it wanted to be recognized by these countries." International recognition was, in fact, a problem for East Germany. In 1967, East Germany was still only recognized by a few fellow communist countries.[68]

IM Thomas had inadvertently hit upon East Germany's central dilemma. Many pastors-in-training, who would interact with fellow Christians around the world, were peddling opinions hostile to the government. They were even ridiculing its foreign policy. There was no doubt in East German officials' minds that the young theologians had been influenced by fellow Christians in West Germany and elsewhere in Western Europe, not to mention the United States. But how could East Germany prevent its Christians from maintaining contacts in the West? Its only option was Department XX/4.

Another particularly thorny issue for the Church Bureau to monitor was, of course, the smuggling of Christian literature. Agents kept filing reports of Western books spotted in seminaries and on opposition-minded pastors' bookshelves. How had they arrived there? Diepold instructed IM Thomas to keep an eye on book-smugglers, too.

In Jena, word about the Austrian theology student who used his passport to help others had reached a group of seven friends, several of them students at the university. They got in touch with Radler. "It has come to my knowledge that a group of students in Jena are planning to illegally leave the GDR," IM

---

68   Craig R. Whitney, "The East Germans: Recognition Comes at Last", *The New York Times*, 1 September 1974, New York Times Archives 1974, http://www.nytimes.com/1974/09/01/archives/the-east-germans-recognition-comes-at-last-eastern-europe-economics.html (accessed 3 May 2019).

Thomas – Radler – reported. Henning Frunder, a 21-year-old physics student, "told me that it would be better if I came by tomorrow at 1300 hours as he had a confidential matter he wanted to talk about, which he couldn't do in public". Swearing him to secrecy, Frunder had told Radler that he and his friends wanted to escape.

The group's most immediate concern was how to come up with money for the smugglers. But they had relatives in West Germany who might be willing to help. It was, of course, crucial that the East German authorities should not intercept the letters. They were hoping Aleksander would help them by posting the letters in West Berlin. Could he help? Of course he could. Aleksander really was a good person, Frunder concluded.

"Dear Uncle, I apologize for the contents of the first personal letter I address to you", wrote Siegfried Rödinger, a medical student and friend of Frunder's. "I regret that we don't know each other. After hearing Aunt [redacted]'s stories about you, you have become somewhat of a role model to me; your courage and perseverance." Recently, Rödinger explained, the Stasi had come to talk to him about his opposition activities; Rödinger had now concluded that he was no longer safe in the German Democratic Republic. Next came the question: Rödinger needed DM2,500 for his escape. "Could Uncle be so kind and send the money to the bank account of Aleksander Radler, my good friend who is kindly posting this letter to you from West Berlin?" Rödinger advised Uncle Rudolf to reply to Aleksander's address.

In his report to his handlers, IM Thomas painted the desperate students in a very different light. "As they assessed that their relatives were petit-bourgeois citizens they felt it was necessary to write a 'hard story' with the content that either you send the money or we have to cross the 'green border'. If something goes wrong [IM Thomas quoted the student as saying] you will next see us dead." And, IM Thomas added, most likely the students were planning to participate in a protest against the upcoming referendum on East Germany's new constitution, which was scheduled for 6 April 1969. Citizens were being asked to approve a new government set-up that guaranteed a ruling position for the Socialist Unity Party.

As 1967 gave way to 1968, university students were reeling from the shock over the killing of Che Guevara, the Cuban communist revolutionary and global youth icon, who had been shot and killed in Bolivia. In Greece, meanwhile, the military had just defeated a counter-coup by King Constantine II. According to *Neues Deutschland*, there was, in fact, only bad news in the West. On 23 January 1968, it reported that an American expert had identified West Germany's president, Heinrich Lübke, as a Nazi-era concentration camp architect and war criminal. *Neues Deutschland* also reported that an American bomber equipped with nuclear weapons had crash-landed on Greenland. But in the GDR there was good news: East Germans could now buy cauliflower in the winter too.[69]

In 1968, Radler transferred back to the Humboldt, though he frequently returned to Jena. He resumed his meetings with Lieutenant Diepold in Conspiratorial Apartment Weser. One day in January 1968, he brought major news for Diepold, who was becoming a trusted partner. The two men weren't friends exactly, but Radler felt comfortable with him. And when talking to Diepold, Radler didn't have to guard his words or put on an act. Bringing the lieutenant conspiratorial news had become like a drug, with its seductive highs. This particular day, 23 January, Radler told Diepold that he had visited a 26-year-old woman who worked in a church bookshop in West Berlin. The bookshop secretly supplied East German theology students and pastors with books, and Radler's acquaintance was in charge of the deliveries.

Now Radler had uncovered one of the smugglers' methods. "She told me that the [West German Lutheran Church] pays DM30 per person [recipient], which is smuggled into the GDR as books," he told Diepold. "In the bookshop

---

69   "Archiv der Ausgaben von 1946–1990: USA-Experte, Lübke ist schuldig", *Neues Deutschland*, 23 January 1968, https://www.nd-archiv.de/artikel/1242063.usa-experte-luebke-ist-schuldig.html (accessed 3 May 2019).

there's a sign mandating that the books never be sent to the GDR alone but always in packages that contain luxury foods." West Germans often sent East German friends and relatives packages containing food products that were hard to get in the East, especially good coffee and high-quality chocolate. Pesky Christians, IM Thomas had thus established, were burying theological books among these innocuous items.

One morning in May 1968, Henning Frunder travelled to East Berlin with his precious cargo of letters and quickly made his way to the Karl-Liebknecht-Strasse, near the Friedrichstrasse station where the S-Bahn tram crossed between East and West Berlin. The Palace of Tears, Berliners called it: it was the place where Westerners travelled back to their free countries while East Germans remained behind.

Frunder walked into the Presse-Café and waited. Located so close to the border, the Presse-Café was a popular location for meetings involving border business. Unsurprisingly, journalists liked to spend time there too, Frunder had been concerned about meeting in a café patronized by journalists, but Radler had recommended it. As previously agreed, Radler entered at 4.30 p.m. Frunder was relieved that the first step had gone according to plan. The two men spoke briefly. Aleksander seemed artificially friendly, Frunder thought, but then again, maybe it was just his anxiety playing games with him. Then the two men discussed the final details. What if the border guards got suspicious? "If the border guards pat you down and seize the letters, I'll go back to Jena right away and we will try to escape via Czechoslovakia," Frunder told Radler. They agreed that if Radler got through the border inspection without problems, he would scratch his head once he emerged on the West German side.

The two men left the Presse-Café and walked to Friedrichstrasse. Inside the station, Radler crossed to the West German side. Standing on the East German side, Frunder saw him disappear. Around Frunder, fellow East Germans were getting misty-eyed waving goodbye to West German relatives. Several minutes later, Radler emerged on the West German side. He scratched his head. Frunder couldn't contain his excitement as he travelled back to Jena. The train journey seemed to last forever. By the time he arrived, Frunder had even forgotten about Radler's strange joviality at the Presse-Café.

But Radler had no intention of posting the letters to the students' relatives – at least not immediately. Instead he delivered them to Lieutenant Diepold. As the days passed, Frunder and his friends got nervous. After several weeks, they had still heard nothing even though Radler had promised to send Frunder a telegram as soon as any of the relatives got in touch with him.

Eventually, a Stasi agent posted the letters in West Berlin but, by now, the Jena students' dreams of escaping were futile. They were arrested and put on trial for attempted escape. Frunder, Rödinger and four of the others were convicted and given jail sentences. Fortunately for the Stasi, one of the friends had agreed to testify against the others. That deflected suspicion from Radler.

Still, the Stasi couldn't be sure. Word of the arrests and jail sentences seemed to be spreading. IM Lorac – Krügel – reported to his handlers that five students in Jena had been arrested, but he hadn't heard any other details. The Stasi quickly decided that Radler was at risk of being compromised. He would have to be moved from the GDR to another country, to the "capitalist abroad". Division XX sent a memo to Erich Mielke himself explaining the plan. But to which country? Sweden was swiftly chosen, as Radler had already visited and even knew Swedes. Given these links, the Stasi reasoned, nobody there would get suspicious if he enrolled at a Swedish university. Besides, Sweden's Lutheran state church, the Church of Sweden, was a powerful global player, representing almost every Swede. Better yet, it maintained particularly close relations with East Germany's Lutherans. Radler, it was decided, would move to Sweden while remaining a Stasi operative. The Stasi would now have an international pastor agent.

Many East Germans would have risked life and limb to get to Sweden, but the idea failed to excite IM Thomas. Especially compared to the bustling Berlin, Sweden seemed sleepy. And if he had wanted to leave the GDR, he could have done so long ago thanks to his Austrian passport. But then again, being sent abroad with the support of the Stasi, with promises of regular meetings in continental European cities, was not bad either.

CHAPTER 6

AGENTS' VANITIES

On 31 July 1968, a 24-year-old student composed a letter to the Stasi from the Swedish university city of Lund. "I'm sitting in a shady park, awaiting the things that shall come," he wrote. The student was Aleksander Radler, IM Thomas. Even though he called himself a socialist, Radler wasn't referring to upcoming protest marches but to future espionage assignments in Sweden. During the summer, the Stasi had expertly managed to dispatch IM Thomas here, far away from potential scrutiny at home. "The things that shall come" would include establishing himself in Sweden and working for the Stasi from there.

Getting to Sweden had been arduous. On 26 July, the Stasi's division in charge of passport matters had helped IM Thomas cross over into West Berlin. He could have crossed the border to West Berlin openly using his Austrian passport, and travelled on from there to Sweden, but that would have left a trace with the West German authorities. Instead the Stasi helped him get to West Berlin, from where he booked a standby airline ticket to Hamburg under his real name.

From Hamburg, he had travelled to the Swedish town of Linköping, where he correctly calculated that he would be able to connect with the parents of Anders Törnvall, an acquaintance from a previous trip. Radler stayed with them for three days. "The father is a lecturer at the teacher colleague in Linköping," a Stasi officer summarized the information provided by IM Thomas. "He has good connections to church circles and members of the Swedish army. He is himself a lieutenant in the reserves and has an ID that allows him to enter army facilities."

Radler went on to Stockholm and met up with a female friend, 'Anita'.[70] On their way to the north of the country, Anita's car had broken down, so they switched to hitchhiking. One of the drivers who had picked them up had introduced the gregarious Radler to a friend of his, a manager at IBM. The IBM manager had promptly invited Radler to the home of his girlfriend, an opera singer, who had allowed him to stay in her apartment for a week and a half. Radler clearly had a gift for charming people. IM Thomas's file does not reveal what happened to Anita.

IM Thomas then made his way to Lund. Despite having only a tourist visa, with the help of the IBM manager Radler managed to get a room in Christian student housing as well as a job as a hospital watchman. The IBM executive also invited Radler to several parties and even offered him financial help. He "is very interested in a closer relationship with [IM Thomas]," a Stasi officer wrote down.

Radler's timing was fortuitous. Across Western Europe and North America, students were demonstrating against capitalism and the Vietnam War, for peace and socialism. Czechoslovakia's reformist leader, Alexander Dubček, was a particular source of inspiration for the students, showing that socialism and freedom could coexist. His experiment, dubbed the Prague Spring, had inspired a feeling of hope among the countless students who had until then mostly been protesting against issues but not presenting many solutions.

---

70   Not her real name.

Lund students were marching too. During the university's 300th anniversary celebrations in the spring, hundreds of police officers had been called in to protect visiting dignitaries from raging students. "Heath go home," they chanted as US ambassador William Heath arrived. Lund was not Paris, where the charismatic German-French student leader Daniel Cohn-Bendit was drawing enormous crowds. But the Stasi was eager to keep an eye on it anyway. Lund academics maintained close links with East German colleagues.

In Leipzig, meanwhile, a few students were protesting in the same vein as their Western comrades. But East German authorities most definitely didn't appreciate these ideological relatives. In fact, East Berlin and its fellow Warsaw Pact capitals were alarmed. In the spring, the Stasi's harried officers had been given a temporary reprieve when student protest leader Rudi Dutschke had become incapacitated. Dutschke was an East German Christian – and former member of Lutheran youth groups – who had been barred from university after refusing to perform military service. He had, however, had the incredible luck of being in West Berlin when the Wall was built. In West Berlin, the charismatic Dutschke had enrolled in the Free University's sociology department and co-founded the Socialist German Students Association, a movement working for the same socialism with a human face that Dubček had introduced in his country. Countless students joined Dutschke's group and the protests. But on 11 April 1968, a young anti-communist tried to assassinate him. Though the gun's bullet failed to kill him, Dutschke was left with severe brain damage.

During the summer things had turned more precarious still for the Stasi. On 20 August 1968, the Soviet Union – assisted by its Warsaw Pact allies Poland, Hungary, and Bulgaria – invaded Czechoslovakia to end Dubček's Prague Spring. (East Germany was willing to participate but, in the end, its troops were not needed.) Within hours, the 250,000 Warsaw Pact troops and their 2,000 tanks had crushed Czechoslovak resistance.

True to form, the following day *Neues Deutschland* ignored the news and instead filled its front page with an open letter to East Germany's citizens from the Soviet Union's official news agency, TASS, explaining the ills of Czechoslovakia's ways.[71] It also led with the story that a new technology had been introduced at an East German cotton factory.

The world, however, reacted with outrage; even Italy's powerful Communist Party condemned the invasion. Across Western Europe students launched protests in support of Dubček. The Stasi found itself trying to prevent any reform ideas from proliferating inside East Germany. "It was explained to the IM that we must identify and prevent developing provocations at a very early stage. Western media is clearly trying to heat up the situation, so we have to assume that the situation doesn't remain unheeded among theology students and other church constituencies", wrote Lieutenant Kunth after a meeting with IM Lorac.

The Prague Spring was over. But across the West and even among Warsaw Pact citizens, the outrage over this violent response to genuine reform efforts was growing. Jürgen Kapiske, a twenty-year-old otherwise loyal socialist, was outraged by the Soviet brutality too. Under the cover of darkness, he snuck down to a train station in his home town in the plains east of Berlin and painted a slogan in support of Dubček.

At the Church Bureau, officers had other headaches as well. Many seminarians were listening to songs by Wolf Biermann, a communist West German balladeer who, in 1953, had moved to East Germany for ideological reasons. He had been bothering East Berlin with his unorthodox interpretation of socialism ever since. In 1965, following the publication of a collection of poems by Biermann in West Germany, the East German government had banned him from publishing or performing in their country.

---

71   "Archiv der Ausgaben von 1946–1990: An alle Bürgerinnen und Bürger der Deutschen Demokratischen Republik!", *Neues Deutschland*, 21 August 1968, https://www.nd-archiv.de/artikel/1276206.an-alle-buergerinnen-und-buerger-der-deutschen-demokratischen-republik.html (accessed 3 May 2019).

And yet East Germans were finding ways of listening to Biermann's recordings and reading his poems. IM Lorac was keeping a vigilant eye on his students. "The IM was told that student [redacted] has duplicated and distributed poems by Biermann on a typewriter. These poems come from the book *Die Drahtnarve*, which has been smuggled into the GDR and comes from a church library", Stasi officer Kunth noted on 10 January. Never missing an opportunity to slander his students and colleagues, IM Lorac explained that the student was known for his childish behaviour. For good measure, IM Lorac also examined the Theological College library's inventory for any books related to Biermann. Fortunately for the college, there was no offending literature.

Though IM Lorac enjoyed the power of being the secret eye watching, reporting and denouncing, he was frustrated that his diligent work for the Church Bureau still hadn't resulted in the professorship or bishop's seat of which he considered himself worthy. Like his fellow officers Alexander and Blümel, Lieutenant Kunth now acted as IM Lorac's "Father Confessor", dispensing advice in between issuing assignments. Soon IM Lorac was again strategically worrying about his professional future and his pension, as his college post didn't come with a church pension. "One really should become a bishop," he sighed to Kunth. The officer listened patiently, as Alexander and Blümel had before him. Not even the Stasi could appoint bishops, but Kunth reassured the agent the Church Bureau would help him get a higher pension. And with IM Lorac now such a long-standing agent, Kunth decided he could give him more demanding assignments as well. He asked IM Lorac to gather similar-minded people "who obey [IM Lorac]" and "systematically influence them to achieve an unsupportive attitude vis-à-vis the diocesan leadership".

What Kunth and his colleagues failed to take into account was that IM Lorac was not the sort of man who could gather disciples, let alone influence them. One morning in 1970, PhD student Michael Beintker was sitting in his office in the theology department in Halle when a man he didn't know turned up. "I'm your new colleague," the stranger said. Although academic theology in East Germany was a small world, Beintker had never heard the name Siegfried Krügel before. Some of his older colleagues were familiar with Krügel, but they certainly had not been involved in his appointment. In fact, there had been no search process, no evaluation of other candidates. In no time, the Halle theologians concluded that the Stasi had placed Krügel there.

"It was immediately obvious that he worked for the Stasi," Beintker tells me. "He was a dreadful academic who was very stiff and had no charm. He didn't really integrate. Let's just say he wasn't someone you would go for a beer with. And the students didn't go to his lectures because they were so incredibly boring. Even so, he had the guts to boss us around."

Several months later, having provided the usual stream of gossip, IM Lorac reported that a theology student at the university had been arrested and handcuffed. After having to endure listening to a recording of a person being tortured, the student had been presented with a confession, which he had refused to sign, IM Lorac had been told. Then, according to IM Lorac's information, the student had been tortured, hung up with his hands tied and with a rope around his neck. Was the account true? As usual, Kunth added the information to the files. It was probably a false rumour; unlike Soviet authorities, East German authorities usually didn't employ brute force. But even if the account was incorrect, it was worrisome that rumours of this kind were circulating among opposition-minded divinity students. That hardly made them inclined to work for the Stasi. In the Normannenstrasse, Joachim Wiegand was now convinced that threats and violence must not be used. Subtle quid pro quo, yes – but East Germany must not be seen as a country that persecuted Christians.

Sitting in Wiegand's living room, I'm reminded of the industrious IM Lorac, who reported anything he came across in the expectation that the Stasi would reward him. There was, for example, the student who had just sat his final exams and delivered his Master's thesis. "Very bad," IM

Lorac judged the outcome in a report to the Church Bureau. The agent proceeded to evaluate the thesis, on the subject of the relation between Lutheran pastoral care and the Protestant reformer Philip Melanchthon, a friend of Luther's. Why on earth would Kunth need an evaluation of a clearly ecclesiastically focused master's thesis? But IM Lorac provided it, and Kunth added it to the files.

In Halle, Krügel's new colleagues had the nagging feeling that he was listening a bit too eagerly whenever they spoke. But then again, they were so used to Stasi infiltration (some of them were in fact IMs themselves) that they would not reveal any secrets to anybody but their most trusted friends.

At Krügel and Kunth's first rendezvous after Krügel had taken up his Halle post, the officer asked for a sample page from a typewriter at the theology department (model *Konsul*, he specified). Kunth also asked the agent to find out, via his son at Karl Marx University in Leipzig – which two female members of the university choir had recently handed out anti-regime flyers. It irked the Stasi that students were somehow having access to typewriters – ownership was granted only to approved institutions and individuals – and that they were managing to distribute their anti-government flyers. The student rebellion could not be allowed to reach the German Democratic Republic.

Producing a sample of the department's typewriter so that the Stasi could see where flyers being distributed had originated, and using his son to spy on fellow members of the university choir were both tasks that a man of the cloth should want nothing to do with. But IM Lorac produced the sample and queried his son. He went even further, documenting in detail all department equipment that could be used to reproduce information. There was, for example, "a new Optima [typewriter] in the secretary's office, delivered in 1970 via Genex". Genex was an official East German retail outlet selling its products only for hard currency. The company, which sold everything from food to vans, was in fact a crucial source of West German currency for the East German government. The West German buyers, in turn, often gave the items to East German friends and acquaintances who had no other means of accessing such high-quality items.

In the summer, Krügel's son would graduate from university. Though he could have gone on to the customary seminary training and subsequent ordination, like many pastors he first wanted to get a PhD. Unfortunately, none of the professors seemed willing to take him on as a doctoral student. IM Lorac brought up the matter with Kunth. "Many places including the ZK [Central Committee of the SED] and the MfS promised they would help," he reminded the officer. As usual, Kunth promised to confer with his colleagues and do his best to help. IM Lorac might not care about the future of East Germany, but his son's predicament had once again made it clear to him that he was doing the right thing by working for the Stasi.

As the spring of 1972 turned to summer, excitement ruled in Munich, where the Olympic Summer Games were about to begin. Soon athletes, coaches, volunteers, and journalists began arriving for the Games. Staff members were finalizing the details, including which hostess would be assigned to which VIP. A 28-year-old German–Brazilian woman, Silvia Sommerlath, trained some of the hostesses and was also assigned as the guide to Crown Prince Carl Gustaf of Sweden. Meanwhile, unbeknownst to nearly everyone, a Palestinian terrorist group called Black September was also making precise plans for the Games.

The Church Bureau had impeccable timing: IM Lorac was already scheduled to go to Munich for a theological conference. He received detailed instructions:

Which church-related institutions in Munich specifically work against the GDR and other socialist countries?

- Detailed information about location and names of the organization
- Names and descriptions of the persons working there

- Goals and tasks of these institutions
- What has been planned by church-related institutions during the Olympic Games?
- Will there be specific church events for Olympic participants and visitors from the GDR?
- Where are these events planned to take place and what is their goal?
- Who is in charge of such events on behalf of the church?

IM Lorac was given several other tasks, along with instructions to be particularly careful so as not to blow his cover. He was also given DM100 – crucially, it was West currency.

If IM Lorac had known about Silvia Sommerlath's existence, he might have tried to meet her. Her uncle, a distinguished emeritus theology professor named Ernst Sommerlath, had served at the Karl Marx University in Leipzig for many years. Thanks to his international stature and dignified persona, he had always managed to steer clear of the Stasi and the SED, but he remained a thorn in the government's eye. IM Lorac had already tried to dig up some dirt on him but failed miserably: there was none.

On 26 August 1972, German president Gustav Heinemann opened the Olympic Games. Immediately, the Americans' star swimmer, Mark Spitz, began racking up gold medals, beating world records in the process. It promised to be the Cheerful Games promised in the official slogan.

At 4.30 a.m. on 5 September, eight members of Black September, dressed in black and armed with assault rifles, pistols, and grenades, entered an Olympic Village apartment hosting Israeli athletes. Soon the terrorists, commanded by a young Jewish–Christian man named Luttif Afif, had shot and killed two of the Israelis and taken nine others hostage, later adding several more. They demanded the release of 232 prisoners held by Israel, along with the release of two German terrorist leaders, Andreas Baader and Ulrike Meinhof of the Baader-Meinhof gang, who were awaiting trial in West Germany. At the Olympic Village, the German authorities initially tried to negotiate with the hostage takers, but Israel's prime minister Golda Meir refused to release any prisoners. The Germans then decided to liberate the hostages. The attempt ended in carnage, as the terrorists killed their hostages and a police officer. Five of the terrorists were killed during the shoot-out.

As the atrocities unfolded, IM Lorac was already back home and had even delivered a detailed report. One of the things that had struck him in Munich was the large number of events organized by American military chaplains. He then delivered another report, this time evaluating fellow professors, especially Professor Traugott Holtz, whom he assessed as being progressive and who "steers a gratifying course" but seemed reluctant to take decisive steps. IM Lorac couldn't know that Holtz, too, worked for the Stasi (code name: IM Prof. Baum).

IM Lorac should have been content now that the Stasi had helped him get the university post he had been pining for. But he was often unhappy. When he felt down about something, when others would talk to their spouse or their friends, he confided in his handler. On 17 April 1973, IM Lorac was feeling particularly despondent. He still hadn't received his travel permit for an upcoming trip to West Germany. What's more, he complained, the Leipzig city administration still had done nothing about his application to move from one apartment to another within the city. Though Krügel was now working in Halle, his wife had wanted to remain in Leipzig. With the two cities at commuting distance from each other, it was a workable arrangement. But the Krügels were unhappy with their apartment. Surely the Stasi could fix that little problem?

Worse still, IM Lorac had heard that the government was planning to close universities' theology departments. "I've thought of asking the bishop for a pastor post," he told Lieutenant Heindke, another case officer. Heindke tried to improve his agent's mood. Like his Church Bureau colleagues, he was skilled at acting like a Father Confessor without going soft on his agents. Just recently IM Lorac had complained about being a mere lecturer while younger scholars were already professors, implying that the Church Bureau ought to do something about it. "In my opinion the IM tends to give up quickly and is susceptible to mood swings," Heindke noted in IM Lorac's file.

It didn't take long for IM Lorac to feel more upbeat again. He had, for example, had a conversation with a West German church official who had recently returned from a visit to the US. IM Lorac had asked his acquaintance about American Lutherans and felt the conversation had yielded good intelligence. "The mentality of American Lutherans is distinctly petit-bourgeois," he informed the Church Bureau. On top of that, the US Lutherans maintained "close links to the industry and the banking sector, primarily by putting their pension funds at the disposal of capitalist major corporations that invest this money in, for example, South Africa". Though the information was clearly conjecture and third-hand information, the Church Bureau recorded it. US Lutherans supporting South Africa's internationally-shunned apartheid regime could be potentially useful fodder, and every piece of information helped an officer advance up the career ladder. IM Lorac also kept watching his colleagues, at one point informing the Church Bureau that the unassailable Professor Sommerlath had been acting in a "politically reactionary" fashion.

IM Lorac had no idea that Sommerlath had recently gained even more importance, though of a different kind. At the Munich Olympics, his niece Silvia and crown prince Carl Gustaf had fallen in love. Now they were dating, valiantly trying to keep their romance a secret from the tabloids. Meanwhile, Carl Gustaf's grandfather had died, making Carl Gustaf King of Sweden.

By 1975, IM Lorac's mood swings had again taken a distinct turn for the worse. "I'm going to reduce my activities," he warned Lieutenant Heindke one

October morning. Heindke was used to agents stalling and negotiating, but he hadn't seen this coming. "I'm not refusing to work," IM Lorac explained. "But I'm still just a lecturer. I feel humiliated when I have to address younger colleagues as 'Herr Professor.'" IM Lorac felt fundamentally let down by the Stasi. Early on, the MfS made promises, he complained, pointing out that he had faithfully served the Agency for many years and that it should now help him. But it hadn't.

IM Lorac refused to be soothed. He told Heindke that he would not accept his remaining quarterly payment (600 marks, the officer noted), though moments later he decided to take the money anyway.

This was tricky. If IM Lorac, an agent for nearly fifteen years, began to spill the beans, it would humiliate the Stasi. IM Lorac didn't know many secrets, of course, but he could reveal his assignments. Making matters worse, his first case officer had been Franz Sgraja, now the head of the Church Bureau.

On 19 June 1976, King Carl XVI Gustaf of Sweden married Silvia Sommerlath in Stockholm Cathedral. The ceremony, attended by heads of state and the royal families of Europe, was broadcast live. One of the officiants was Professor Ernst Sommerlath, whom the East German authorities had grudgingly granted a travel permit.

Back in East Germany, Lieutenant Heindke informed the head office in Berlin about IM Lorac's state of mind. *Oberleutnant* Conrad, the head of the Church Department's Leipzig office, noted: "On 24.8.1976 [I] was informed by Comrade Captain Heindke that he has been asked by IM Lorac to inform us that said IM is immediately ending the cooperation as a result of lacking support by the MfS."

Conrad called IM Lorac. The attention from a higher-up worked: the agent declared himself willing to meet. At the meeting, the disgruntled agent once again recited his complaints: he had pursued his career on the Stasi's instructions and the Stasi had promised him that getting certain professional advantages would be no problem. But, he continued, the Agency hadn't kept its part of the bargain. As he had already lamented to Kunth and Heindke, IM Lorac told Conrad that he was still having to call younger colleagues "Herr Professor". "I have a feeling that the MfS doesn't need me any more," IM Lorac whined. "I've been relegated to a sidetrack." Why do you think so? Conrad asked, whereupon the irate agent detailed how Heindke had failed to turn up to several meetings and, at one meeting, had failed to bring the full amount of his – IM Lorac's – stipend. Conrad knew that the promises of certain career advantages were not true, because the Church Bureau was not in a position to make such guarantees, but he also knew better than to contradict the angry agent.

Then IM Lorac dropped a bombshell: he had drafted a letter that he was planning to send to Erich Mielke, the feared Minister for State Security. He was just waiting to see how the conversation with Conrad went, he informed the officer.

Conrad immediately knew what IM Lorac was saying: give me a professorship or I'll write to Mielke that the Church Bureau is incompetent and treats its agents shabbily. Department XX/4 was being blackmailed. This is the risk every intelligence agency runs. At the drop of a hat, agents – its most important assets – can turn into its worst enemies.

In truth, IM Lorac was a second-rate agent, as the Church Bureau knew well. For years, while lobbying the Church Bureau for a professorship, IM Lorac had disingenuously been telling Kunth that he'd previously been offered a professorship at the University of Halle but turned it down for reasons of "operative necessity", that is: in order to serve the Stasi. But Conrad also knew that it was better to keep a mediocre agent happy than to alienate him. "How can we help you?" he now asked. IM Lorac had come prepared with a long list. Among his demands, in addition to the professorship, was a job for his son's fiancée as a day care teacher, and a visit to a spa resort.

Oberleutnant Conrad quickly concluded that the relationship was salvageable. "I will conduct the next meetings," he told IM Lorac. They decided to meet again on 9 September. The agent's threats had worked.

At least, Conrad thought, he'd defused the crisis. He was wrong. Despite Conrad's concessions, IM Lorac wrote to Mielke. The letter was passed on to one of Mielke's assistants, who brought it up with the humiliated Church Bureau.

The atmosphere was decidedly awkward when Conrad and IM Lorac reconvened in Conspiratorial Apartment Sonneneck a few days before Christmas 1976. "It has to be pointed out that even though this wasn't written down, at the previous meetings the IM always got to describe his personal matters," the officer noted, once again listing IM Lorac's demands, which now also included a place at a good high school for his youngest son.

But IM Lorac remained especially irate over his main complaint, the elusive professorship, where he insisted the Church Bureau had still done nothing. "I won't hesitate to write a second letter to the Comrade Minister," he threatened. Besides, he added, it would be very useful for the Stasi if he became a professor. Conrad knew that was nonsense. On the contrary, it would be damaging to the Stasi as everyone would quickly identify the struggling academic as an IM. But Conrad said nothing. Unlike a foreign intelligence agency, a domestic intelligence can't pull its agents out. All Conrad could do was to keep flattering Dr Krügel and help solve his problems. That was the bargain.

CHAPTER 7

CUNNING INFILTRATION

It was 10 p.m. on 20 September 1970 and already dark at the train station in Köthen. The town, located about half an hour from Halle, isn't the sort of place that attracts a lot of visitors. The few people who visit mostly come to pay their respects to Johann Sebastian Bach, who once served here as a musician to the local prince. But on this evening, a young man was waiting for the train. He was a student at Halle University and had been spending the evening drinking with a friend. Now, in his drunken state, he had wandered onto the tracks.

"Come with me," the stationmaster demanded. Otherwise, he informed the student, there would be a fine. The student refused. "You're crazy," he shouted. In East Germany, you didn't address an official in such a manner. The stationmaster called the police, and two officers quickly arrived. Approaching the student from behind, they pulled his arms back to arrest him. The student, an accomplished judo fighter, irately tried to escape the officers' grip, hitting one of them. But the cops were not only stronger but sober as well. In no time they had subdued the student and brought him to the hospital.

Several days later, at the university dorms in Halle, the student – named

Detlef Hammer – went to see his friend Gerhard Gabriel. Gabriel was a theology student of true clergy stock: when ordained, he would be a fourth-generation pastor. Gabriel immediately noticed his friend's bruises and asked what had happened. Hammer explained that he and a friend had been at the train station when, standing in the station building, they had seen the police beat up several travellers on the platform. Leaning out of the windows, they grabbed the officers' rubber batons, Hammer told Gabriel. The officers beat him up. Gabriel was proud of his friend who had dared to leap to the defence of fellow citizens unjustly attacked by the police.

Gabriel would have been shocked to learn that, after speaking with him, Hammer called Sergeant Falk Kuntze at the Stasi office in Halle. Hammer needed help, knowing full well that punching a police officer was bound to result in immediate expulsion from university. Could the officer speak to the university administration and ask them not to take action? But Kuntze demurred. "You must behave as if there's no contact with the MfS," he instructed the student.

In reality, there was significant contact. On 21 May, Hammer had presented himself, out of the blue, at the Stasi's Halle office and volunteered his services. He had brought with him information about Wolfram Tschiche, a troublesome theology student whom the Stasi already had under surveillance. Hammer had befriended Tschiche and had exclusive information. Though walk-ins were unusual and even suspect, the Halle officers had quickly sensed that the twenty-year-old law student had potential. Six days later he had committed himself to the Stasi. "I, Detlef Hammer, declare myself willing to give the Ministry for State Security my support in the reconnaissance of enemy groupings. I will maintain deepest silence about this collaboration as I am aware that the fight against hostile persons is only possible through secrecy", he wrote in his own hand on 27 May. He chose a straightforward codename: Detlef.[72]

It didn't matter that the Stasi had quickly learned from other IMs that

---

72   Harald Schultze and Waltraut Zachhuber, *Spionage gegen eine Kirchenleitung*, (Magdeburg: Evangelisches Büro Sachsen-Anhalt, 1994), p. 10.

Hammer didn't believe in socialism and, in fact, read the *Bild-Zeitung*, a West German tabloid notorious for its hatred of East Germany. In his meetings with Kuntze, Hammer had hidden any such leanings. On the contrary, he had explained that he wanted to fight groups that were hostile to the government. But the Church Bureau was not an ideological outfit, instead signing up agents of all persuasions, as long as they could deliver information and keep secrets.

In Halle, the officers had quickly concluded that IM Detlev should infiltrate the university's Lutheran student group, the *Evangelische Studentengemeinde*.[73] Not only were its members of interest to the secret police; the group was led by Wolf Krötke, who had served a prison sentence back in the 1950s for writing an anti-government poem. "Establish a position of trust with student chaplain Krötke", Kuntze instructed.

Now, a couple of days after Hammer's drunken train station brawl, the Stasi discreetly intervened with the university. It would have been disastrous to lose this promising young agent just as he was hitting his stride. Hammer got away with a warning. "He seems to have learned his lessons from the negative incident and realized what a serious situation he got into," Kuntze noted on 2 October. Fortunately for Hammer, other IMs who had been asked to provide information about him returned only positive findings. Detlef was safe.

I've come to visit Wolf Krötke in Pankow; Christoph Demke has joined us. Demke, another opposition-leaning East German pastor, was bishop of the Church Province of Saxony in the eighties.[74] Gerhard Gabriel, Detlef Hammer's friend dating back to their student days, has arrived as well. In the Lutheran student group in Halle, Gabriel was one of Hammer's closest friends. I ask Gabriel to summarize Hammer's life as a student. "He studied little and drank

---

73   The official English translation is Student Christian Movement. The vast majority of German universities have an *Evangelische Studentengemeinde* and a *Katholische Studentengemeinde*, the Roman Catholic counterpart.

74   The Church Province of Saxony (Kirchenprovinz Sachsen) was the Lutheran diocese based in Magdeburg. There was also a Diocese of Saxony (Landeskirche Sachsen) based in Dresden.

a lot, and he was always cheerful," Gabriel recalls. "He survived on very little sleep. He was devout but tended towards excess." "Was he intelligent?" I ask. Extremely so, Gabriel explains: "He was far ahead of us. We had philosophy study groups with Pastor Krötke and the people participating were all very intellectual. We studied writers such as Kant, Marx, Feuerbach. Detlef always grasped things before everybody else."

Another thing stood out about Hammer: at the age of twenty, he already had a wife and a child. Though marriages were not uncommon among East German students – there was even student housing for married couples – Hammer's marriage seemed odd. He lived the life of an unmarried student, with lots of partying, little sleep and lots of interest in other women. His family didn't even live with him in Halle. "He was into money, whisky, and women," says Gabriel. "Those were basically the pillars of his personality."

By late 1971, Hammer was safely in the Stasi's fold, and with university expulsion no longer hanging over his head, he could delve into his agent duties in the Lutheran student group. Almost every member came from a Christian home, and many were theology students. Hammer, by contrast, came from an atheist home; his father was a factory foreman and a member of the SED. Even so, Hammer was warmly received by the group. Recognizing his debt to the Stasi, and enjoying the thrill of his secret identity, he further increased the speed of his impressive reporting. Not even Krötke's philosophy gatherings were safe. IM Detlev energetically provided Kuntze with lengthy reports about matters such as the "anthropological foundation of the perception of God".

As a law student, Hammer was also extremely unusual in Pastor Krötke's group. No institutions of higher education in East Germany were more loyal to the government than the law schools, which trained their students in communist jurisprudence. And yet, here he was, the atheist-raised Detlef Hammer, who hadn't even been confirmed, showing keen interest in Krötke's philosophy meetings and volunteering to represent the student group at nationwide gatherings. With few others volunteering for such tasks, Krötke selected Hammer.

Krötke was not so naïve to think that the Stasi had forgotten about him. On the contrary, he operated on the assumption that at each student group event there's at least one IM. "Only say things that you would also be able to say in public," he advised the students. He just didn't think that Detlef might be one of the informants. In fact, Hammer's unusual background endeared him to Krötke and the rest of the group: it happened so rarely that someone with no church background joined the flock. "He enjoys the full confidence of the student chaplain," the Stasi noted. Krötke noticed how the Christian faith grew on Hammer, and soon the young man announced that he would like to be confirmed. That's a major step in the Lutheran Church, one that requires lessons over many months. But Krötke waived that requirement and instead gave Hammer private lessons. At least that's what Hammer told the Stasi. When asked about it years later, Krötke – who otherwise possesses an admirable memory – had no recollection of having confirmed Hammer, let alone waived the requirement for confirmation classes. Did Hammer lie to his officers? If so, he was far from the only one. Like intelligence officers everywhere the Stasi's seasoned handlers knew that agents got creative in order to make a better impression.

And there was calculation behind Hammer's devoutness. The Church Bureau had quickly decided that, upon graduation, IM Detlev would be well-positioned to infiltrate the church not just as an informant but as an employee. The road to that goal went through Pastor Krötke. Hammer had to impress him.

Hammer also kept reporting on him. Keeping the former political prisoner under surveillance was, of course, one of the Stasi's objectives with IM Detlev. One day, Pastor Krötke discovered that the student group's radio was missing. It was an expensive radio, but what particularly worried Krötke was that the radio had disappeared from the student group's rooms in a church-owned building. Only Krötke and a small number of students had the key, and they all swore that they had not been there. Who had taken the radio? Krötke told Hammer that he didn't want to call the police. "Then we'd risk the police investigating the rooms," he told Hammer. The student delivered the news straight to the Stasi. "Personally, I don't understand student chaplain Krötke's reasons for not reporting the case to the police," he deviously added. "What does he have to hide?"

Hammer's dedication to the Halle student group soon had the desired effect. Krötke mentioned the promising student to the Church Province of Saxony.[75] In 1972, when Hammer had less than year left of his law studies, the diocese inquired whether he might be interested in a position as a lawyer at the diocesan headquarters. Of course he would, Hammer responded. In reality, he wasn't interested at all, especially since the church paid far lower salaries than other employers. Indeed, the Stasi noted that Hammer's monthly income at the diocese would be less than half of what he would earn working in the court system. But having their own man inside the church administration would be an outstanding opportunity. The Stasi would pay the salary difference. As instructed by his handlers, Hammer feigned interest in the job. "On the part of [Hammer] there is complete readiness to work in the [diocesan headquarters] on behalf of the MfS", Stasi officer Jonak noted in Hammer's file. "It will allow the IM to learn of all indications, plans and intentions of the Protestant Church in Saxony and the entire Lutheran Church."

In fact, the Stasi desperately needed to infiltrate the Church Province of Saxony. It was a rebellious body that "generally works against our socialist development", and did so "under the direction and approval of [its leading clerics] and in consultation with bodies and persons in the West", Jonak noted.

---

75   Like the Roman Catholic church in Germany, the Lutheran church is divided into dioceses, though in the Lutheran Church they're known as "regional protestant churches". The only exception was the diocese based in Magdeburg, the Church Province of Saxony, which contained both Lutherans and Reformed Christians.

Indeed, "the church leadership in Magdeburg, led by Bishop Krusche, forms a political–operative focus in the GDR". What's more, the diocese was large, influential and well-connected abroad.

The Church Bureau decided it was time to let Hammer's wife and parents in on his secret. Otherwise, his parents – committed communists that they were – were certain to disown him when he told them that he was going to work for the church. The Stasi also promised to more than double IM Detlev's annual agent pay, from 6,000 to 16,000 East German marks.

The diocese offered Hammer the job, with a starting date of 1 January 1974. The Stasi would provide him with a car, a cassette recorder, a container for transportation of church documents, a secret address to which to send information, and of course his monthly salary. It would also give him a generous life insurance policy. IM Detlev would, in turn, report everything he saw at the church, including "negative and hostile clergy". It was a thrilling task for the colourful Detlef Hammer.

"How does a Stasi officer infiltrate the church?" I ask Joachim Wiegand. Recruiting agents is one thing, but Stasi officers were outsiders. How could they insert themselves into church circles, where most people knew each other and would naturally become suspicious of an inquisitive newcomer? Wiegand explains: "The way I decided to go about it was: you go and find an intelligent young man attending university. You contact him and say, 'you'll get whatever you want from me, money, everything. You'll quit your degree course and switch to theology.' Of course you have to know lots of things beforehand: for example, what kind of family does he come from? You can make it look like he had to switch to a different degree, for example saying that he had problems with his professors and was expelled. So he switches to theology, the church believes him, and I train him in things like information-gathering, how to behave, how to cover your tracks. After five years, he finishes his degree. He gets a job in the church and rises through the ranks. After ten years, he's in an excellent position." But Wiegand won't tell me the names of any of those clerics.

In 1974, Wolf Krötke moved to East Berlin to teach at the Sprachenkonvikt. Detlef Hammer, for his part, was immersing himself in his work at the Church Province of Saxony's main offices in Magdeburg. Just a few days into his new job, IM Detlev had submitted his first report to his handlers, informing them of, among other things, his daily schedule: the workday began at 7 a.m. and ended at 4.15 p.m., with prayers at 11.45 a.m. and communal lunch at noon. The industrious agent had even visited the local university's Christian student group.

Though he didn't yet have access to any particularly sensitive diocesan information, IM Detlev forwarded whatever reached his desk. Meanwhile, he impressed church leaders through his cheerfulness and diligent work. His manager often asked him how he was feeling and if he liked the apartment the diocese had arranged for him. Even the bishop was excited. Talented lawyers rarely wanted to work for the church.

Soon IM Detlev was sent to meet Major Sgraja himself – the head of the Church Bureau. During a weekend at a safe house in East Berlin, Sgraja and other officers taught the young agent the finer points of church espionage and gave him strategic tasks. He was to establish friendships with leading clerics; work towards a top position in the church; make sure the Stasi's viewpoints were adopted by the diocese without arousing suspicion; prevent "provocations" against the government, "negative appearances" by leading clerics, and "open agitation"; and establish and expand relations with the World Council of Churches. The Stasi also changed Hammer's codename to IM Günther. "Thanks to the good groundwork and the preparation in [the Christian student group] in Halle I have been well received," Hammer summarized to his handlers after two years in his diocesan post.

As Gabriel had noticed early on, his friend had a taste for the good life and knew how to achieve it. In 1976, Hammer sold his early-version computer to the diocese, pocketing 35,000 East German marks – an enormous amount in a country where a university-trained engineer earned an average monthly salary of 950 marks.[76] But how could a mid-level East German church bureaucrat own such technology? He couldn't. The computer had been a gift to the diocese by a Christian organization in West Germany. That sort of disloyalty didn't bother the Stasi because IM Detlev kept delivering highly useful intelligence: which positions the diocese was planning to adopt on hot issues; problems with particular clergy; international contacts.

Hammer also passed along information about a member of the church youth group in Zeitz (a nearby town) who had been asked to work with the police. Now the Stasi knew not to pursue the young man further: he had already unmasked their recruitment attempt. Hammer made full use of the micro camera, the hidden microphone, and the two Sony recording devices he had been given.

In East Berlin, Joachim Wiegand was now deputy head of the Church Bureau. Though IM Günther was still run by the Stasi's Halle office, he had become so important that Wiegand, too, was involved in deciding his assignments. In fact, the lawyer had become a pillar of Church Bureau intelligence. That motivated the Stasi to take a highly unusual step: it promoted him to *Offizier im besonderen Einsatz* (OibE), officer on special duty. Hammer would be elevated from agent to undercover Stasi officer.

At the diocesan office, Hammer was becoming a well-liked member of the staff. He had an exuberant personality; colleagues often commented on his loud and ready laughter. One day, Gerhard Gabriel, visiting Magdeburg, impulsively decided to go and see his old friend. He announced himself to the receptionist. "No, Herr Hammer hasn't arrived yet," she informed Gabriel. "I can't hear his laughter." And Hammer went beyond his official duties as a diocesan lawyer. Friends and acquaintances regularly came to him when they were in trouble with the law.

I know about Marion Staude, another undercover Stasi officer – code names Anke Brandt and Elke Köhler – who like Hammer infiltrated the

---

76   Schultze, *Spionage gegen eine Kirchenleitung*, p. 36.

Church Province of Saxony. How many other undercover officers did the Church Bureau have in the church? I ask Wiegand. Like the other times I've tried, Wiegand won't be tricked into revealing cases I don't already know about. All he'll say is two other undercover officers worked as lawyers for the church. They have not yet been identified. "There was one in Thuringia and one in Mecklenburg," Wiegand says. Then – stop. Wiegand won't name or further describe them. That means that somewhere in Germany, there are at least two high-ranking church officials who were undercover Stasi officers and have not been unmasked.

Though many Church Bureau's agent recruits were students and others already in the workforce, some of the best recruits were even younger. "The best thing is when you find a promising person, say a young man who has a positive attitude towards the GDR, who wants to get somewhere, who wants to study," Wiegand explains. "You approach him and say, 'you will attend university'. He gets a party book [membership in the SED], but secretly. Then he develops into, for example, a church lawyer, because church lawyers are the people you get the most and best information from. Then you let his wife in on the secret. Sure, there are some complications along the way. The church obviously has an effect on you mentally. But that's the classic approach."

In April 1977, it had been a month since IM Günther was made an undercover officer – Detlef Hammer was now OibE Günther – and it was time to set his new objectives. IM Günther's handlers had decided he could continue to collect information about the church's plans, but one of his new tasks as OibE Günther was to make sure he was included in the diocese's executive committee sessions and gained access to all meeting minutes. He was also instructed to get himself included in all the internal information sent from clergy and parishes around the diocese, and to gain access to the personnel files of all clergy and ordained theology professors. Among his other tasks: to initiate active measures against the bishop. Bishop Werner Krusche was a respected cleric who had been severely wounded as a young

Wehrmacht soldier drafted to fight in the Soviet Union, and had later left West Germany to serve as a pastor in the GDR. He was also chairman of the Lutheran Church in East Germany and a vocal opponent of the government. His stellar reputation within the church needed to change, the Stasi had decided. OibE Günther's job was to discredit the valiant bishop.

The Church Bureau was just as efficient as any foreign intelligence agency. And, like them, it operated on the assumption that one agent is never enough. In East Berlin, no fewer than forty-three agents – including members of the vestry and the congregation, as well as fellow pastors and a dear friend named Wolfgang Schnur – reported on the rebellious Pastor Rainer Eppelmann. At the headquarters of the Diocese of Berlin-Brandenburg, top lay official Manfred Stolpe fed the Church Bureau a steady stream of invaluable information – much of it in an official capacity, but some rather more secretively. But others, in turn, reported on him. In May 1975, the issue of Stasi bugging had come up during a meeting for officials from different dioceses. Shouldn't we get a West German technical expert to come and examine all East German church offices for bugging equipment? one of the participants suggested at the meeting. "We've already had one here in Berlin, and he removed two or three such devices," Stolpe responded. "But the MfS equipment is so sophisticated that it's almost impossible to detect it. Besides, the MfS uses many other sources of information in addition to bugging devices. The best way to protect yourself against bugs is to play radio music." Stolpe added another thought: "Personally I consider the MfS one of the world's best, both when it comes to their equipment and the character of their work."

"Other sources of information": Stolpe could afford to taunt his church colleagues. But unbeknownst to him, Hammer had reported the exchange to the Church Bureau, thus further increasing Stolpe's standing.

OibE Günther never missed an opportunity to report, and thus to raise his own standing. When he travelled to Geneva as part of a diocesan delegation, he naturally shared the details from the delegation's meetings with his case officers. When the Synod (the German Lutheran Church's central decision-making organ) convened, OibE Günther reported on their discussions too. When pastors came to him (by now the diocese's top legal representative) with questions about how to deal with the authorities or getting permits for foreign travel, he passed the information to the Church Bureau. And when pastors told him about Stasi recruitment efforts in their youth groups, he naturally forwarded that information to his handlers as well. He passed along internal memos by other diocesan officials without knowing that they, too, worked for the Stasi. He reported about upcoming meetings with West German churches. "The purpose of the meeting is an agreement about potential assistance by the Evangelical Church of Kurhessen Waldeck," he informed the Stasi in January 1976, referring to an upcoming meeting he was to attend. "The focus will be on the transfer of money." Such transfers of hard currency by West German churches were a red flag to the Stasi.

"The large number of applications by pastors for permission to leave the GDR has become a problem for the church leadership," OibE Günther reported in August 1975, adding that the church leadership had now decided to stop giving pastors permission to work in West German churches. In essence, the situation had become so desperate that the diocese would penalize any pastor wishing to leave the GDR. The move was good news for the government, which would now escape some of the embarrassment of having despairing pastors leave the country.

As before, Hammer recorded the contents of letters between bishops and other clerics: the draft of a statement to be read in all churches on a particular Sunday; a letter about a pastor suspected of raiding the church coffers.

All the while, Hammer maintained his cheerful façade, laughing and whistling as he went about his work. Like the students back in Pastor Krötke's group, Hammer's co-workers loved having him around. Some of the diocesan workers, however, had started wondering about their colleague's apparently superb cash flow. "Look at his car," they whispered. Cars were very hard to come by. Only after many years of diligent saving could most East Germans buy a car, and then only a Trabant. But in 1977, at the age of only twenty-seven, Hammer suddenly turned up at work in a Shiguli. The Shiguli was a Soviet car known in the West under the brand name Lada. While most Westerners turned up their noses at the slow and clunky vehicle, the Lada was a major step up from the Trabant. Now Hammer had one. When his colleagues inquired, he told them it was a gift from his father. In reality, it has been purchased by the Stasi.[77]

In 1983, Bishop Krusche retired and was succeeded by Christoph Demke. As a member of the diocese's executive committee, Hammer now began working closely with Demke too. "I'm so cheerful, I don't know why," he often told the new bishop. Demke thought nothing of the comment: on the contrary, it was good to have a cheerful staff member given the complicated and burdensome task of running a church under constant scrutiny and discrimination. But sometimes Hammer also mentioned his "shabbiness" to Demke. Perhaps, the bishop thought, Hammer was simply referring to his weakness for women and alcohol.

At any rate, Hammer was an invaluable aide. He kept an eye out for clergy and others who might need a pep talk with the bishop. Indeed, Demke quickly concluded that his top lawyer was pastorally talented, a man who spotted people's personal issues and tried to help even though it was not part of his job description.

---

77   Schultze, *Spionage gegen eine Kirchenleitung*, p. 36.

CHAPTER 8

AN EXOTIC FOREIGN ASSIGNMENT

The Warsaw Pact's invasion of Czechoslovakia, which had launched in August 1968 and led to mass protests against the Soviet Union, was the perfect moment for IM Thomas to enrol at Lund University. Lund is conveniently located in Sweden's southernmost region, near the continent, and the university's theology department had for generations enjoyed an international reputation. From this vantage point, IM Thomas would be able to track Lund's well-known theology professors as well as his fellow students, and his studies would connect him with the globally influential Church of Sweden.

In November 1968, his Swedish skills rapidly improving, Radler thus presented himself at the theology department, located in a medieval street near the university's grandiose white main building. He introduced himself to Professor Gustaf Wingren, the department's most famous scholar and an international authority on the theology of Martin Luther. Wingren's reputation had already attracted several international students, so the Austrian's motivation was not surprising. Besides, international students brought a flair of the big world to this charming city, and Radler had been recommended by Professor Fritzsche in Berlin. Although the Lund theology department suffered from the competition and academic politics endemic at every university, its scholars inhabited a genteel world. They were, of course, extremely familiar with the plight of Christians behind the Iron Curtain, but it would never have occurred to them that they themselves might be drawn into the murky side of the Cold War.

Wingren welcomed Aleksander Wolfgang Clifford Radler as a student in the undergraduate programme that both pastors and academic theologians attended, and Radler quickly began studying for the course in systematic theology and other mandatory modules. Professor Wingren couldn't know that IM Thomas quickly filed a report – about the professor himself. "Wingren is generally very easy-going and is popular among the students. He is very vain. He likes to dramatize when retelling events and situations", the agent informed the Stasi.

Radler's fellow students quickly came to enjoy the company of their jovial new friend from East Germany. In letters to secret Stasi addresses back home, he provided information about his fellow students' political activism and – quite considerable – drinking. But apart from explaining that his mother was in a care home, he revealed little about himself.

Radler was also busy with his other life, making the rounds in Lund and acquainting himself with its colourful cast of characters. There was a documentary film-maker preparing a film about deserters in West Germany's armed forces and the US Army; a female student moonlighting as a crew member on the ferry between Sweden and East Germany who "sleeps with every man" although she told Radler that her fiancé worked for Swedish counter-intelligence. The fiancé notwithstanding, she kept inviting Radler to spend the night. Though Radler may have been interested it was not a good idea, because whilst the woman was attractive (as Radler informed the Stasi), the person Radler should really get to know was her fiancé.

Other intriguing characters appreaing in Lund: the former editor-in-chief of a "counter-revolutionary newspaper in the CSSR [Czechoslovakia]"; an East German theology student living the good life, massively in debt and shirking every lecture; a Polish student suspected of working for Poland's foreign intelligence agency; a Brit claiming to have worked for British military counter-intelligence in East Berlin. In Lund, the Briton was maintaining close connections with both Israelis and Poles. He frequently travelled to West Germany and was constantly on the lookout for people who could carry out missions in Poland. "In Lund he's always with his brother-in-law, who reportedly works for Israeli intelligence", IM Thomas reported. Such scattered information was not what the Stasi really needed, but IM Thomas was finding his feet as a foreign agent, and this was good practice.

There was also a 35-year-old woman, formerly married to a Czech, who was "very generous and is interested in a closer relationship with [Radler] and is prepared to [financially] support him". Radler also met a former journalist for East Germany's official news agency, ADN, who had recently defected to Sweden in protest against the invasion of Czechoslovakia. But the journalist told Radler that he hadn't just been angered by the Soviet invasion; he had also defected because he was disgusted with East Germany's embassy in Stockholm. The journalist told Radler that 70 per cent of the embassy's staff worked for the MfS. In Frankfurt an der Oder, whose Division officers still haunted Radler, IM Thomas's handler Böhm made careful notes. All kinds of people with intelligence connections clearly were tumbling around in Lund. IM Thomas, meanwhile, enjoyed the attention he was getting from the MfS, but he also liked its regular money transfers. The Stasi reimbursed many of his expenses in Sweden and regularly sent him a stipend.

But, in September, Böhm received an urgent message from IM Thomas requesting an emergency meeting. A friend of his was under investigation by the Security Police, Sweden's counter-intelligence agency, and Radler had been interviewed as well. He was extremely nervous. Böhm instructed him to travel to the Polish port city of Świnoujście. Radler did so, using his own passport, and checked into a hotel under his real name. The two men discreetly convened in a guest house and painstakingly went through Radler's interview with the Security Police. Böhm was reassured: the officers had apparently interviewed Radler only as a witness. Besides, Professor Wingren had told the Security Police that Radler knew the suspect from Berlin, so there were no suspicious links.

The handlers at Division XX had decided that the emergency meeting also presented a good opportunity for a longer conversation with IM Thomas. Böhm had brought with him a forged passport, to allow IM Thomas to travel from Sweden to the Stasi's preferred rendezvous spots without attracting the attention of the Swedish Security Police. The officer had also brought a coding machine, code books, and a container for messages – necessary equipment for secret communications with Frankfurt an der Oder. Patiently, the seasoned officer taught the jumpy seminarian how to use them, letting IM Thomas practise the procedure over and over until there was no risk of accidents.

IM Thomas was still worried; he suspected that somebody had been shadowing him. And he was concerned about his future: what would happen once he finished his degree and was ordained? Would he have to remain in Sweden? Böhm reassured his agent. But the reality was that while IM Thomas hoped to return to East Germany, the Stasi wanted him based in Sweden.

In fact, the Stasi was investing heavily in IM Thomas, its rare agent on permanent foreign assignment. Three months later, Böhm's boss, Major Radziey, travelled to Szczecin on Poland's Baltic Sea coast for another long session with Radler. Radziey reviewed the practicalities of IM Thomas's life in Sweden: his studies and living arrangements, which East German documents he still needed. Since Radler's girlfriend Monika still had some of those documents in East Berlin, the Stasi had arranged for her to rendezvous with Radler in Szczecin.

But there was another important reason for the meeting with Radziey: IM Thomas had failed to use the codes that the Stasi had issued him. Since no country's officers can always travel to gather information from their agents, using codes is fundamental. Like Böhm before him, Radziey painstakingly drilled IM Thomas on how to send his reports, how to set up personal meetings with his handlers, and how to plan a meeting using a courier.

"Which people in the GDR are you still in contact with?" Radziey asked. The officer wanted to make sure Radler stuck to his cover story: a devoted disciple of Professor Wingren. He reviewed IM Thomas's contacts and friends in Sweden and any gaps in his cover story: "How are West Germans in Sweden reacting to your presence there?" Based on their reaction he could gauge IM Thomas's performance as an agent. It would have been hugely damaging to East Germany if rumours began circulating about a Stasi spy at a Swedish theology department. IM Thomas had already made his own observations about his country's standing: "Swedish public opinion has started to turn against the GDR," he told Radziey. "Even in circles that used to be positive towards the GDR there has been a radical change. More and more often they compare the politics of the GDR with a fascist dictatorship." That, of course, made it easier for West Germany to influence public opinion in Sweden. It also increased IM Thomas's value.

At the safe house in Szczecin, Radziey once again tested whether IM Thomas was at risk of being unmasked, going through the standard list of questions used by Stasi to determine whether an agent had been compromised. IM Thomas revealed that he was worried about a former theology student who had fled East Germany and now lived in Lund:

"He tells people that I was born in Moscow and am Russian, that I speak German with a Russian accent and that, in Berlin, I was constantly visiting Karlshorst." Karlshorst was the Soviet Armed Forces' East German headquarters. This account was so far from the truth that Radziey told IM Thomas not to be alarmed. But the officer reiterated that Radler's safety depended on his cover remaining intact. "Whatever you do, always stick to the cover story," he instructed him. "If Swedish security agencies approach you, tell them that your pacifism prevents you from working for them."

Then, suddenly IM Thomas dropped a bombshell: in Berlin, another theology student suspected that he, Radler, was working for the Stasi. To his surprise, Radziey was not alarmed: he knew that all around the GDR, people were suspecting one another of working for the Stasi. "It happens all the time at the theology department," IM Thomas agreed. Far from harming the Stasi, such widespread suspicion helped it. Uncertain which of their friends, colleagues, and family members worked for the Stasi, for the most part East Germans refrained from voicing any opinions critical of the regime outside their own four walls. Students usually assumed that one member of their seminar groups – the class-size groups university students were assigned to – was an informant. How to identify the informant? Many students simply decided that the class member they least liked must be working for the Stasi.

Radziey sensed that he also needed to remind IM Thomas of his mission in Sweden. The Stasi was, after all, paying for some of the agent's expenses in the expensive country. IM Thomas was expected to investigate public personalities in Sweden: their positions in society, their attitudes towards East Germany, their connections to West Germany. The agent was to pay particular attention to "operationally interesting characteristics that could potentially be used by our agency," Radziey explained. The two men had been conversing and having meals together for two days now and were ready to part ways. "Do you promise to get in touch once a week?" Radziey asked. IM Thomas agreed, bade farewell and walked towards the city centre, where Monika was waiting.

The truth was that while IM Thomas had written his handlers a few postcards and sent some photos of his new surroundings, the Stasi had grown disappointed with his performance. On 7 January 1969, one of the officers made a note of what needed to be communicated to IM Thomas: "Extensive explanation of why a visit to Hamburg is necessary. Write postcards more frequently. Keep the notification appointments." IM Thomas was, in fact, becoming a bit of a loose cannon. Though an energetic spy, he had become careless and wasn't following instructions. He was failing to contact handlers at the agreed times and often forgot the appointments altogether. When he did write, he often revealed details that could unmask him if others intercepted the message. And he spent more money than the typical student-cum-hospital watchman. People might conclude that a foreign intelligence agency was funding him.

Once again, IM Thomas needed to be given detailed instructions. On 28 January, he was asked, among other things, to report on the atmosphere in Lund with regards to "Prague" – the Prague Spring. "Continuous reports on all problems required", his instructions read. One week later, his handlers told him to proceed with a February trip to Hamburg as planned and instructed him to make contact with a couple there. But the officers also advised caution: "Which persons from [West Germany] come to you? Take care in such situations."

Then, on 4 March: "Open information must under all circumstances be avoided in letters," the cable explained. "Do not accept invitations abroad. Cover story: need to study." By now, the Stasi had concluded that it was too risky to let IM Thomas use the espionage equipment it had provided. On 11 March, an officer cabled: "Meeting absolutely necessary. Arrive 20–24 March. Confirm exact date and time to the cover address. Bring [the] secret writing material, [the] code, [the] passport with you. No trips to West

Berlin [or] West Germany." The Agency no longer even trusted IM Thomas to use his false passport to travel.

IM Thomas did nonetheless produce some useful reports. On Christmas Eve 1968 he cabled that a British former counter-intelligence officer now living in a town near Lund had been recruited by Polish intelligence. "Congratulations on your success", a handler responded.

It was enormously useful to the GDR to have a student spy trolling around in European student networks, especially those connected to the church. The students all seemed to know one another and to exchange visits and ideas – sometimes dangerously so. They were also constantly finding new ways of smuggling Soviet bloc citizens to the West. In October 1969, IM Thomas reported an East German being smuggled by Danish students to West Germany via Hungary. Equipped with a Lebanese passport, the man was now helping other East Germans escape, IM Thomas informed his handlers.

A new smuggling method was also spreading. It worked like this, as explained by IM Thomas: Person A travelled to Bulgarian capital of Sofia, where he was given a false passport with an exit visa for Denmark. Person B boarded the same flight but with a city in another Soviet bloc country as his final destination. Because trips from Sofia to the Danish capital of Copenhagen required several stopovers – there were few flights between the communist world and the West – passengers had to wait in a transit room at the Budapest airport, where they were given transit cards. Person A and Person B met in the transit room, where they surreptitiously exchanged transit cards. Person B could continue to Copenhagen with a valid transit card, while Person A would travel on to the city in the other Soviet bloc country and make his way home.

The officers in Frankfurt an der Oder had done well in choosing Lund as his base: despite his frequent lack of attention to detail, they received good intelligence even when their agent remained in the city. In March 1970, he detailed the presence of a Yugoslav spy in Lund. The Yugoslav was a most exotic character even among Lund students experienced in rebellion, anti-bourgeois living, and free love. IM Thomas informed his officers that the Yugoslav made porn films in a Christian student dorm, "mostly group sex". A fellow theology student, married to another Yugoslav, had further told IM Thomas that the porn director was also a spy, though IM Thomas wasn't sure for which country.

Given his involvement with such sordid tales, Radler could have been expected to flounder in his academic studies. But by now he had already completed the first courses of his degree.

Not surprisingly, the separation had killed his relationship with Monika. But soon he met Ulla, a Swedish nurse. By 1972, they were married; later that year, Radler finished his theology degree and was accepted to the theology department's doctoral programme. Ulla, a local woman, shared his interest in church though less so in politics, East Germany, and academic theology. Better still from the Stasi's perspective, Ulla provided IM Thomas with credibility and stability in his new home country. In September 1973, the Radlers welcomed a baby daughter; two years later, they welcomed another daughter. IM Thomas had succeeded in going completely undercover in Sweden.

Although he had delivered the occasional gem such as the porn director, IM Thomas's mediocre intelligence-gathering continued. In Berlin and Jena, and in the early days in Lund, he expertly and energetically infiltrated people-smuggling operations. Now most of his reports instead consisted of little more than accounts of conversations with church officials or summaries of articles he had read in Swedish newspapers. But he did get around, turning up at seemingly every major church event. It didn't enter the minds of the pastors, bishops, and officials in the Church of Sweden that they should watch their tongues. But Radler was losing the drive to pursue sensitive information, the kind that would help the Stasi form an accurate picture the Church of Sweden. And Böhm and his colleagues still had to remind IM Thomas not to reveal personal details in the letters and postcards he sent to cover addresses.

While IM Thomas's espionage was deteriorating, his undercover persona was by now flawless. Depending on the context, Radler told his friends and colleagues that his father had been a Viennese surgeon or high-ranking Austrian official with the last name Radler-von Reichenau. To some friends, Radler explained that his mother belonged to the Russian aristocratic Shuvalov family. Now, he told friends, she was mentally ill and in a care facility. Of course they had sympathy with his frequent visits to East Germany to visit her. Despite maintaining several different stories about his background, he expertly stuck to the same story with each person, never trapping himself in storylines. He even kept Ulla in the dark.

Radler was making inroads in local politics, too. Soon after joining the centre-right Moderate Party, Sweden's largest opposition party, he was selected to run for local office in Lund. More fitting would have been the Social Democrats, Sweden's long-time ruling party. But the Social Democrats maintained a friendly attitude towards the GDR. Having a source in the Moderate Party, even at the local level, was much more useful to the Stasi.

But Böhm was waiting in vain for exclusive insights into politics or matters such as whether a vacant bishop's seat would be given to a cleric who supported the East German regime or to a candidate who sided with dissidents. At the Lund theology department, a church historian who specialized in bishop appointments was surprised at how often Radler wanted to talk to him about this or that upcoming appointment. But then again, Radler was a chatty fellow.

"He was a congenial man," Radler's boss in Lund, church historian Professor Ingmar Brohed, recalls.[78] The Brohed family socialized with

---

78   Brohed passed away in 2019.

the Radlers, and Brohed tells me of Radler's prowess as a runner. To his colleagues, Radler lived the steady, bourgeois life of an academic.

Like many other agents, IM Thomas developed a habit of treating his handlers like a Santa Claus, an entity that could grant wishes. While careerism had motivated pastors such as Siegfried Krügel to sign on in the first place, Radler had by all accounts been motivated more by adventure and a sense of belonging. By now, however, he was frustrated with his career. In 1972, he had completed his undergraduate degree in theology and had, like most theology students in Sweden, been ordained a pastor in the Church of Sweden. Five years later, he completed his doctoral degree in theological ethics with a dissertation on the role played by German Enlightenment theologian Schleiermacher in Swedish theology. In its preface, he thanked his supervisor Professor Wingren and colleagues at the Lund theology department, as is customary in academic publications. But he also thanked Professor Fritzsche in Berlin, the man who had first put him on the Stasi's radar.

After completing his doctorate, Radler had been appointed lecturer at the University of Lund – a good post, but it didn't bring him closer to the East German professorship Radler felt he deserved. He told his handlers and East German theologians that he was eager to return to East Germany. "I'm truly attached to my home country," he had already told them.

Ulla, meanwhile, had remained so loyal that Radler felt at liberty to maintain flirtatious relations with other women. By the late seventies, he was no longer the striking man of his youth; his hair was thinning and he had gained weight. But, as in Berlin and Jena, women fell for him. A few colleagues felt sorry for Ulla and the girls, but who were they to meddle?

CHAPTER 9

TARGET: INTERNATIONAL ORGANIZATIONS

Although he was an exceedingly rare pastor on permanent foreign assignment, Aleksander Radler was not the Stasi's only far-flung cleric. East Germany's foreign intelligence agency, the HVA, was, of course, in charge of foreign espionage – but when pastors travelled abroad, the Church Bureau took advantage of the opportunity. Travelling abroad gave pastors a chance to meet and network with Christians from other countries. They would naturally maintain these friendships upon their return, and perhaps even be influenced by them. At the same time, the Church Bureau knew it could use foreign-bound pastors. The fact that every East German needed a permit for Western travel helped the Church Bureau utilize pastors' trips. The travel permits were, in fact, designed exactly for such control. They not only helped the regime limit the number of foreign trips by its citizens; in exchange for a permit, the traveller was usually obliged to produce a report about the trip for his employer, and often for the SED and the Stasi as well.

"How do you entice a pastor who is not an IM to bring back valuable information?" I ask Joachim Wiegand. He gives me an example; a young pastor in the northern university city of Greifswald whom we will call Schmidt. Pastor Schmidt, the Church Bureau knew, was moving to Geneva for a three-year assignment at the World Council of Churches. "We were always interested in the WCC, so we went to see him," Wiegand explains. "We introduced ourselves to the family as foreign ministry officials. As it happened, the only way we could meet up with him was by having lunch with his family. They had made duck roast, and we all had a nice time. These things were simply very human."

Major Sgraja had sometimes questioned the value of Wiegand's long meals with pastors: what did they spend three hours talking about? In other departments, meetings lasted half as long. But, as Wiegand reminds me, "with a pastor you can't rush things". When the pastor said grace before the meal, Wiegand would politely explain that he had been brought up differently. But the pastor still got to bless the food.

Over lunch in Greifswald, Wiegand and his colleague didn't mention anything about information – they didn't want to discuss sensitive matters in front of the cleric's wife and children. But the three men agreed by phone that the pastor would come to see Wiegand in Berlin. "He told his family that he had to go for a meeting at the foreign ministry in Berlin, which was obviously a logical thing to do," Wiegand explains to me. "If you move to an important foreign posting, it makes sense to be in touch with the foreign ministry."

As agreed, the pastor delivered information from Geneva to Department XX/4. He didn't spend a career with the Stasi, but the Church Bureau was at any rate only interested in his reports from the WCC. Founded one year before the German Democratic Republic, the WCC had long been a crucial stage for world politics with a Christian angle. The KGB and its Warsaw

Pact sister intelligence agencies had, for years, placed priests there – not only to gather information but to steer the body's decisions in a communist-friendly direction as well. The Russian Orthodox Church had only joined the WCC in 1961, when the KGB permitted it to do so.

In 1975, Metropolitan Nikodim of Leningrad became one of the WCC's six presidents after the Soviets had heavily lobbied developing countries to vote for him.[79] The veteran KGB agent already had several years as a WCC delegate under his belt, and he had used that time just as the KGB intended. Thanks to East Bloc clergy like Metropolitan Nikodim and their Western comrades, the WCC hadn't condemned the Soviet invasion of Czechoslovakia, instead choosing to focus on the eradication of racism – an issue where it was easy to single out the United States for criticism. When, in 1975, the WCC discussed a resolution on religious liberty, especially in the Soviet Union, a KGB agent on the drafting committee softened the language.[80] Later, Soviet bloc intelligence agencies managed to secure the election of Bulgarian church history professor Todor Sabev as the WCC's deputy secretary-general.[81] The pastor agents performed well, managing to turn the WCC into a reliable critic of American actions while for the most part remaining silent on communist states' discrimination of Christians.

But the Stasi operated more reticently. The pastors selected for the WCC by the Lutheran Church in East Germany were, at any rate, not the kind who would have liked – or been able – to cajole other countries' representatives in a particular direction. Instead, Department XX/4 focused on gathering information. In 1979, Wiegand signed an agreement with his Warsaw Pact

---

79   Mark D. Tooley, "World Council of Churches: The KGB Connection", *Frontpage Mag*, 30 March 2010, http://www.frontpagemag.com/fpm/56261/world-council-churches-kgb-connection-mark-d-tooley (accessed 3 May 2019).

80   Andrew and Mitrokhin, *The Mitrokhin Archive*, p. 641.

81   Tooley, "World Council of Churches", *Frontpage Mag*. See also "Prof. Dr Todor Sabev", *World Council of Churches*, 15 September 2008, https://www.oikoumene.org/en/resources/documents/general-secretary/tributes/prof-dr-todor-sabev (accessed 3 May 2019).

counterparts agreeing to share information gathered from the WCC, the Lutheran World Federation, the Ecumenical Council of Churches, and other international church bodies. Back in December 1962, the industrious IM Lorac had delivered to the Church Bureau the Lutheran World Federation's preparation notes for its upcoming World Congress. With the new agreement in place, such information would automatically be shared between the sister agencies.

"Did you worry about Warsaw Pact pastors spying?" I ask Konrad Raiser, a West German Lutheran pastor and veteran WCC official who worked with Sabev. As Raiser explains, WCC officials were aware that representatives or delegates from churches in Warsaw Pact countries at the WCC had links with the respective intelligence agencies: "It was a regular pattern. All church officials from the socialist states were obliged to report back to the authorities upon their return." But, Raiser says, the East German pastors were more independent than their fellow clergy from other socialist countries. "They did receive 'general instructions' from the government authorities but did not necessarily consider these as conditions for their participation." Some of the East German delegates, of course, didn't just follow general instructions but were Stasi informants.

CHAPTER 10

INTERCEPTING BIBLE SMUGGLERS

Korntal is a charming town near Stuttgart in south-west Germany, known for its medieval castle once inhabited by a prince-knight. For generations, it was also a one-industry town, with Christianity as the industry. At the beginning of the nineteenth century, King Wilhelm I of Württemberg, realizing that enormous numbers of Protestant Christians were leaving his majority-Catholic kingdom for religious freedom in the United States, had decreed that they would be free to practise their religion in Korntal. Württemberg Protestants would be allowed to settle in the small market town as long as they were members of the *Brüdergemeinde*, a denomination linked to the Lutheran Church. Korntal immediately established itself as a centre of religious activity featuring publishing houses, homes for the sick and the elderly, orphanages, and educational institutions.

By 1973, Korntal residents no longer had to be members of the *Brüdergemeinde*, but the town had remained a Christian entrepreneurial hub. *Licht im Osten* ("Light in the East") was now based in Korntal, too. Founded in Germany after World War I to evangelize Russian POWs in German camps, *Licht im Osten* soon became a pioneer in supporting Christians in the Soviet Union and elsewhere in Europe's East. By the 1970s, the group had developed special expertise in smuggling Christian literature to believers behind the Iron Curtain.

For *Licht im Osten*, operating from Korntal was not just practical but prudent. With its activities closely monitored by Warsaw Pact secret police agencies, the organization had to keep an extremely low profile. And the bucolic town near Germany's border with France definitely had a lower profile than West Berlin or Bonn.

It was a spring day when *Licht im Osten*'s doorbell suddenly rang. A secretary opened the door and the visitor outside introduced himself as Gerd Bambowsky, a pastor from East Germany. He had already written to *Licht im Osten* offering to assist in their book-smuggling work. The secretary brought Pastor Bambowsky in to see Erwin Damson, a new member of staff in charge of the book-smuggling. Bambowsky introduced himself to Damson. After a bit of small talk, Bambowsky got down to business. "I need Russian Bibles," he told Damson.

Damson was dumbstruck. Given the risk of being arrested behind the Iron Curtain, not enough people were willing to smuggle books behind there, and fewer still were suitable. Many Americans and Western Europeans were eager to do it, but they were so closely monitored during their visits that having them carry illicit cargo posed enormous risks. The small number of Soviet bloc citizens allowed to travel to the West were mostly not suitable mules either.

In fact, getting any books across communist countries' borders, let alone delivering them to persecuted Christians, was extraordinarily challenging. East German Christians might have fit the bill. A number of them – including the occasional regime critic – did of course get permission to visit the West, and as citizens of a fellow communist country they had easier access the Soviet bloc. Unsurprisingly, however, they were wary of smuggling items back.

But, at *Licht im Osten* on this spring day, Gerd Bambowsky offered his services. The extremely outgoing man, who looked to be in his early forties, was eager to begin immediately, offering to take Russian Bibles with him on his way back to East Berlin. "That's really something," Damson thought to himself. "An East German pastor."

Damson couldn't know that Bambowsky was hardly a typical East German pastor. Despite already serving as an evangelical preacher, Bambowsky hadn't even passed his final exams for Lutheran ministry. Instead, he worked for the *Märkische Volksmission*, a Christian charity in East Berlin. But Bambowsky knew that introducing oneself as a pastor opens doors. He also had the highly unusual habit of immediately switching from the formal *Sie* to the informal *Du*. It lent his conversations an instant air of intimacy.

Although Pastor Bambowsky had arrived on his own, he was not operating alone. As IM Gerd, he had for several years been an agent for the Church Bureau.

Let's, for a moment, travel back to 1962. That year, East Germany introduced compulsory military service for men, only to discover that many young Christians would rather go to jail than serve in the armed forces. But jailing thousands of Christians solely because they refused to carry weapons would have caused major international embarrassment. Two years later, the government had introduced a Solomonic solution: weapons-free military service where conscripts served as construction soldiers, toting spades instead of guns. Nonetheless, the Stasi had to keep a close eye on such recalcitrant young men. And to do so, it needed informants.

In April 1965, Bambowsky – who had spent the past several years as a travelling preacher – was about to join the *Märkische Volksmission* as an evangelist. But he had also entered the world of the Church Bureau and been given a test assignment. On 26 April, he delivered his inaugural report. On the Stasi's behalf, he had attended a church-organized meeting for construction soldiers. Though he hadn't been able to convince the conscripts to reveal anything useful, Bambowsky brought back the leaflets handed out by Siegfried Ringhandt, an influential pastor who had attended the meeting. "It is clear in the materials that construction soldiers' religious feelings and attitudes are being exploited against our state", noted Lieutenant Heinritz in that initial report. On the same day, *Neues Deutschland* led with a story about youth attending an international gathering of anti-fascists, who had proclaimed that the GDR gave them confidence.[82] The German Democratic Republic took youth matters seriously.

Satisfied with Gerd Bambowsky's test assignment, Department XX/4 had taken him on as an agent. While signing his acceptance papers on 13 May 1965, he had informed Heinritz that several of the *Märkische Volksmission*'s staff members had served in the "fascist Wehrmacht". Although the Wehrmacht, Germany's armed forces, had served under Hitler, far from all its troops were fascists – especially since many of the soldiers and officers were draftees. As for his own father, Bambowsky had described him as a talented painter who was fluent in Russian and several other Slavic languages. Though Bambowsky hadn't mentioned it to the Church Bureau, his parents had also been itinerant actors. At any rate, they were now both dead. With his long wild hair, Bambowsky himself seemed to cultivate an artistic flair. And rather unconventionally, early on he had told Heinritz that his preferred meeting times were between 10 p.m. and midnight, alternatively between 7 and 8.30 a.m.

Early on, Bambowsky had also told Heinritz that he had been engaged for a long time – but had made no mention of his fiancée's name. "The

---

82   "Archiv der Ausgaben von 1946–1990", *Neues Deutschland*, 26 April 1965, http://www.nd-archiv.de/ausgabe/1965-04-26 (accessed 3 May 2019).

question will be put to him during the next meeting", Heinritz had noted.

Lieutenant Heinritz had, as always, instructed the new recruit in the basics of espionage: don't call us from your own phone but from a public phone; identify yourself by your code name only. Bambowsky had eagerly informed the officer that all was clear and promptly chosen his first name as his code name. He was now IM Gerd.

Heinritz had started IM Gerd off with simple tasks:

• Who sits in rooms 326–328 of the Georgenkirchstrasse 70 in Berlin, where Westerners often visit?

• Visit Bishop [redacted] to congratulate him on his sixtieth birthday and clandestinely urge him not to retire.

• Check out family [redacted]: the husband allegedly belonged to the "fascist RSHA!"; examine the family's finances, passions, intelligence; who visits them; has IM Gerd already noticed anything suspicious? ("The light is often on until the middle of the night!")[83]

In those early days, IM Gerd continued to be tasked with routine espionage on bishops, pastors, employees of Christian charities, and ordinary church members while pursuing his Lutheran seminary studies. Things were going well. But Lieutenant Heinritz didn't manage to learn the identity of IM Gerd's former fiancée. Whatever the identity of the mysterious woman, Heinritz had soon concluded that she no longer existed, if she ever did. IM Gerd was gay, and rather flamboyantly so.

Several days before Christmas 1971, a new handler, Major Otto, visited IM Gerd at his apartment. Though agents and officers were supposed to meet in safe houses, IM Gerd usually insisted on meeting at his home. On this day, the agent was again impatient, eager for more work; he felt he had perfected church intelligence in the Berlin–Brandenburg area. "He

---

83   RSHA, *Reichssicherheitshauptamt*, was the intelligence agency operated by the SS during World War II.

would like to do more for our organization", Otto wrote in his file. "The IMV [Bambowsky] has often given such promises." An IMV was an IM with direct access to enemies: a particularly valuable and trustworthy IM.

IM Gerd had, in fact, evolved into a star agent who consistently delivered high-grade reports. Yet Bambowsky also took after his itinerant actor parents: he always craved the limelight and got an adrenaline push from being on the move. Reporting on church meetings in the Berlin area was far too dreary. IM Gerd would much prefer international activities and infiltration.

Major Otto had recognized IM Gerd's natural talent for undercover work, especially assignments that involved convincing strangers of his genuineness. Rather unsurprisingly, the actors' son was also an outstanding preacher, whose sermons dazzled especially the female members of his congregations. In the Brandenburg villages near the Polish border where he often preached, older women routinely checked the announcements for upcoming services: if Bambowsky was preaching, they'd attend the service.

Major Otto finally complied with IM Gerd's wishes. After consulting with his colleagues he had, in fact, already decided to insert IM Gerd into the Poison Spider operation, which targeted Western charities smuggling Christian literature behind the Iron Curtain.

Otto initially assigned IM Gerd an easy target. The *Gustav-Adolf-Werk*, a small charity with branches in both East and West Germany, helped fellow Christians behind the Iron Curtain – a bit like a mini-*Licht im Osten*. Small though it was, the *Gustav-Adolf-Werk* was on the radar of both the Stasi and the KGB. The KGB didn't appreciate the visits organized by the group, especially since some of the visitors – unsurprisingly – abandoned their government-issued routes and minders. "Why did Gernot Friedrich, a pastor from Jena, regularly turn up close to sealed-off military zones?" the KGB asked the Stasi. He must be spying for the West, the sister agencies concluded.[84]

84   Rossberg and Richter, *Das Kreuz mit dem Kreuz*, p. 107.

The Church Bureau spoke with Gernot Friedrich's superior, Bishop Werner Leich, and with the *Gustav-Adolf-Werk*.[85] Klaus Rossberg then met with Friedrich himself, and the Stasi made sure the pastor's travel permit was revoked, but Friedrich was undeterred. A pastor agent was brought in to spy on him.[86]

Now, in 1972, it was IM Gerd's turn. For the outgoing preacher, infiltrating the *Gustav-Adolf-Werk* was an easy task. And once involved with the organization, he easily expanded his network to include larger West German organizations such as *Licht im Osten*. The Bible-smuggling world is, by its very nature, a close-knit group.

By now, the Stasi was not only well aware of Bambowsky's sexual orientation; it had decided it could even be useful. Major Otto gave IM Gerd another assignment too: try to infiltrate your boyfriend into the inner circles of the East German YMCA. Bambowsky's much younger boyfriend, Knuth Hansen, was training to become a pastor in East Germany's tiny Mennonite Church. The Church Bureau wanted to infiltrate the YMCA because it attracted West German students willing to smuggle – for pay – Christian books to the East. The Bureau had already had some success. IM Lorac's son had, for example, unwittingly spied on the YMCA simply by answering his father's questions about the group. Bambowsky himself was far too old for the organization, but Otto strategized that Hansen could gather intelligence and pass it to Bambowsky. It would be the young man's admission test.

I ask Erwin Damson about the moment in 1973 when Bambowsky appeared at *Licht im Osten*'s door. Damson describes how he gave Bambowsky Russian Bibles and told him that he looked forward to working together. Even

---

85   After East Germany's collapse, Leich said that Church Bureau officers had repeatedly tried to enlist him as an agent, but failed. U. Schwarz and P. Wensierski, "Ich war zu änstlich", *Spiegel Online*, 13 April 1991, https://www.spiegel.de/spiegel/print/d-13679417.html (accessed 21 May 2019).
86   Christoph Gunkel, "Kaltblütig, raffiniert, verschlagen", *Spiegel Online*, 11 May 2012, http://www.spiegel.de/einestages/ddr-bibelschmuggler-kaltbluetig-raffiniert-verschlagen-a-947576.html (accessed 3 May 2019).

now, decades later, Bambowsky remains the most painful chapter in Damson's life, and he can effortlessly recall every detail of their cooperation. "I was naïve," he repeats.

But he was not alone. After Bambowsky took his leave after that first meeting in 1973, Damson briefed his colleagues on their conversation. The other staff members, too, were thrilled at the spectacular opportunity. Thanks to Bambowsky, hundreds of suffering Christians in the Soviet Union would soon receive much-hoped-for book deliveries, Damson and his colleagues were sure. Though they didn't know much about the pastor, they were reassured by the fact that he had already worked with the *Gustav-Adolf-Werk*. At any rate, as with all smuggling volunteers it would have been offensive to conduct in-depth scrutiny or due diligence. If people volunteered their services and were not well-known proselytizers who would attract communist authorities' attention, it sufficed.

Damson was ecstatic at the new addition. But the situation was even worse than simple Stasi involvement. The KGB had asked East Berlin for assistance, and IM Gerd's information about *Licht im Osten* would now be sent to Moscow as well.

The KGB had known for years that Christian books were being smuggled into the Soviet Union but, despite putting couriers under surveillance and inspecting vehicles, it had failed to stop the smuggling. For example, the Dutch group Open Doors had lots of staff members and the means to buy and retrofit minivans with secret compartments for hundreds of books. US-based organizations with names such as Campus Crusade for Christ, Mission without Borders International, and Operation Mobilization were likewise well-funded and maintained offices in Europe. From his office in Korntal, Damson envied the wealthy organizations and their sophisticated methods, especially their expertly rebuilt vehicles.

The clandestine Bible deliveries, in fact, posed a delicate and seemingly intractable dilemma for the communists. Officially, their countries didn't persecute Christians – though the worldwide public was well aware of pastors and other citizens being jailed simply on account of their faith. Or, put more precisely, they were not jailed for being Christians. That would have been illegal and attracted Western scrutiny. Instead, the Christians were put under surveillance until they committed an infraction, however miniscule. Searching every Western tourist entering their countries for hidden Bibles would have caused diplomatic clashes and a worldwide PR nightmare. Detaining Western couriers found transporting religious books would have had similarly embarrassing results.

Moscow needed to infiltrate and disrupt the smuggling network itself. Could Division XX help? Department XX/4 director Sgraja had proposed Bambowsky, who thus became an agent for the KGB as well as the Stasi. East Berlin would forward his reports to Moscow.

Sgraja's amicability in lending the Soviets his agent masked an irony. During World War II, as a young draftee fighting on the brutal Eastern front, Sgraja had been captured by the Red Army – a fate he shared with 3.15 million other German soldiers.[87] It was an atrocious fate and an easy way for Soviet dictator Josef Stalin to take revenge on his former ally, Adolf Hitler.

After being captured, German soldiers were forced to march long distances in freezing temperatures while still wearing their torn clothes. Those who couldn't keep up were immediately shot, while those who survived were dispersed to camps around the country. Many were brought to Siberia, where they had to work in temperatures of up to minus 40 degrees.[88] Of the German POWs captured by the Soviets, 90

---

87   Of the 5.5 million Red Army troops captured by the Wehrmacht, two thirds died.
88   "Bis Kriegsende geraten drei Mio. deutsche Soldaten in sowjetische Gefangenschaft", Focus Online, 17 February 2016, https://www.focus.de/wissen/videos/1943-kriegsgefangene-bis-kriegsende-geraten-drei-mio-deutsche-soldaten-in-sowjetische-gefangenschaft_id_5289838.html (accessed 3 May 2019).

per cent perished.[89]

But POW Franz Sgraja was fortunate: he was selected for instruction in a Soviet "anti-fascism school". After the war, he was sent back to East Germany – by now a dedicated communist. Like Joachim Wiegand and many other officers, Sgraja didn't work for the Stasi merely because it was a secure job. He truly wanted socialism to triumph.

Now Sgraja and his Soviet counterpart agreed on a plan for Bambowsky. The preacher would travel to the Soviet Union, ostensibly on a smuggling assignment for the *Gustav-Adolf-Werk* but, in reality, to report to the KGB on the charity's operations. If Bambowsky succeeded with this trip, it could be the first step towards unmasking the entire book-smuggling network and helping the KGB solve a troublesome headache. And, by helping its Soviet big brother, the MfS would look good.

Bambowsky soon boarded a plane from East Berlin's Schönefeld airport to Moscow, equipped with the addresses of the *Gustav-Adolf-Werk*'s contacts in the Soviet Union. Visiting each of them at their home or their office, Bambowsky handed over books and letters, as well as a bit of money from the *Gustav-Adolf-Werk*. He inquired about each person's Western contacts and the ways in which they usually received smuggled literature. Bambowsky the actor smoothly feigned interest in their predicament asking, for example, what sort of support they received from global Christian bodies such as the World Council of Churches. He found out who acted as the unofficial leaders of the Soviet Lutherans and Baptists and who their Western contacts were.

Bambowsky's Soviet trip was a smashing success. Hounded Christians, including Lutheran Archbishop Alfred Tooming of Estonia, gratefully

---

89   "Sowjetunion ließ deutsche Kriegsgefangene frei", *Spiegel Online*, 22 July 2008, http://www.spiegel.de/einestages/deutsche-kriegsgefangene-a-947365.html (accessed 3 May 2019). Towards the end of the war, conditions improved somewhat as the Soviet authorities kept German POWs alive for use in rebuilding the Soviet Union. Of Germans captured near the end of the war, 30 per cent survived.

shared their secrets with the unexpected Good Samaritan and invited him back. At Department XX/4, Major Otto was predictably pleased. Archbishop Tooming could be brought into closer cooperation with the *Gustav-Adolf-Werk*, he instructed IM Gerd. Information unwittingly provided by Tooming could add crucial pieces to the puzzle as the KGB and the Stasi tried to identify and eliminate underground networks of Soviet Christians.

Soviet authorities were acutely aware of the diplomatic dangers involved in breaking-up Bible-smuggling networks. On 21 June 1972, a British pastor named David Hathaway had driven a bus belonging to his Christian travel company Crusader Tours across the border from Bavaria to the Czechoslovak town of Rozvadov. His van was, in reality, also a Bible-smuggling vehicle. Its luggage compartment was divided into a visible part for standard luggage and a secret part for clandestine books. On this trip, the secret compartment contained Bibles and hymnals in Russian, Hungarian, Slovak, and Czech, various religious leaflets, five tape recorders, two electric shavers, and forty-eight cassette tapes. Pastor Hathaway had already carried out dozens of such missions, by his own calculations delivering 50,000 books to Christians behind the Iron Curtain. But this June, his fortunes changed. Meticulous Czechoslovak border guards discovered Pastor Hathaway's secret cargo and arrested him. The interrogation report reads:

During routine customs control, an elaborately concealed space was discovered in which a large amount of religious literature with political overtones was found, as well as anti-state propaganda leaflets and other materials. The contents of the printed material show that it represents materials belonging to a sectarian Protestant church residing in the capitalist West. The conclusion was that these materials were to be used by a thus far unknown method for hostile activity against the Republic. On the same day, the State Security

decided to prosecute and on June 23, they officially accused
David Gordon Hathaway of "attempted sedition and attempted
violation of customs regulations".[90]

On 27 October, a Czechoslovak court convicted Hathaway of attempted "violation of the regulations on the circulation of goods in connection with foreign countries", sentencing him to two years in prison. A British diplomat observing the trial made the following report:

The prosecutor launched a vigorous, but, on the whole, fair
attack against Mr Hathaway. The main burden of his speech
was that Mr Hathaway was an enemy of the Czechoslovak
Socialist Republic and he called on the court to impose
a heavy sentence as a deterrent to others who might be
tempted to emulate him.[91]

Bible smugglers could expect tough conditions.

The British government was left in a bind: should it intervene on behalf of its citizen, as Christian activists and a growing number of newspaper commentators demanded? Or should it respect the judicial process of a country whose laws its citizen had violated? Intense backchannel diplomacy ensued, with the British government discreetly pleading with the Czechoslovak government to release Hathaway. On 17 April 1973, Hathaway was expelled and put on a plane back to Britain.

By now, Major Otto had made sure that IM Gerd was properly equipped for successful infiltration. Were the *Gustav-Adolf-Werk* to suspect that the Stasi had penetrated its ranks, it would naturally minimize information and courier trips. On Otto's instructions, IM Gerd had already studied

---

90   Francis D. Raška, "Bibles for Communist Europe: A Cold War Story – Part 1", *Hungarian Review*, 14 May 2015, http://www.hungarianreview.com/article/20150514_bibles_for_communist_europe_a_cold_war_story_part_1 (accessed 3 May 2019).
91   Raška, "Bibles for Communist Europe", *Hungarian Review*.

Protestant groups in the Soviet Union, written scholarly reports on the topic and researched the *Gustav-Adolf-Werk*'s publications.

By early summer, IM Gerd had managed to gain so much credibility with the *Gustav-Adolf-Werk* that its members of staff began to reveal the organization's routes: elaborate schemes involving nocturnal transfers of books at deserted highway rest stops; daytime transfers featuring drivers seemingly busy changing tyres; deliveries to nondescript garages. IM Gerd had also assembled a chart of seven secret book depots used by the smuggling networks in East Germany for deliveries en route from West Germany to communist countries. The smugglers transported non-literary items, too. According to IM Gerd's calculations, 20 per cent of the goods around this time were typewriters, transistor radios – necessary for underground work – and clothes. He estimated that 25 per cent of the books were anti-communist literature.

But in a meeting with Major Otto's colleague, Lieutenant Gerhardt Bartnitzek, on 18 June, IM Gerd reported that the smugglers seemed suspicious. What to do? As usual, Bartnitzek provided good advice: IM Gerd was to tell the smugglers that he was willing to work with them but only on a basis of mutual trust. On the upside, the Soviet recipients had taken to their new pastor friend from East Germany. IM Gerd handed Bartnitzek a letter from an elderly lady in Moscow thanking him – Bambowsky – for the "kind gifts". She was referring to Bibles.

With *Licht im Osten* now also in Bambowsky's portfolio, news of the willing Bible-runner spread quickly in underground Christian networks. At an evangelist conference in West Berlin in October 1974, two representatives of Britain's Bible Society approached him. The three men had several long conversations, the two Britons confiding that they needed more accurate information about Soviet Christians' situation, the size and strength of their congregations, and most importantly their fellow Christians' addresses and personal needs. "Can you help us get that information?" they asked. Of course he could; he would soon be going to the Soviet Union again. The men agreed to meet immediately after his return.

On 21 November 1974, IM Gerd embarked on the trip he'd mentioned to the Britons. Like his previous trip to the Soviet Union, it was organized by the Stasi and the KGB but officially carried out on behalf of the *Gustav-Adolf-Werk*. Flying from East Berlin to Moscow, the colourful cleric secretly met with Christians in the Soviet capital, giving them Bibles and religious songbooks. He also visited a pastor's widow in Moscow who functioned as a communications central for Russian Lutherans and met with leaders of Moscow Baptists as well as the Soviet Baptists' secretary-general. He then travelled to Tallinn, the capital of the Soviet Republic of Estonia, where he again met with local Christians including Archbishop Tooming. Next he went to Riga, the capital of the Soviet Republic of Latvia, where he met with Lutheran archbishop Matulis. Tooming and Matulis led churches that were barely tolerated. Their dire situation was compounded by the fact that they lived in previously independent countries that had been occupied by the Soviet Union since World War II. Both were considered brave opponents of the KGB.

Send Tooming and Matulis our greetings and ask them what else they need, the *Gustav-Adolf-Werk* had instructed Bambowsky. The organization also wanted him to find out how the "brothers and sisters" were doing, learn about their problems with Soviet authorities, the size of their congregations, congregational leaders' names, and contact details. With post censored by the authorities, Western charities struggled to keep in touch with those they wanted to help. Couriers were crucial links, not just delivering goods but gathering knowldge as well. The KGB and the MfS, meanwhile, were after the same information.

As usual, IM Gerd immediately relayed his findings to the Church Bureau. "The trip was conducted according to the wishes of the Soviet security organs within the framework of operative process Poison Spider. The deployment of IMV Gerd was directly led by Comrade Lieutenant Bartnitzek, HA XX/4, and by comrades at the Soviet security organs in Moscow and Tallinn", Department XX/4 logged.

As word got around that Bambowsky was successfully managing to enter and leave the Soviet Union with the precious goods, more Bible-smuggling groups approached him, some also offering to fund his trips. The UK Bible Society asked for a debriefing after the November 1974 trip: the atmosphere, the congregations' addresses, size and location.

The November trip had yielded valuable intelligence for the MfS and the KGB. Archbishop Tooming had, for example, told him that another local Christian had for a long time maintained close links with Open Doors. The Dutch group had already managed to smuggle 40,000 Bibles into the Soviet Union, Tooming said. Furthermore, one of the Baptist leaders in Moscow had told IM Gerd – in a "very conspiratorial meeting" – that 4,200 Christian books and anti-Soviet literature had been delivered to him by a Dutch smuggler using a car with a secret compartment. That autumn, the KGB destroyed the secret printing shop that IM Gerd had helped locate.

But even though losing the printing shop was a heavy blow to the Latvian Baptists, religious literature was still being printed. IM Gerd again provided clues: an Estonian contact had told him of a modern underground printing shop in Estonia. Bambowsky picked up further news: the parts for the printing presses at the illegal printing shop in Latvia had been smuggled into the country by the UK Bible Society as well as groups of Belgians. Another contact told Bambowsky that Open Doors had given him books and typewriters as well. Though seemingly trivial information today, that was crucial information for Major Otto and his KGB counterparts: ordinary Soviet citizens could not buy typewriters, as the authorities – like their East German colleagues – feared they could be used to disseminate information critical of the regime. Smuggler-missionaries, the Church Bureau learned, had even managed to deliver the occasional copy machine to the harassed Christians.

By its very nature, clandestine work requires extraordinary trust among those involved with it. Gerd Bambowsky had proven himself phenomenally skilled at establishing such trust. His new Christian friends in the Soviet Union had already invited him to return, while the Western aid groups increasingly depended on the industrious Bible courier. At one meeting, an Open Doors representative gave Bambowsky 325 Gulden as a thank-you gift – and offered him a station wagon fitted with a secret book compartment. That was excellent news: Open Doors was Europe's leading Bible-smuggling organization. But Bambowsky didn't show his excitement. Instead he upped the ante: "We could also build a permanent smuggling channel to me," he told the group.

Major Otto had, in fact, determined that it was time for IM Gerd to infiltrate Open Doors. Also among the agent's new tasks, though further down the list, was to establish the identity of the Bible Society's Soviet contacts. Meanwhile, staff and helpers at Open Doors, the UK Bible Society, and *Licht im Osten* had been put under observation by MfS Division XII, the Stasi's surveillance arm.

IM Gerd had already discovered that Open Doors often used Dutch students to transport its books to East Germany during their university breaks, paying them a fee for their services. And, thanks to IM Gerd, the Church Bureau knew that the organization frequently also enlisted Dutch tourists travelling directly to the Soviet Union, who would each bring forty Bibles in their personal luggage. Of ten tourists who had recently travelled to the Soviet Union, only one had been apprehended. It was a time-consuming method, but it worked pretty well for small quantities.

Tourist smugglers greatly annoyed the Soviet security services. Were it left up to the security services, the Soviet Union would have no Western tourists at all. But the country needed hard currency, and many officials also saw tourism as an opportunity to educate Westerners about the glories of the Soviet Union. So the Kremlin operated a schizophrenic policy: it permitted visits by Western tourists, but they had to adhere to officially organized itineraries that focused on famous sights and precluded contact with ordinary people. Soviet customs officials were well aware that some tourists tried to smuggle Christian books, and arrested a few every so often. As IM Gerd had relayed to Department XX/4, in many cases these tourists were not individual do-gooders but part of a larger Bible-smuggling operation.

IM Gerd had also discovered a smuggling route that had previously eluded the Stasi: several US soldiers stationed in West Berlin had brought Bibles to East Berlin in their luggage. Here the Stasi was powerless, as Western troops were allowed to enter East Berlin at Checkpoint Charlie without luggage inspection. Worse still, the Stasi had learned that Western diplomats occasionally sent Bibles in the diplomatic pouch. And IM Gerd delivered news of yet another innovative scheme: a PanAm flight attendant bringing Bibles on board the airline's flight to Moscow. The pioneering direct flight from JFK in New York, launched in 1968, was a potential goldmine for small-quantity Bible smuggling. The flight attendant had twice delivered book packages to the Baptist leader in Moscow. But now, in 1974, she was sick, so Open Doors asked Bambowsky to arrange a trip to Moscow as soon as possible to tell the Baptist leader not to worry about the stewardess's absence. Without irony Major Otto logged: "In this context [name redacted] warned the IM of the staff member at the Baptist central office in Moscow and the secretary at [redacted]. Both are thought to be working with the Soviet security services." The staff at Open Doors was clearly aware it had been infiltrated in Moscow – but didn't have the slightest suspicion regarding its East German courier.

After Bambowsky's return from one of his Soviet trips, a West German pastor involved in book-smuggling asked for a meeting. The two men convened at the post office by Friedrichstrasse station. Though the West German was excited about the successful Bible delivery, he was clearly anxious: "Were there any particular occurrences?" Bambowsky feigned ignorance. The pastor elaborated: "Did you hear anything about arrests or house searches?" Nothing at all, Bambowsky reassured him. The pastor was relieved. The reason for his concern, he explained, was that a Christian illegal printing shop in Riga had recently been raided by the police. What a blessing that nothing seemed to have happened to the people involved with it, he said.

Bambowsky was excited about the news: it was verification that his cover had not been blown. The West German pastor explained that the raid only meant that his group and the Belgian Christians who supported the printing shop would have to come up with new methods. Bambowsky heartily agreed. The two men agreed to meet a couple of months later.

By now IM Gerd had an extremely busy courier schedule. But since it was sometimes difficult to collect the books in West Germany, the underground network engaged other runners who smuggled the books to him in East Germany. One evening in February 1975 – Department XX/4 gives precise details: 8 p.m. on 6 February – a journalist doubling as a runner appeared at Bambowsky's door with twenty-two sets of books in Russian and eleven sets in Polish. Should Bambowsky be interested, the journalist-courier said, there were unlimited quantities of these publications. Bambowsky meticulously took down the titles, for the benefit of the intended recipients, the journalist assumed. Instead, he, of course, shared the titles with the Church Bureau: *Life After Death*; *Holy Scripture*; *What Do You Know About the Fourth Commandment?*; *The Parable of the Prodigal Son*. As always, dutiful Church Bureau officers recorded the details.

In most cases, the recipient of IM Gerd's findings was Lieutenant Bartnitzek, on whose desk a multitude of tracts ended up. One entry reports: "The IM handed the staff member [Bartnitzek] 800 Bibles in the Russian, Estonian, and Latvian languages, which had been sent to him from Holland via the American married couple [name redacted]. As with the January operation of destruction of illegally imported literature, these Bibles will be centrally stored with us, for the purpose of pulpification."

Here's how Bambowsky's book deliveries worked: he brought a few books to Soviet Christians, to keep his cover and further infiltrate the underground networks. Delivering the books rather than just infiltrating the Western organizations spreading them also helped him identify the Soviet citizens receiving the books so that the KGB could arrest them.

But most of the books entrusted to Bambowsky never made it anywhere near their intended recipients. The Western charities were unknowingly filling Stasi and KGB storage rooms with religious literature, all the while rejoicing in their smuggling triumph. And with the smuggling operations recording such seeming success, supporters donated even more money.

"What was Bambowsky like as an agent?" I ask Wiegand. "He was very eager," Wiegand explains – and then reveals that the pastor's smuggling activities were in fact not his real assignment. "The background with him was that we wanted intelligence [about Christian groups]. Bible-smuggling was the by-product. We knew that the East Missions [Bible-smuggling groups] were no friends of the GDR; that there were people who were hostile to the GDR and the Soviet Union." "Are eager agents good?" I ask. "No," Wiegand says, "it's not good if agents are too eager; it means they exaggerate their findings and then you have to go back and verify their information."

But IM Gerd was eager mostly in a good way. In April 1975, he embarked on yet another visit to the Soviet Union, again as a courier – though, of course, officially, he went as a tourist. The third layer, the most secret one, was his undercover mission for the Stasi and the KGB. No Westerner would be able to travel to the Soviet Union with such ease. This time Bambowsky travelled on behalf of *Licht im Osten*, Open Doors, the *Gustav-Adolf-Werk*, and the Working Group for Russian Church History, an academic group he had also infiltrated. Among his objectives was to establish links with several additional Lutheran and Baptist leaders.

By now, Bambowsky was collecting regular incomes from *Licht im Osten*, the *Gustav-Adolf-Werk*, Open Doors and the Stasi. He lived extravagantly, his fellow Bible smugglers had noticed. Money, in fact, seemed to interest him greatly. But as Erwin Damson had initially sensed, Bambowsky also craved recognition. The not-yet-ordained Lutheran cleric was thrilled when Bartnitzek informed him that the MfS had decided to award him a medal.

On 7 October 1975, the twenty-sixth anniversary of the German Democratic Republic, Gerd Bambowsky received the Merit Medal of the National People's Army in silver. The ministry's official commendation, signed by Minister Mielke, credited Pastor Gerd Bambowsky with "particular achievements, responsible activity, initiative and high personal operational readiness in fulfilling tasks for the purpose of strengthening and securing the Worker and Peasant Power". The Worker and Peasant Power was, of course, the German Democratic Republic.

A short time later, IM Gerd was considered ready for in-depth undercover training. Bartnitzek had scheduled a meeting at a safe house for 19 February 1976, shortly before IM Gerd was to depart for West Germany again. Assisted by a colleague, Lieutenant Bartnitzek taught his agent how to detect whether he was under surveillance and, if so, how to act. Bartnitzek also detailed how to behave if border guards decided to check his luggage or question him, and how to behave if arrested. IM Gerd learned the procedures to follow if he had an accident or fell ill during a mission. "It can be assessed that the IM correctly understood all the situations that were addressed and shown and knows how to interpret the correct behaviour", Bartnitzek notes in his log.

Almost on the side, Bambowsky was conducting his studies for Lutheran ordained ministry. Although he was undeniably a charismatic preacher, he was certain that parish work wasn't his vocation. In ordained ministry as in undercover work, Bambowsky liked to be on the move. But his career plans in the church would have to be sorted out a little later.

He and the Church Bureau were planning yet another trip to the Soviet Union, even more audacious than his massive book deliveries. On this trip, again underwritten by Western charities, Bambowsky would smuggle offset printing machines. "The Soviet comrades should decide which measures should be performed with regards to the Soviet Union", a Church Bureau memo reads. That meant that General Paul Kienberg, Division XX's boss, would ask his KGB colleagues what they would like IM Gerd to do while in their country. The Church Bureau also asked Kienberg for permission to "liquidate the book smuggling channel". The time had come to stop observing and reporting – the Church Bureau had enough intelligence to shut down the illegal book transport.

CHAPTER 11

A LITERARY UNDERGROUND RAILROAD

On the morning of 18 August 1976, Oskar Brüsewitz, a dissident pastor in the town of Rippicha some two and a half hours south-west of Berlin, asked his daughter to play a hymn for him. He then put on his cassock, drove to the nearby town of Zeitz and parked in the town square. On top of his car, he placed a poster protesting the government's harassment of Christian youth. "The church in the GDR accuses communism! Repression of children and youth in schools", it read.[92] Then he poured gasoline over himself and set himself on fire. As passers-by tried to save him, he ran towards the assistant bishop's office, while police officers removed his protest signs. Some 300 residents witnessed Brüsewitz succumb to the flames. He left behind a farewell letter to his fellow pastors: "I loved you all.

---

92   Carsten Dippel, "Die Selbstverbrennung von Pfarrer Oskar Brüsewitz", *Deutschlandfunk*, 15 August 2018, https://www.deutschlandfunk.de/die-selbstverbrennung-von-pfarrer-oskar-bruesewitz-allein.2540.de.html?dram:article_id=423832 (accessed 19 May 2019).

Oskar. In several hours I will discover that my redeemer lives."

The regime was shaken. The idiosyncratic pastor was now in the hospital, unlikely to survive. He had been popular with local children and teenagers but not at all with the authorities. The Church Bureau, as well as some church officials and pastor colleagues, were convinced that Brüsewitz was mentally unstable. The Church Bureau even suspected him of being a Western agent provocateur.

During one of my conversations with Wiegand about Detlef Hammer, he mentions Brüsewitz. "Somebody like Hammer has a completely different connection to me, to us," Wiegand explains. "Hammer told us all the dirt that was going on in the church. Thanks to him, we knew exactly what Bishop Krusche in Magdeburg had in his files. We knew everything about him. Krusche had a complete Brüsewitz file in his cabinet. We couldn't act on that information as it would have exposed Hammer, but we had the information, we knew that Brüsewitz was mentally unstable. When he burned himself to death there was a big brouhaha, but the truth is that he was having problems with the church as well, not just with the government."

Major Western news outlets immediately reported on the self-immolation, which appeared inspired by Czech student Jan Palach's death seven years earlier. From Honecker to Wiegand, anxiety spread: would more dissidents humiliate the regime by setting themselves on fire?

On 22 August, Pastor Brüsewitz died of his injuries. That put the diocese in an acute dilemma. Brüsewitz had been an infuriatingly difficult man, but he had died fighting oppression and deserved recognition. Besides, the whole world was watching. Numerous West German newspapers and TV stations had already announced they would report from the funeral. "The aim is to shape reporting in such a way that it's not seen as incitement against the GDR," Detlef Hammer reported to the Church Bureau, summarizing the diocese's internal discussions. Church representatives, the diocese had decided, would give no media interviews. West German news media had been understanding, but the Christian Democratic Union – one of West Germany's two largest parties – was not. It had already told the diocese it was planning to make human rights violations in East Germany an issue in the upcoming national elections.

On 26 August, Brüsewitz was buried in Rippicha. Thanks to Hammer, the Church Bureau knew beforehand that a crowd of more than 500 was expected. The Stasi, meanwhile, dispatched five officers led by Joachim Wiegand, by now the Church Bureau's deputy chief.

"It was a huge event, with all kinds of Western journalists, with flyers being distributed," he recalls. "We had walkie-talkies. I was Eagle 1. I called Eagle 3, who was sitting in a shed in the graveyard. 'What do the flyers say?' I asked. 'It's not a flyer, it's a hymn sheet,' my colleague answered. 'Well then, sing!' I told him." The officer began singing, with his walkie-talkie still on. "A mighty fortress is our God", Wiegand heard. In East Germany even secret police officers knew their Lutheran chorales.

The Stasi had been keeping Rippicha and Zeitz under surveillance since the morning. West German correspondents had arrived, including the two national television networks with camera teams, on whom the officers kept a trained eye.

Back at their desks, Wiegand's team wrote a detailed summary of the events: "Representatives of the Lutheran Church, local pastors, family and acquaintances of the family, among others, arrived in 110 cars", they noted and described some of them: Mrs Brüsewitz and the two Brüsewitz daughters; two brothers living in West Germany who had arrived with their wives; an aunt also living in West Germany.[93] Wiegand and his men counted 370 participants, among them seventy-two pastors wearing clerical robes. The service itself was fine, they logged, with none of the pastors or participants causing trouble.

---

93   "Zur Beisetzung von Pfarrer Brüsewitz am 26.8.1976 in Pippicha, Kreis Zeitz", *Stasi Mediathek*, p. 3, https://www.stasi-mediathek.de/medien/zur-beisetzung-von-pfarrer-bruesewitz-am-2681976-in-rippicha-kreis-zeitz/blatt/12/ (accessed 3 May 2019).

Not even two well-known dissidents had caused any trouble, the team noted – that is, the two men had refrained from criticizing the regime during the funeral. However, as Wiegand's team noted in the post-funeral brief, IMs had told them that two pastors had considered whistling during the sermon because the preacher had not sided with Brüsewitz, while another had complained about the heavy police presence.[94]

While most pastors were consumed by Brüsewitz's fate, Gerd Bambowsky was getting excited about the prospect of another undercover trip to the Soviet Union, and especially about his new minivan. Open Doors, grateful to its star smuggler, had bought him a Barkas, East Germany's version of the VW minivan.

Though the Barkas was manufactured in East Germany, it was only available to people who absolutely needed it – say, plumbers and carpenters whose equipment wouldn't fit in a Trabant. For a steep price, however, Westerners could purchase a Barkas through Genex, the East German government-run company selling high-quality products for Western currency.

Thanks to Open Doors, Bambowsky now had the much-desired vehicle, complete with secret compartments that could fit 900 Bibles. "They don't want to limit themselves to Bibles but also send office equipment, typewriters, etc.", Bartnitzek noted. "They will then send specialists from Holland who will build one or more compartments in this vehicle." The Church Bureau requested surveillance.

Open Doors had also promised Bambowsky a new station wagon, with which he could easily transport Christian books in plastic sacks and bury them in a designated place; another courier would unearth them and conduct the second leg of the journey.

---

94   "Zur Beisetzung von Pfarrer Brüsewitz am 26.8.1976 in Pippicha, Kreis Zeitz", *Stasi Mediathek*, p. 5, https://www.stasi-mediathek.de/medien/zur-beisetzung-von-pfarrer-bruesewitz-am-2681976-in-rippicha-kreis-zeitz/blatt/14/ (accessed 3 May 2019).

Lieutenant General Kienberg did not approve Department XX/4's request to liquidate the book smuggling network. So the smuggling continued, with IM Gerd retaining his starring role. That meant even more contact with Erwin Damson at *Licht im Osten*. Every time Bambowsky met with Damson, he took pains to thwart surveillance. There were, for example, the cushions that he insisted on placing on top of the telephone. It was unusual, to be sure, but Damson considered Bambowsky the expert. Beyond their undeniable professional results, Damson enjoyed Bambowsky's personality. He had also discovered that the East German had humour, of the dry and irreverent Berlin kind. And after he heard Bambowsky in the pulpit he was blown away. "No eye remained dry," he told his wife.

But even though Damson liked the pastor and appreciated his precautions, he fretted about some of his more unusual requests. Why did Bambowsky request so much non-religious literature? But Damson remained convinced of his trustworthiness. And he needed him. Still, when Bambowsky asked him for the addresses of Soviet underground printing shops, Damson demurred. Such information was simply too sensitive to share, even with an East German man of the cloth.

Thanks to the Barkas, Bambowsky's value as a smuggler skyrocketed: he could now transport much larger shipments in the van's secret compartments. (Never missing an opportunity to use an ideologically flavoured adjective, the Stasi referred to such compartments as "conspiratorial compartments".) To open and close the hatch, Bambowsky just pressed a well-disguised button. Thanks to the van, he even had capacity to transport disassembled printing presses. Several groups were, in fact, already asking him to transport printing presses and books to the Soviet Union for them too.

At their next meeting, IM Gerd related to Lieutenant Bartnitzek that one group had already arranged a delivery of books and a printing press to Christians in the Estonian capital of Tallinn using him – Bambowsky – and his Barkas. Bartnitzek took down the planned trip schedule, October and November 1976. Leaving nothing to chance, he added details about the printing presses that were to be delivered: "Paper size A4, can use regular typewriter paper." Such information helped the KGB officers to track down and destroy the machine.

IM Gerd had further crucial news: to minimize the risk of detection, Open Doors had found an American diplomat who had already helped the organization and was willing to bring the delivery from West Berlin to Bambowsky's home.

Just a few months earlier, in the summer of 1976, Open Doors had also asked Bambowsky for help with its printing presses in Kiev. "The Dutch mission firm", as Department XX/4 called Open Doors, had managed to smuggle the printing presses there via Romania and Poland, but now the printing machinery was sitting idle because none of the local Christians had the expertise to assemble it. "Perhaps we could train you to assemble the printing presses?" an Open Doors employee had asked Bambowsky. And since he was going anyway, Open Doors asked, could Bambowsky also bring Bibles, money and printing press parts to the Soviet Union? Of course he could. Ever ambitious, IM Gerd in fact planned to ingratiate himself with Open Doors' chief executive and hatch deals far above the lower-level members of staff who had so far been his contacts.

IM Gerd had been cultivating other contacts too. Recently, an American couple had turned up at his house with some 800 Russian Bibles. In a fortuitous turn of events, the couple was involved with one of the US groups Bambowsky was trying to infiltrate. A US military chaplain from the US Army base in Kaiserslautern had also come to visit. When Bambowsky described the challenge of getting the books across the border from West to East, the military chaplain was alarmed at the couriers' lack of security. "I'll help you establish a better connection," he promised.

The American connections were, however, rather tricky. Unlike *Licht im Osten* and other European veterans of the Bible-smuggling underground, the US groups often seemed unaware of the dangers and almost cavalier about the consequences if anything went wrong. But they were expanding their activities. On 16 March, two young members of Campus Crusade for Christ (the Church Bureau referred to the organization as *Campus Christi*) came to see Bambowsky. He had reported the upcoming visit to Bartnitzek, who dispatched another IM for surveillance outside the building. The IM took down the visitors' licence plate number and "conspiratorially photographed" their car, Bartnitzek noted in his log.

In Bambowsky's living room, the two Americans explained Campus Crusade's activities in great detail: 5,000 staff, 350 of whom were based in Europe, primarily in Britain and Vienna. One of the men told Bambowsky that he had attended divinity school in Chicago, his studies underwritten by Campus Crusade, and that he was now based in Vienna. He confided that Campus Crusade was having trouble establishing a network in Europe's socialist countries. In fact, the group lacked a single contact. Could Bambowsky help?

Bambowsky whipped out his standard response: of course he was happy to help. But in his report to Bartnitzek, he scoffed at his inexperienced visitors, dismissing them as having naïve views about religious life in European socialist countries. Campus Crusade for Christ, Bambowsky explained to Bartnitzek, had four principles, which he delivered to Bartnitzek translated into German:

1. God is Lord of all people. Everyone needs him!

2. One can't establish contact with God because he's a sinner!

3. The contact between God and the people can be established through Christ!

4. One has to say yes to it, when one has been told about it one can tell others![95]

---

95   Translated back into English by the author.

Had the Americans recited these principles to Bambowsky in German or had he translated the principles from English himself? He didn't tell Bartnitzek, but the experienced officer could be forgiven for wondering what this American organization was about. "One can't establish contact with God because he's a sinner!" (*Man kann mit Gott nicht in Verbindung treten, weil er ein Sünder ist!*) Did Campus Crusade really consider God to be a sinner? Or had somebody mistranslated? Given its apparent lack of German skills, how was the organization hoping to build a courier network in East Germany? Still, Bartnitzek wrote the down the principles.

Around the same time, Bambowsky set off on a two-week trip to West Germany with the goal of further infiltrating *Licht im Osten*, "the political-clerical diversion central", as Department XX/4 called it. The pastor's additional Church Bureau assignment was to "establish contact with politically-operationally important people, for example Bischof Scharf". Kurt Scharf, the Lutheran bishop of Berlin, was the top-ranking cleric among both East and West Germany's Lutherans. Unusually, Scharf was an East German who had ended up in the West simply because he happened to be in West Germany when the Berlin Wall went up. When he tried to return home, the East German authorities refused him entry. Scharf was a key target to win as an ally of East Germany, and IM Gerd succeeded in establishing contact, meeting with the bishop twice during his trip.

IM Gerd was, in fact, increasingly reaping the benefits of his legwork in Bible-smuggling circles; his connections created further connections. Bishop Scharf, IM Gerd relayed to Major Otto on his return, had said that he valued Bambowsky's judgment and told him that if he ever needed anything, he could simply contact him. More problematically, though, the bishop also inquired about Pastor Brüsewitz.

Soon after, Erwin Damson again welcomed his industrious friend. As always, he gave Bambowsky more books for East German destinations, but this time he also suggested that Bambowsky go on yet another trip to the

Soviet Union. The East German immediately accepted the offer – but he was quietly disdainful of Damson. Indeed, he didn't think very highly of his fellow literary missionary. "[Damson] is possessed by great ambition and his wife supports his efforts to get a top position soon. For this reason, he also wants to strengthen *Licht im Osten*'s activities into the Soviet Union and personally make a visible contribution", he reported to the Church Bureau.

The Bureau summarized Bambowsky's intelligence from the meeting with Damson: "The main reason was clearly that [Damson] wants to strengthen his own position within *Licht im Osten* through the help of the IM and his activities." "[Damson] points out everywhere that it was him who managed around 80 deliveries last year, whereas it used to be only 10 annually."

IM Gerd also reported that Damson was planning to further strengthen his position in *Licht im Osten* by conducting an "inspection tour" in the Soviet Union and would undertake the trip looking a bit different [in disguise] and perhaps using a false passport as well. "He will get the required false passport with the help of people at the BND", Department XX/4 noted in IM Gerd's report. Apparently the *Bundesnachrichtendienst* – the West German intelligence agency – was willing to aid West German Bible smugglers. Once again, IM Gerd had delivered invaluable insights.

Major Sgraja and his staff had been keeping a close eye on *Licht im Osten* for some time, They worried that Erwin Damson was trying to establish another smuggling channel through East Germany, this time using Western diplomats, military personnel, and journalists. But they were not overly alarmed at the new smuggler network: Damson had decided that Bambowsky would receive the deliveries. Damson also wanted Bambowsky to take on a larger role in getting the books to the Soviet Union and Czechoslovakia. "I depend on your support," he had told Bambowsky.

Now *Licht im Osten* just needed more depots in East Germany. Damson asked Bambowsky to identify barns, farmsteads and former bakeries that could receive the deliveries, and promised to increase Bambowsky's compensation. It had been a good day for IM Gerd.

Indeed, while Bambowsky greatly enjoyed his regular trips to West German cities, he also rather liked his comfortable existence in the East. Besides, as *Neues Deutschland* reported as Bambowsky returned from his visit to Korntal, "millions of primarily young people are being denied the right to work".[96] In East Germany, by contrast, *Neues Deutschland* reported that industrial production was steadily increasing. On the same day, *Neues Deutschland* readers further learned that Chile's fascist junta had "bestially tortured" and killed a communist former mayor, while a representative of South Africa's ANC had condemned NATO countries' support of Southern Rhodesia's white prime minister, Ian Smith. Smith's government was fighting communist-backed black guerrillas. In Bucharest, meanwhile, reconstruction following a recent earthquake was proceeding well, *Neues Deutschland* reported. Any reader of the newspaper would inevitably conclude that the West was a brutal place.

Conspicuously absent from *Neues Deutschland*'s reporting was, however, coverage of Czechoslovakia's Charter 77 movement and its growing international prominence. The newspaper also didn't mention that a Soviet Jewish human rights activist named Anatoly Shcharansky[97] had just been detained in his home country and charged with espionage on behalf of the CIA. But the busy Bambowsky would, at any rate, have had little time to consider the fate of Soviet dissidents. Indeed, with more Christian dissidents to locate and report to the KGB, further career advantages beckoned for IM Gerd.

---

96   "Archiv der Ausgaben von 1946–1990: Millionen auf Stellensuch in den Landern des Kapitals", *Neues Deutschland,* 18 March 1977, http://www.nd-archiv.de/ausgabe/1977-03-18 (accessed 3 May 2019).

97   Later known as Natan Sharansky.

CHAPTER 12

AGENTS AND THEIR REWARDS

Siegfried Krügel, the theology lecturer, had artistic tastes. Fortunately, he didn't have to worry about missing an opera or theatre performance in Leipzig: he could simply ask the Church Bureau for help. One day, Stasi officer Alexander thus arrived at Conspiratorial Apartment Balkon, bringing with him twenty-four tickets to five upcoming performances. In IM Lorac's file, Alexander had meticulously noted the price per ticket and the total for each performance. In total, the tickets amounted to 140.20 East German marks. The Stasi had already agreed to pay 100 marks, but IM Lorac might be willing to pay a little bit himself. Alexander wasn't sure. For now, he simply gave IM Lorac the tickets. "Can you please check if I should accept money from him at the next meeting and if not, how much I should request from him?" he wrote to his superior. The Church Bureau always kept good order.

And it rewarded its agents. The agents, though, didn't expect to become wealthy. Like IM Lorac, they received concert tickets and consumer goods that were hard to come by, and sometimes a modest amount of money. "In light of his good work the GM was handed a monetary reward amounting to

150 MDN [East German marks]", Alexander logged after a meeting with IM Lorac.[98]

Products from the West were a particular boon. So, of course, were trips to West Germany. "The IM brought up the next subject and reminded me of the planned spa visit", reads an entry in IM Lorac's file. Extended spa visits for health purposes are a big thing in Germany. But IM Lorac didn't want to visit one of East Germany's austere spas. Instead it would, he argued, be a much better idea to visit one in West Germany because there he could both visit BND's headquarters in Pullach, near Munich, the Lutheran Church's external relations office in Frankfurt am Main, and attend a Christian conference in the Bavarian town of Neuendettelsau. Oddly, the eager agent was unaware of the fact – or chose to ignore it – that Pullach is situated almost four hours away from Frankfurt am Main and some two hours from Neuendettelsau. Besides, an East German pastor without connections to West German espionage would have minimal chances of gathering intelligence about the BND, the country's intelligence agency. But Siegfried Krügel wanted his spa cure in West Germany. He also wanted a job for his wife, "preferably as an editor in a publishing house," he informed Lieutenant Kunth.

What IM pastors like Krügel preferred not to understand was that the Stasi was not a fount of limitless gifts. But as so often, Department XX/4 had a solution: it advised IM Lorac to ask the church to arrange the spa visit on the grounds that he could use the trip to acquire West German passports that East Germans could use in order to escape. Learning more about how East Germans got their hands on West German passports would be useful. IM Lorac agreed to the assignment.

On another occasion, IM Lorac was eager to attend another theological conference in West Germany to raise his professional profile. But the government's Church Department turned down his application for a travel

---

98   Geheimer Mitarbeiter (GM), secret collaborator, was an early label for MfS informants. It was later changed to IM (including IM subcategories).

permit. The Church Bureau spoke to the Church Department, which settled the matter. Lieutenant Kunth even drove IM Lorac to the agent's appointment with the Church Department official handling the matter. Suddenly, the pastor began worrying: what should he tell his colleagues and the Lutheran Church officials who had supported his travel application in the first place? It would be hard to explain to them why the stern Church Department bureaucrats who had initially turned down the application had suddenly changed their mind. "Tell them that you complained about the denial [of the application] and requested a review, and that after some back and forth the permission was finally granted," Kunth advised.

As predicted, Krügel's colleagues asked about the sudden reversal. "I was asked countless times how I managed to get the permission," he told Kunth. "I told them that the word 'scholarship' means something here." Ever vain, IM Lorac explained to Kunth that he had told his colleagues that he had gone directly to the Interior Ministry, which – valuing serious scholarship – had approved his application.

A successful travel application: hardly a king's ransom. But just like a CIA officer doubling as a KGB agent could blow his cover by living beyond his means, Church Bureau agents could also risk exposing their true identities by the perks their espionage provided. People would draw their own conclusions if the government suddenly reversed a denied travel request.

I ask Joachim Wiegand about agents' rewards. He gives me an example. "One bishop wanted a [special traffic permit] and a lamp from the West [West Germany]. That's the way people are." The Stasi helped the bishop get his lamp – although such gifts by no means meant that he was a favourite. The bishop was himself watched by other pastor IMs. "Through our IMs we would, for example, have the draft of a pastoral letter or announcement by him before it was made," Wiegand explains. "Then I could go to the bishop and say, 'in your announcement you're criticizing Honecker. That's not OK. Leave it out and you'll get your lamp, or get your visa for the West or whatever.'

They had countless things they were keen to have: books, medication, cars, construction permits. Of course we knew in advance exactly what [perks] they were keen on."

That's the way people are. Wiegand wasn't cynical about it during his career, and he isn't now. He's just very familiar with the deficiencies of the human character. If a bishop is willing to trade his integrity for a lamp, why should Wiegand not take advantage of it?

Indeed, early in his career, Wiegand already learnt that a great deal of people could be cheaply bought, especially in the German Democratic Republic, where even bishops yearned for West German lamps. Several pastor IMs enjoyed fine cigars. Lieutenant Blümel in Leipzig, for example, knew that cigars never failed to put IM Lorac in a good mood. Sometimes Blümel brought a surprise gift. "He was served coffee, cookies, and cigars and received a new release from the *Verlag der Wissenschaften* [a government-owned East German publishing house] with the title *Marx or Sartre*, for which he expressed cordial thanks," Blümel logged after a meeting in August 1965.

And, like many other agents, IM Lorac wasn't shy about articulating his needs. In 1965, he asked the Church Bureau to expedite the installation of a phone line at his house: an outrageous request, considering that most East Germans lacked a phone connection and IM Lorac had no urgent reason to place calls from home. Slyly, he instead motivated his request with espionage reasons: he couldn't "call conspiratorially" from his office, he informed Blümel.

At almost every meeting, Lieutenant Blümel also provided IM Lorac with theological handbooks the agent had requested; the Church Bureau was not above supplying the Word of God if it served its interests. And the department was flexible in other ways too. "[IM Lorac] asked us to help him get the medicine Gerioptil 3H. It's a West medication that's not yet available here", logged Officer Alexander after a meeting with the pastor. Though the officer had confused the 3 and the H, he had taken the drug's name down correctly. Gerioptil H3 was a new medication against dementia. For whom did IM Lorac need it? He didn't say. Another time, Alexander handed him five seat reservations for the train to the Baltic Sea resort of Warnemünde, where IM Lorac was about to go on vacation. "He was very excited to receive them", Alexander wrote in the agent's file.

All around East Germany, Church Bureau agents were asking for – demanding, even – similar favours. At his second meeting with the Stasi in Halle, Detlef Hammer had to be reminded that turning up early for a meeting was a very bad idea as he could be spotted waiting idly. But when it came to money, Hammer was less naïve, insisting that the Stasi reimburse even his expenses for the first meeting. A couple of meetings into the game, he was already receiving monetary thank-yous. "In accordance with the confirmed suggestion he received 50 marks", Officer Kuntze duly wrote in Hammer's file after one of the first meetings.

IM Gerd was initially mostly content with small rewards. "During the meeting tobacco products were supplied and corresponding baked goods were served with the coffee, which [IM Gerd] gratefully accepted", now-Captain Heinritz noted after a late-morning meeting with the agent. Later on, though, IM Gerd grew to like his regular agent monetary gifts more and more, which provided him greater material comfort than he would have had as a run-of-the-mill pastor.

Meanwhile, IM Thomas (Aleksander Radler) wasn't doing too shabbily working for the Stasi, and made sure to also send the Firm receipts for sundry expenses.

One of the good things about being an agent in your home country, rather than abroad, is that your employer can relatively easily help make your life more comfortable. An agent or undercover officer operating abroad can't usually turn to his employer to help sort out his children's problems in school. But Stasi agents could. During one of his meetings, IM Lorac – having, as usual, enjoyed coffee and cigars – brought up the issue the Thomas-Oberschule; he wanted the Church Bureau to arrange for his son to get a place at the school. The problem was that the son lacked the prerequisite grades. The boy was not to blame, Krügel insisted: there were simply too many rowdy kids in his class who prevented studious ones from excelling.

Oh, IM Lorac added, he and his family were going to spend their summer vacation at a church retreat centre in the town of Ilsenburg. Could Blümel help arrange the permits? Because Ilsenburg was located near the border with West Germany, the Krügel family would need the border permits required of all East Germans wishing to spend time near the border. Blümel promised to speak with his colleagues at the police. Within a month, the Krügels received the permits.

But getting an under-performing youngster into a popular high school posed a challenge even for the Stasi. The following summer, with the academic year approaching its end, no school transfer had materialized. IM Lorac was visibly annoyed. "Can you take care of it, otherwise there will be trouble at home," he complained to an officer. What he conveniently forgot was that every measure by the Stasi on his behalf increased the risk of him being exposed. Of course, the Church Bureau could talk to the school authorities in Leipzig and even pressure them into accepting the boy, but not even government officials had much sympathy for Stasi agents. And lots of children wanted to attend the Thomas-Oberschule.

In late August, with the new school year fast approaching, Pastor Krügel still hadn't received news about a school place for his son. The youngster would, of course, get a place somewhere else, but Krügel was adamant that he must attend the Thomas-Oberschule. Krügel had also been lobbying the city's school administration, but to no avail. "We will help you according to our abilities to make sure the matter gets resolved quickly," Lieutenant Kunth assured him. Most secret police agencies are a bit like the Lord Almighty: when agents are in a pinch, they can always plead for help. The Church Bureau came through for IM Lorac: the boy got the place. "He's the only child in the class who doesn't belong to the FDJ," IM Lorac proudly informed Kunth. But his father served the Stasi.

Unfortunately for the much-tested Lieutenant Kunth, that was not the end of IM Lorac's school needs. Sometime later, he was back with another school request. IM Lorac had again been pestering the Church Bureau about it, complaining that his phone calls to city officials had yielded no results. "Speak your points on tape and we'll try to help you," Lieutenant Heindke – another handler – advised him. IM Lorac did so, detailing his son's intellectual prowess and adding that the only reason he would be rejected is because of "my [i.e. Siegfried Krügel's] profession". "I would again like to ask the MfS to help me in this personal matter," he concluded, conveniently not having mentioned that his son's grades may simply not have been good enough. The Stasi proved a reliable ally. "Initiate measures for the son's acceptance", the Church Bureau logged.

Indeed, unlike foreign intelligence agencies with their often-lavish rewards, the Stasi acted more like a good friend. How an agent was rewarded for his services was determined solely by the handler's judgment and each agent's motivations in serving the Stasi. Agents who spied in support of East German socialism and were motivated by ideology, and required little monetary incentive or career support. Many other IMs, in turn, loved the intrigue, the flattering of their egos, the feeling of being in on a secret; they didn't need financial or material rewards as motivation. But most agents did want something concrete in exchange for their services: Western goods, a new telephone line, assistance getting a new apartment, career advantages. Large sums of money would, at any rate, not have been particularly useful in East Germany, where most desirable goods were usually only available in the country's Intershop shops for Western currency.

The Stasi's friend services were highly useful. In 1977, when IM Gerd wanted to move to a new apartment, finding one proved difficult and involved trading in another apartment. Rather than turning to his own family or friends, he asked the Church Bureau for help. In fact, by now he felt the Church Bureau should do much to secure a comfortable life for him. "The IM expressed his disappointment that the MfS is not in the position to materially guarantee his espionage activity. He said that he considered this a disparagement of him and that at age 47 he finally wants to have a long-term residence solution", Lieutenant Winkler dutifully wrote down.

Pastor Richard Schröder was, for some time, Gerd Bambowsky's superior in a suburban East Berlin parish soon after Bambowsky's ordination into the Lutheran Church. Visiting Schröder, I ask about Bambowsky's relations with the Stasi. Schröder has followed up on the doings of his former assistant. "The Stasi was like family for him," Schröder says. "But if your church, rather than you personally, gets advantages, is it also wrong to cooperate with the secret police?" I ask later, during a conversation with Wiegand. Wiegand is telling me about one of the churchmen he considered to be an exemplary faith leader. Wilhelm Pusch was the "apostle", the leader, of East Germany's tiny New Apostolic Church. "The New Apostolic Church had a church building near the MfS," Wiegand explains. "The original one had been demolished, but they built a new one. We sorted everything out with Apostle Pusch. He got construction materials, everything. In exchange, he led the church in a responsible way. He didn't agitate against the GDR. New Apostolic people are pacifists, but Pusch made sure that they didn't refuse to do military service." A religious leader who talks to the Stasi to get construction material for a new church, that can't be unethical, I reflect. But then again, where to stop if you get construction materials just for talking a bit? Do you get even more advantages, including career leaps and personal perks, if you talk more? In the GDR, you did.

Wiegand mentions another case. "I met with a bishop in a conspiratorial apartment. Of course he realized that I was not from the Interior Ministry. It was just before Christmas, and I brought porcelain from Meissen. His wife was very excited about it. I told him, 'we're pulling on the same rope.'" Wiegand mentions another bishop, in the city of Görlitz. Görlitz – I think for a moment. Then the bishop must be Joachim Rogge. "Was it Rogge?" I ask. "Yes, Rogge," Wiegand says. "He's dead; if he were alive I wouldn't tell you. Rogge was very helpful. He frequently came to see us, had hot chocolate with us; we gave him Stollen and presents for Christmas." If Wiegand had threatened the clerics into collaborating, they would have baulked. But some porcelain, Christmas bread and a friendly Christmas visit had the desired effect. It occurs to me that every example he mentions illustrates human weakness or vanity, or both.

Manfred Stolpe – the top church official in the Diocese of Berlin-Brandenburg – for his part, secured travel permits. In 1973, the German Democratic Republic was admitted to the United Nations. For the GDR, it was a seminal moment; countries outside the Soviet bloc that had been reluctant to recognize it now did so. East Germany joined other UN bodies as well, along with other international organizations. That meant lots more travel for East German representatives – and more work for the Stasi.

Stolpe was well on his way to becoming one of Department XX/4's most prominent agents, having combined his stellar church career with a life as Stasi IM Sekretär. So important was IM Sekretär that, even after taking over at the helm at the Church Bureau, Wiegand often got personally involved in his assignments. Like all church leaders, Stolpe of course had official dealings with Department XX/4 – but he mixed them with undercover ones. "For example, he'd let me know that somebody's mother [in the West] was old and ailing, and I'd arrange for that person to get an exit permit," Wiegand tells me. IM Sekretär also received West German currency, a total of 16,684 Deutschmark by the time East Germany collapsed. "Stolpe did as much as was possible for us," Wiegand explains. "Not everything was doable, not everything could be prevented, but we managed to prevent a whole lot for the benefit of a sensible coexistence."

CHAPTER 13

SPYING AND DOING ONE'S PART FOR EAST GERMANY

On 15 June 1973, Ditmar Heydel drove to Erkner, a small town outside East Berlin. After parking in a spot by the train station where he couldn't easily be seen, Heydel sat back to watch. At 1.30 p.m. sharp, a young man walked up to Heydel's car. "He behaved as required by conspiracy and took the appointed route. He was neither accompanied nor watched by others. His behaviour was irreproachable, secure, and deft", Heydel noted in his file.

The young man got into Heydel's car, and together they drove to the nearby town of Bad Saarow, where they sat down in a low-key eatery. Ditmar Heydel was a lieutenant in Department XX/4. The young man's name was Jürgen Kapiske. A somewhat shy 25-year-old, of medium height with a round, boyish face, he was studying to become a pastor in the Lutheran Church.

Kapiske's parents had wanted him to work at the post office, and he initially trained as a post office telephone operator, but the pastor in his home town of Jacobsdorf was an engaging man who had encouraged young Jürgen to pursue ordained ministry. Being musical, young Jürgen had also learned to play the organ, and often accompanied Sunday services in Jacobsdorf. The pastor was grateful, since the church couldn't afford a professional organist.

Disembarking from the S-Bahn in Erkner to see Heydel, Kapiske had been feeling rather down. At the restaurant, he told the officer that he felt like the odd man out at the Sprachenkonvikt in East Berlin. Originally founded by brave Christians in the Third Reich as an underground alternative to the Nazi-dominated official seminaries, the Sprachenkonvikt had remained open after the war, teaching future pastors the languages of theology – Hebrew, Greek, and Latin. By the time Kapiske enrolled in 1972, the Sprachenkonvikt also offered a full-fledged theology degree programme. The students were mostly taught by opposition-minded professors like Wolf Krötke, the pastor who had been jailed as a student for having written an anti-regime poem. English instruction was provided by Horst Kasner's wife Herlinde, who also taught Latin. The government didn't allow her to teach at state schools or institutions, but the Sprachenkonvikt had welcomed her. The Konvikt, as everyone still calls it, operated on the outer edges of East German legality, barely tolerated by the authorities and awarding degrees and doctorates not recognized by the government.[99]

But Kapiske, the son of collectivized farmers, wasn't critical of the regime. On the contrary, he fully supported the political system that had given him opportunities otherwise out of reach to a working-class boy. Kapiske had, in fact, enrolled at the Sprachenkonvikt almost by accident. He had already been a theology student at the Humboldt when he was called up for military service – but when he returned to East Berlin after having completed his military service, he discovered that the Humboldt did not have room for him.

So now he was an odd bird at the Konvikt. "So many of the other students are pastor's sons," he told his parents. "Some even come from real

---

99   The *Sprachenkonvikt* still exists and is located at the same address. Today it functions as student housing.

pastor dynasties." Consciously or unconsciously, Kapiske was exaggerating. Though some of the seminarians were pastors' sons, many others came from backgrounds similar to Kapiske's. In fact, the Stasi had precise information about East German seminarians' background. Another agent had provided the Church Bureau with an internal church survey of current seminarians: 31.5 per cent came from pastor families, 21.2 per cent came from blue-collar worker families and 16.2 per cent stemmed from white-collar worker families. Those figures worried the Stasi. Despite its best efforts, Christianity was clearly reaching East Germans far from the church circuit.

In their political tastes, though, the students at the Sprachenkonvikt differed from Kapiske. Many of his classmates listened to Western radio stations and openly discussed the global situation, often with critical comments about their own country. And with some eighty-five students living in the Konvikt building, there was plenty of opportunity to discuss current events. The rest had to live elsewhere in East Berlin, granted they had a government permit for residence in the capital. Krötke and other teachers had to negotiate with the authorities for permits for themselves and their students, and even for staples for the school canteen.

Ditmar Heydel, Kapiske's lunch companion this summer day, had a talent for engaging people in conversation. He was already familiar with Kapiske's disillusionment. Always on the lookout for friendly contacts in theology departments and seminaries, Heydel knew that despite his piety, Kapiske was also a committed supporter of the GDR. And from the outset, Kapiske had known the identity of the fatherly man sitting across from him. Introducing himself to Kapiske at their first meeting, in a parking lot behind the train station in Frankfurt an der Oder, Heydel had showed the young man his Stasi ID badge. Doing so violated official recommendations, but Heydel had done his homework and knew that Kapiske would not run away at the sight of a Stasi officer.

Kapiske wasn't sure why Heydel had contacted him in the first place, but he assumed it had something to do with the fact that Soviet officers had caught him taking photographs in a deserted area near his home; as he later found out, the area was home to Soviet military installations. The Soviet officers had questioned Kapiske and turned him over to the East German authorities.

At their brief first encounter, Heydel had told Kapiske that he would enjoy meeting to talk about current issues. Kapiske didn't hesitate. Kapiske had been interested in world politics from an early age; perhaps it could hardly be otherwise for a boy from Jacobsdorf, a small town in Brandenburg, east of Berlin. The young man devoured literature about World War II, which had ended only three years before his birth. Towards the end of the war, Soviet troops advancing from Poland had captured Jacobsdorf, too. Though many residents had fled westward, Kapiske's parents were not alarmed by the Red Army. Anything would be better than the Nazis, and most importantly, Germany's defeat meant there would finally be peace, they contended. After being wounded in an air raid, Kapiske's mother had been rescued by a Red Army officer. No, the Kapiskes were not afraid of the Russians.

Unlike most pastor agents, Kapiske is willing to talk about his work for the Stasi. I have come to visit him in his parental home in Jacobsdorf, where he now lives with his girlfriend. The village comprises two streets and a restaurant (the grocery store recently closed), as well as a train station. Jacobsdorf's church – Lutheran, of course; there are almost no Catholics in this part of Germany – is next door, but Kapiske attends services only occasionally.

It's not that he's lost his religion entirely; it would simply be awkward. When Kapiske's Stasi past came to light, the church defrocked him. Though the current pastor has invited him to serve on the parish council, Kapiske has declined. "I don't believe I'm credible, and most people would see it the same way," he explains. Together with his girlfriend, however, he writes and edits the parish newsletter, a surprisingly polished publication for such a small parish.

Growing up in this very house, this is not the future Kapiske imagined, but he's at peace with his life. "Why are you willing to talk when others won't?" I ask. "It has taken years of reflection and inner struggle to get to this point," he responds. It's a shame other Stasi pastor agents won't talk. If they won't explain their past, their motivations and perhaps their regrets, how can we even begin to understand how the church espionage could be so successful? Joachim Wiegand has excellent insights into his agents' motivations, of course, but he can't speak on their behalf.

That's why Jürgen Kapiske's testimony matters so much. Although he has considered writing his memoirs, he has decided against it: he senses that it would lack the necessary objectivity. So he has agreed to talk to me and has set no conditions.

I ask him about that first long meeting with Ditmar Heydel. "The conversation was very open," he tells me. "I told him about my heroes, for example Richard Sorge [a Nazi-era German diplomat who spied for the Soviets]. As a result, we were able to talk on a sensible basis. He told me little about himself; it was obvious that he couldn't reveal much. But he had an interest in me, and my impression was that it was sincere."

As they began their collaboration, Kapiske particularly appreciated the fact that Heydel had immediately revealed his identity. Kapiske trusted him. Besides, Heydel was a good conversationalist who seemed to share his interest in World War II. As they got up to leave, they made plans to meet again.

Travelling home after the meeting, Kapiske reflected on the unusual meeting and felt strangely upbeat. Finally there was someone with whom he could share thoughts and ideas. But the next morning, it was back to the Konvikt's improvised lecture hall and seminar rooms. Kapiske had become more and more disaffected with his studies. In fact, he had concluded that some of the other students wanted their country to develop closer links with West Germany or even cease to exist altogether.

"What about the church?" I ask Kapiske. "It was moving in the wrong direction," he says. "Many of the students at the Konvikt dreamed of the resurrection of the Weimar Republic or even the Kaiser. Most of them didn't like the GDR."

None of the other students had in fact suggested that the Weimar Republic should be reinstated, but that's how Kapiske interpreted their views. He concluded that the Lutheran Church posed a threat to the German Democratic Republic.

Kapiske and I are sitting in his warm study. It easily gets chilly here on the Brandenburg plains, and Kapiske's home lacks central heating, but the heating in his study works. He tries to explain the conflict he saw between the church and the government in East Germany: "The church and the state didn't understand each other at all. The older pastors didn't understand the communists, and the communists didn't understand the pastors." There were only a few exceptions, he adds, mentioning Emil Fuchs, a brave opponent of the Nazis who went on to teach theology at the Humboldt. "His books made a lot of sense to me," Kapiske says. Fuchs's son, Klaus, enjoyed hero status in East Germany thanks to his atomic espionage for the Soviets; streets were named after him.

But among the Konvikt's professors and other seminarians, Kapiske felt there was nobody he could confide in. Among the pastor dynasty sons at the Konvikt was Markus Meckel, Ernst-Eugen Meckel's son. Rebellious Meckel Junior had been expelled from high school for questioning the regime. After graduating from a church-run high school he had enrolled at the Konvikt, all the while challenging communist orthodoxy, and he seemed to be getting away with it. Kapiske concluded that Meckel was shielded by his father. He couldn't know that Meckel Senior was a Stasi agent.

Ernst-Eugen Meckel's motivations in working for the Stasi were, in fact, very different from Kapiske's. Like his son, Meckel Senior disapproved of his country's regime. But the Stasi had given him the dreaded HWG designation and presented him with the choice of working for the Firm or having his transgressions reported to his bishop. Meckel Senior had chosen the Stasi. Kapiske would soon learn that, in espionage, nothing is what it seems.

Heydel kept his word. Following the meeting at the restaurant, he contacted Kapiske at the dorm at the appointed time to arrange another meeting. But he had been too optimistic. Kapiske's disaffection with his fellow pastors had turned into doubts about his career vocation. He told Heydel that he no longer wanted to become a pastor.

Heydel leaped into action. "I told him that he will be able to use his knowledge to unmask enemy powers operating under the cover of church work", Heydel wrote in Kapiske's file and shared the news with his colleagues. Lacking the luxury of a long courtship with his prospective agent, he simply told Kapiske that, as a pastor, Kapiske could help the MfS and the country.

Heydel convinced him. Kapiske, such an unremarkable theology student that his Konvikt professors would later have trouble recalling him, quickly proved himself a model student of Heydel's. He also began taking his Konvikt studies seriously. Though Kapiske had dearly wanted to return to the Humboldt, the Church Bureau preferred the Konvikt, especially since the Bureau had already infiltrated the Humboldt. By 1973, some two thirds of the Humboldt theology department's professors and a number of its students were informants.[100]

Long after East Germany was no more, Kapiske would fondly remember his Humboldt lecturer in church history. Rosemarie Müller-Streisand was half-Jewish, the daughter of a Marxist bookkeeper. Despite losing most of her family in the Holocaust, Müller-Streisand hadn't fled Germany but remained in her home city of Berlin, an ardent supporter of the new East Germany and its regime. Kapiske liked Müller-Streisand's husband, too. Professor Hanfried Müller taught systematic theology, the philosophy of religion, and was as committed to East German communism as his wife.

---

100   Krötke, "Die Theologische Fakultät der Humboldt-Universität 1945–2010".

Indeed, he argued that the role of the church in the world was to embrace Marxism-Leninism. Both husband and wife worked for the Stasi. "A real fanatic," Wiegand later described Rosemarie to me. "She was really on the extreme left."

At the Sprachenkonvikt, a newly motivated Kapiske began cultivating connections with leading clerics. Previously adrift, he now thought of himself as fulfilling an important function. Heydel reported that Kapiske, reporting under codename IM Walter, was completing intensive MfS studies, too, reading the books necessary for "Chekist [secret police] duties", joining extracurricular Christian groups, and learning English for future foreign assignments.[101] At one meeting, Heydel and Kapiske discussed the book *Schild und Flamme* (Shield and Flame), an account of "the hard struggle" suffered under the Soviet Union's first secret police agency, the Cheka.

At a meeting in the autumn of 1973, Heydel taught his new recruit the ABCs of undercover work. He provided a cover address and phone number to be used when Kapiske needed to get in touch. He also instructed his agent in how to choose a meeting place, how to ascertain that he was not being watched, and what to do if he was being observed. "At the agreed meeting time, you arrive at the train station," Heydel explained. "As soon as we've spotted each other, you start walking towards the central square, making sure that you're not being watched." When he reached the square, Kapiske was to wait for a certain car – driven by Heydel or another Stasi officer – and get in. If urgent, IM Walter would receive a telegram at his parents' house with the words "please preach sermon on..." – with an inserted date – which meant that IM Walter was expected at the Jacobsdorf autobahn exit at 10 p.m. that day.

IM Walter soon began delivering useful information. Some Konvikt seminarians supported pro-Israeli, anti-Arab, racist views, he reported.

---

101   The Cheka was the Soviet Union's first secret police agency. It was later succeeded by, for example, the KGB.

On another occasion he informed Heydel that a leading pastor had once worked for Nazi Germany's counter-intelligence agency. He kept close tabs on the "Jesus People", a US-based revivalist youth movement. Though East Germany's atheist regime certainly had no obligation to allow mission-minded American Christians into the country, it did so nonetheless, with good reason: the Americans brought in the badly needed US dollars. The government only allowed visiting Christians to deliver personal greetings at events, not sermons, but the Jesus People visitors shrewdly turned their greetings into moving testimonies. Alarmed, the Church Bureau observed the Americans' charismatic style catch on in a country accustomed to stiff Lutheran sermons.

At the Sprachenkonvikt, meanwhile, West German student groups frequently came to visit. Friendships with such visitors could plant rebellious thoughts among the East German students, IM Walter warned Heydel: "Students like [redacted] are in my opinion capable of committing acts that are hostile to the government." He was certain it was a case of subversion directed by the West German government.

One day, the Konvikt's dean asked if Kapiske – the only trained telephone operator among the seminary's students – to install a new phone line in his office. It was "not registered with the post office, so illegal," Kapiske informed Heydel: "I told Pastor [redacted] about the character of this phone line!" But, at times, Kapiske was slightly frustrated with the Stasi, hoping for faster action and more demanding tasks. Heydel reminded him that accelerated tasks would involve much bigger risks for him.

Kapiske dutifully also attended his seminars and lectures. And, in between all these activities, he had even managed to get married. It was a marriage based on love. Like Jürgen, Heidi Kapiske was a committed socialist.[102] For some time, Heydel and Kapiske had been discussing the possibility of Heidi working at the Konvikt after gaining a degree in library

---

102   Not her real name.

studies. That would clearly be a win for all. To Heydel's delight, Heidi quickly landed a job as a librarian at the Konvikt.

Kapiske struggled with a dilemma common to agents who are married: should he reveal his double life to Heidi? Heydel strongly advised against it. Each person let in on the secret posed an additional security risk. What if Heidi couldn't be trusted? But Kapiske insisted. "I really can't keep this from her," he told Heydel. "Among long-term partners you really can't keep such secrets." Jürgen told his wife. At first, she was taken aback – not surprisingly, given the magnitude of the revelation. But Kapiske painstakingly explained everything, detailing his motivations. Eventually Heidi, too, became convinced that he was doing the right thing.

Heydel, meanwhile, had helped IM Walter choose a topic for his final thesis: East German church newspapers. Just as the officer had predicted, the dissertation's timely topic got Kapiske noticed among East German church publications. In November 1974, Kapiske passed his exams. That meant he would go on to studies at the Gnadau seminary some two hours from Berlin, where pastors received their practical training.

Following Heydel's instructions, IM Walter charted the entire seminary. On the assignment brief, Heydel had written down detailed requirements:

1. Investigate the facilities; the contents, extent and methodology of the education.

2. Obtain conceptual opinions and intent of the church leadership.

3. Reconnaissance of reactionary clerics' plans of falsifying and enforcing the CSCE's imperialist intent under clerical flag.[103]

4. Use your time as a student to:

- Examine the students and their goals and plans.

- Examine Gnadau (personnel, teaching staff, drawings of the facilities and the location).

---

103   The CSCE was the Conference for Security and Cooperation in Europe; its name was later changed to Organisation for Security and Cooperation in Europe.

- Examine subversive propaganda literature, literature smuggling, secret courier systems, etc.

5. Act to combat the subversive trade in human beings and illegal departures from the GDR; aid counter-intelligence and the prevention of terrorist acts, protesters, and subversion.

6. The objective of your time as a student is to pass your exams with the best possible results, to fully exhaust your protection potential, and to create contacts for further penetration into the conspiracy.

Ever diligent, IM Walter even produced an exact drawing of Gnadau's facilities. He also established how large quantities of West German books and periodicals reached the seminary (a pastor in East Berlin coordinated smuggling of the literature) and documented the nature of the literature. To the Stasi's relief, most of the books were theological rather than political ones. IM Walter even went so far as to examine Gnadau's bathroom cabinets, to see if anyone was using West German medications. They had been sent by friendly Christians in West Germany, but to the Stasi the gesture was far from friendly. If East Germans used West German medications, they might begin to complain about their own country's inferior medicine, and that could quickly snowball into protests against the regime itself. There were to be no unauthorized West German prescription drugs in the German Democratic Republic.

The Church Bureau suspected that Western intelligence agencies were operating not just at Gnadau but at every church institution in the GDR, and Heydel had convinced IM Walter of this complete penetration. Later, after East Germany's collapse, Kapiske would consider the mindset absurd. But, mirroring Western fears of communists lurking under every bed, in the mid-seventies Kapiske sensed an imperialist lurking in every pulpit.

After graduating from Gnadau, Kapiske promptly landed an internship with a church newspaper. The Church Bureau hadn't been involved in getting Kapiske the internship, but it was excellent news since Heydel was hoping Kapiske would develop into a church media leader. Eventually, Heydel wanted to place his protégé with the media department at the World Council of Churches. He suggested to his colleagues that IM Walter be given a cassette recorder as a Christmas present.

That August, Oskar Brüsewitz's death shook East Germany. Even though the government denounced Brüsewitz as mentally ill, his death threatened to destabilize the regime. Western governments and citizens would now pay even closer attention to the human rights situation in East Germany. "There's an urgent risk that this will turn into a martyr anniversary," Kapiske told Heydel. "Some circles… are certainly capable of using this case for anti-communist slander."

RIAS, the American radio station in West Berlin, had already broadcast a programme about church-based East German opposition groups. Now the Stasi and the government were worried that church leaders would begin speaking out. They knew that many Americans would definitely listen, and if Jimmy Carter won the election in November, Christians behind the Iron Curtain would have the ear of the world's most powerful man. Ordinary Americans, the Stasi knew, didn't think about communist countries every day – but they cared about the persecution of Christians and were willing to try to do something about it.

IM Walter had generated additional value for the Church Bureau. In late 1976, Heidi was recruited by the MfS. As with most agents, it had been a long process. Heydel had spotted Heidi's potential early on and had begun adding observations regarding her in Kapiske's file. After some time, she had been invited to join the two men for meetings. In February 1975, Heydel had noted that Heidi brought "fundamental political convictions, which are the basis for a sacrificial collaboration. She will work on expanding her position at the Konvikt". Crucially, he had added in that early assessment, "her attitude is honest and characterized by the effort to prevent abuse of the church for enemy purposes." She even enjoyed reading socialist books about the resistance against the Nazis. "Antifascist books", Heydel called them, using official East German terminology. Heidi's parents had raised her well, the officer concluded.

Still, Heydel had been concerned about her reliability. Heidi was "surrounded by negative and hostile elements" including the ubiquitous packages with high-quality coffee and chocolate her family, like many other East Germans, received from West German friends and relations. Receiving such care packages could weaken a Stasi agent's resolve. Heidi Kapiske was, however, a determined woman, capable of separating East German ideology from West German coffee. In late 1976, Heydel invited her to become an agent. She was now keeping a close eye on the Western literature illicitly sent to the Konvikt. "After initial distance, she has been able to considerably contribute with valuable information", Heydel reported in November 1976.

I ask Jürgen Kapiske about his wife's cooperation with the Stasi. He seems unaware that it ever happened. "As far as I know she had no official function [with the Stasi]," he tells me. "She simply knew about my work and covered my back. You need somebody who tells people, 'he went to visit relatives'" [when you're on Stasi assignments]. Is he trying to protect Heidi or did he truly not know about it? I can't tell.

In January 1977, East Germany had just expelled punk singer Nina Hagen; Jimmy Carter had just been sworn in as the thirty-ninth President of the United States. Jürgen Kapiske was ordained in Cottbus, a city an hour and a half south-east of Berlin. As the bishop laid his hands on him, Kapiske felt at ease. He had no hesitation embarking on two paths where one identity would be fighting the other.

When I visit Kapiske in January 2017, forty years have passed since his ordination. "I felt that we desperately needed understanding between the church and the state; that was the most important thing," he tells me. "Ordination meant being part of the church operation, the spiritual operation. You have to use that position responsibly. I thought this was precisely my responsibility. I remember my ordination service very clearly. I had no doubts."

By 1977, however, the confrontation between the West and the Soviet bloc was intensifying. Carter was already angering Soviet officials by focusing on human rights in their country. One month into his tenure, the US president sent a public letter of support to Andrey Sakharov, the Soviet nuclear scientist turned dissident. Furious, Soviet leader, Leonid Brezhnev, dispatched a letter taking Carter to task for corresponding with a "renegade who has proclaimed himself an enemy of the Soviet state".

Meanwhile, Sakharov and other Soviet bloc dissidents took consolation in the Helsinki Accords, signed in 1975 by thirty-five countries including the United States, Western European countries, and Soviet bloc states. In the Accords, the signatories vowed to observe human rights. Brave dissidents like Sakharov, Orthodox priest Gleb Yakunin, and Czech playwright Václav Havel intended to hold communist leaders to account. So, indirectly, did the Conference for Security and Cooperation in Europe (CSCE), the intergovernmental body formed at the Helsinki summit. In January 1977, Havel and some 240 other Czechoslovaks signed a petition they called Charter 77, asking the government to recognize basic human rights.

As they tried to deliver the appeal to the government in Prague, Havel and several other signatories were arrested. But, in a clever move, they had already arranged for copies to be smuggled to the West, resulting in widespread Western media coverage of their appeal. The KGB and its sister agencies across the Soviet bloc suddenly found their workload much larger.

To alleviate the burden, the agencies resolved to help one another. Three years previously, sensing increasing dissident activism in their countries, Warsaw Pact secret police agencies had begun collaborating in a more structured fashion. Following a conference for all the agencies in the Cuban capital of Havana devoted to the matter of "ideological diversion", Division

XX and the KGB's Fifth Directorate launched regular consultations.[104]

But at the Normannenstrasse, the Church Bureau was getting anxious. The Helsinki Accords had emboldened many opposition activists within the Lutheran Church. IM Walter's planned work as a church newspaper journalist-cum-Stasi agent was desperately needed in order to influence the Lutheran Church's own news coverage. But for now, the Stasi had decided that he should earn his clerical credentials by serving in a parish for a couple of years. The young pastor's new parish, Gross Neuendorf, was located on East Germany's border with Poland. From this perch, IM Walter would be able to build contacts with dissidents in nearby Czechoslovakia, Lieutenant Heydel calculated. Kapiske would also freelance for church newspapers.

Kapiske's contacts in Czechoslovakia illustrate why it made sense for the Church Bureau to occasionally work outside East Germany, even though foreign intelligence was the brief of the HVA. Because a theology student – and especially a pastor – engenders trust, Kapiske had already managed to deliver reports on Czech underground opposition church groups; on artists, scientists, and actors active in Prague's dissident underground, and on pastors suspended for anti-government activities who secretly defied the ban.

He had also met an East German pastor who maintained extensive contacts with Czech opposition activists. On 23 February 1977, IM Walter filed an explosive report: the pastor had clandestinely travelled to Czechoslovakia to collect a copy of Charter 77 along with a report by Václav Havel and two other dissidents. Possession of a copy of the Charter was in itself a criminal act, and numerous signers had by now been jailed or fired from their jobs for subversion and "hostility to the socialist state and social system".[105]

---

104   Auerbach et al, *Hauptabteilung XX*, p. 25.
105   "Charter 77 After 30 Years", The National Security Archive, 6 January 2007, https://nsarchive2.gwu.edu/NSAEBB/NSAEBB213/index.htm (accessed 3 May 2019).

The East German pastor had boldly suggested to Kapiske that something like Charter 77 ought to be possible in the GDR as well. That was the sort of chain reaction that the Politburo most feared. "They were also afraid that a movement like this could establish itself in the [Socialist Unity] Party," Kapiske tells me. "And they were afraid that there were some communists who would see such a movement as an acceptable way of dealing with the churches. That was one of their worst nightmares."

With complete trust in Heydel, Kapiske risked an opinion: "I think the GDR should liberalize a bit like the Czechs did in 1968," he told him one day. Now, nine years after the Prague Spring and with a rigid communist regime in place in East Germany, Heydel agreed with Kapiske; he was not an apparatchik.[106] Or maybe he was, and he was simply an excellent officer who knew how to instil loyalty among his agents.

On Heydel's recommendation, the Church Bureau gave IM Walter its official recognition. On the occasion of the German Democratic Republic's twenty-eighth anniversary – 7 October 1977 – the MfS awarded him the Merit Medal of the National People's Army in bronze. He had "successfully completed his theology studies and created the conditions for penetration of reactionary clerical circles," the commendation read.

Back in Gross Neuendorf, Jürgen Kapiske wasn't much enjoying his pastoral duties, although he was aware that it was only a temporary sojourn. Heydel, who was becoming a real friend, told him as much. As in most successful officer–agent relationships, Heydel didn't issue commands to the young man. Instead, the two men were confidantes, sharing a secret that it was neither in Heydel's nor in IM Walter's interest to reveal. Kapiske was on good terms with his parents, and they, too, supported the regime, despite having lost their farm to collectivization. But he hadn't told them that he now worked for the Stasi. Apart from Heydel and his superiors, only Heidi knew.

---

106   Apparatchik, a term that originally described a member of a Socialist Party bureaucracy, is often used to describe a bureaucratic-minded official.

I ask Kapiske about his relationship with Heydel. "It was a very strong bond," he reflects. "We never exerted pressure on each other, and it wasn't necessary. If one of the two starts putting pressure on the other you get a threshold between you. That doesn't work."

CHAPTER 14

AN INDISPENSABLE BIBLE SMUGGLER (AND STASI SPY)

The Church Bureau officers had proceeded with deliberation, giving Gerd Bambowsky several years to establish his credentials. And the Bible smugglers had unknowingly aided his efforts by recommending him to one another. On 23 April 1976, one of these new acquaintances contacted Bambowsky. They met near Friedrichstrasse station. Dr Otto Teigeler, a theology lecturer near Bonn and an expert on Christianity in Russia, related a predicament to Bambowsky.[107] His organization had previously worked with *Licht im Osten*, but that cooperation had ended. Teigeler had approached US military chaplains at the US Army base in Kaiserslautern near Frankfurt am Main asking for help and, a few weeks previously, he had spoken with the US Army's chaplain at Tempelhof, the West Berlin airport. Tempelhof is known for its crucial role during the 1948 Berlin airlift, when Soviet authorities closed all ground access to West Berlin, and in 1976 it was

---

107   Teigeler worked at the Pastoral Theological Institute in Bad Godesberg.

still used by the US military. The chaplain, Teigeler told Bambowsky, "has received many high rewards and has a lot of influence." Bambowsky noted to himself that the chaplain seemed very well informed about transport options in both West and East Berlin.

But Teigeler had a problem: the chaplain couldn't help. "For diplomatic reasons the Americans don't want to get involved," he explained. "There are said to be Baptist soldiers in the US Army who until recently conducted transports to the GDR, but these were cancelled after the soldiers were stopped at the border crossing and told by the East German border guards to either open the trunk or turn around." The soldiers had turned around. Someone had clearly alerted the East German authorities to their activities.

There was, however, good news: the chaplain had found a German–American woman living in West Berlin who often visited East Berlin. She could get the books across the border. Teigeler's dilemma, which he presented to Bambowsky, was how to transport the books onwards from East Berlin. Could Bambowsky help?

In his subsequent debrief with Lieutenant Winkler, Bambowsky remarked that Teigeler hadn't been carrying a bag at their meeting. According to Bambowsky, that suggested that the West German worked for US intelligence, though he didn't explain why that would be the case. Indeed, he seemed to enjoy the thrill rather more than the gathering of basic information. If Bambowsky were a cautious sort of agent, he would have been extremely tense after such a close call. Instead, this encounter with US intelligence, even if it was just a product of his imagination, animated him.

Meanwhile, Campus Crusade for Christ was intensifying its efforts to gain a foothold in East Germany. From there it hoped to expand to other communist countries. One of its members came to see Bambowsky with the manuscript for an introductory booklet in German, and together the two men conducted a final round of edits. Bambowsky had clearly perfected the art of developing personal relationships.

In May 1976, IM Gerd returned from another mission to Moscow, Tallinn, and Riga. The KGB was pleased. The pastor had introduced another undercover agent to the Soviet Christians. It had been a highly complex trip where, in preparation, Lieutenant Bartnitzek had met with IM Gerd no less than nine times. But the other agent's infiltration had succeeded splendidly. "No deconspiration was observed", the Church Bureau noted. "Deconspiration", a crucial word in the MfS vocabulary, referred to outsiders noticing an operation: if they did, it had been compromised.

But IM Gerd's Soviet mission had not been compromised. The KGB's Church Department informed their Stasi colleagues that their agent would receive two golden cups as a thank you. The Soviets kept their word. One day in June, the pastor arrived for one of his usual meetings – and found to his surprise not only Bartnitzek but also Church Bureau boss Franz Sgraja and Klaus Rossberg. The KGB had asked them to personally present IM Gerd with the cups.

And the KGB had reason to rejoice in its new undercover placement. Despite the secret police's brutal and far-reaching power, many Christian groups were managing to outfox it through informal underground networks. Colonel Borönkin, the KGB's deputy head in the Estonian Soviet Republic, told his Stasi colleagues that IM Gerd's mission was the first time that the KGB had succeeded in infiltrating certain Christian circles.[108] Though the KGB had a host of Orthodox priest agents, it was ill-equipped to infiltrate the Soviet Union's many Protestant and Catholic groups. With the former, the Stasi was clearly of significant help.

IM Gerd had also brought an Estonian Baptist preacher named Peter along to his meetings with underground Christians who were receiving smuggled literature. Peter was a KGB agent but, despite being an Estonian himself, he

---

108   After being occupied by the Soviet Union during World War II, Estonia – and its Baltic neighbours, Latvia and Lithuania – were integrated into the Soviet Union and renamed Soviet republics.

hadn't managed to infiltrate Estonia's Christian circles. IM Gerd provided the necessary introductions. After meeting Peter in Tallinn, a thrilled Estonian church leader concluded that the preacher was "a very honest and completely trustworthy Christian". The KGB asked Department XX/4 to deepen Peter's infiltration into the Estonian circles.

With Peter, Lieutenant Bartnitzek had another ball in the air: IM Gerd wasn't told that Peter worked for the KGB. Gerd Bambowsky thought that he was simply introducing another smuggler to the network. Like other agents throughout the centuries, Bambowsky presumed too much – that he alone guarded the ultimate secret, that apart from his handlers all others were dupes. But to his handlers, IM Gerd was simply a part of the game – a man with a secret among many other men and women with secrets.

Peter, for his part, was likewise unaware that Bambowsky worked for the Stasi. And if Bambowsky had known that he was dealing with a potential rival in the Christian book-smuggling business, he would not have been as generous in connecting Peter with underground Christians. But, suspecting nothing, Bambowsky willingly introduced Peter to his contacts. If they seemed to consider Peter trustworthy, IM Gerd should continue infiltrating him into the Christian groups, but if they seemed wary of a new smuggler, he should immediately abort his efforts, Bartnitzek had advised.

With his highly developed nose for competition, IM Gerd was keenly aware that he was not the only show in town. He guarded his turf. In an effort to impress Stasi headquarters, he often whined about his workload – but when case officers offered to add other IMs to operations he always declined the offer. "He declined the offer with flimsy excuses", Lieutenant Winkler wrote after one meeting. Indeed, as soon as Winkler suggested using additional helpers, IM Gerd volunteered to do even more. "He offered me consultations on church-related subjects for the purpose of better understanding the problems", Winkler logged. The officer was onto something. Gerd Bambowsky needed to feel indispensable not just to the Bible smugglers but to the Stasi as well. As was his wont, after complaining to Winkler, IM Gerd unleashed a charm offensive, telling the officer that he considered their relationship very close and trusting.

But not only did he want no helpers; he wanted to be the only Stasi agent on the book-smuggling circuit. "The IM is showing that he wants to block every competition in the literature business," an officer recorded. IM Gerd even kept secrets about the literature business from the Church Bureau. "He keeps precise records of all book deliveries but has only reluctantly and partially given the MfS these lists," the officer noted.

In parallel with inserting Peter into smuggling circles, Bambowsky was deepening his own infiltration into Soviet Christian groups. Recently, he had discovered that PanAm stewardesses were no longer being used ("abused", Bartnitzek wrote) as couriers to the Soviet Union. More than one stewardess had, IM Gerd learned, been involved in the Bible smuggling on the airline's New York–Moscow route, but the Bible charities had closed the channel after discovering that someone along the smuggling chain had been skimming a profit. IM Gerd made another discovery too: two staff members at the organ builder Sauer in Frankfurt an der Oder smuggled books in finished organs destined for Warsaw Pact countries.

Back in Korntal, meanwhile, Erwin Damson at *Licht im Osten* needed Bambowsky's help in establishing new ways of storing Soviet-bound deliveries in East Germany. "We can't make handovers in the open air," he told Bambowsky. "We need more depots." It was too risky to accelerate use of the group's existing secret depots, which included a property near Soviet military barracks in the town of Oranienburg, half an hour north of Berlin, as well as homes, sheds and basements belonging to several Baptist families. The families worked with other organizations in addition to *Licht im Osten*, which made Damson reluctant to ask them to do even more. In short, he needed Bambowsky's help scouting out other "enclosed locations", as he described them – ideally sheds, basements, and unused farm buildings. A further idea:

he and Bambowsky could find ways to engineer handovers during trade shows at the Leipzig Fair, which attracted plenty of international visitors.

As always, Bambowsky was eager to help. But first he drove to the property in Oranienburg and to a family in the town of Reinsdorf near the Czechoslovak border, where *Licht im Osten* also already had a depot. Displaying his affable demeanour, he tried to make the families reveal which other organizations used the depots. But the families were prudent and knew not to reveal such secrets even to fellow activists. Bambowsky left empty-handed. Meeting on 18 June, Bartnitzek asked IM Gerd to try again. "Which individuals bring deliveries to these depots, and which individuals receive the literature?" he wrote in IM Gerd's assignment list. The reconnaissance mission's goal: "Elimination of both depots."

Bambowsky wasted no time. Within a month, he had identified three smugglers who delivered books to the depots: a Dutchman, a Briton and a Swiss man.[109] And he had managed to gather details on how they conducted their deliveries. Their first step, he explained to Bartnitzek, was to collect books in West Germany then drive towards West Berlin. They left the autobahn near West Berlin and took the delivery to a nearby family whose house served as a depot. Then on to West Berlin, where they collected a new load of books. After that they headed north to Oranienburg, where they again left the autobahn and unloaded the delivery at the depot there.[110] They then continued on to Sweden, where they collected a new load at the Slavic East Mission, a Swedish book-smuggling organization. The secret depots were in constant use.

Learning when and how the depots were used was important to the Stasi and the KGB. It might never be able to stop the smuggling altogether, but if it could identify and eliminate the depots, the quantities the smugglers were

---

109   Bambowsky's file does not identify the person(s) who gave him this information.

110   Bambowsky's file does not mention whether the Westerners had permits to leave the autobahn or whether they did so risking arrest.

able to transport would plummet. It would also demoralize the smugglers' efforts.

By late 1976, IM Gerd had become so valuable that he had been transferred from Lieutenant Bartnitzek to more senior officers, primarily Major Schramm and Klaus Rossberg. For particularly important assignments, now-Lieutenant Colonel Sgraja himself worked with IM Gerd.

But Bambowsky's housing situation kept aggravating him. For some time, he had been feeling that he should be living in more spacious and upscale quarters than his East Berlin apartment, and he had made his desires well known to the Church Bureau. In July 1977, Bambowsky was informed that his garage would be seized by the local authorities to make space for a new government-run company. Although the church had managed to find Bambowsky a new property, he didn't like the idea. Instead, he wanted the Stasi to arrange a new house for him. "I'm very disappointed that the MfS apparently isn't capable of materially ensuring my future services by means of appropriate housing. I'm forty-seven years old; I finally need a permanent home," he told Lieutenant Winkler, who had already heard the spiel. The officer recognized the threat: give me a house or I'll tell my entire Bible-smuggling network what you're up to.

Bambowsky was hardly alone in having dubious motivations. Recently he had learned from an Open Doors staff member that another member of the smuggling network had in fact not been delivering the books to Soviet Christians. Instead, the smuggler had been selling the books to a local middleman, pocketing the profit. The middleman had, in turn, been selling them to local Christians, also at a profit.

During a visit by the German smuggler – whom we shall call Dieter Funke – a local pastor had grown so desperate about the vanishing Bibles that he took Funke for a drive in his ramshackle car. But it wasn't just any ride; it was a ride up the local mountains. As they drove higher and higher, the pastor accelerated – and then accelerated again. Soon the pair were whizzing up and down the mountain at what Funke later recalled as 100 kilometres an hour. The terrified Funke pleaded with the pastor to slow down. "Not to worry, we're in God's hands," the pastor replied with a wink – and accelerated even more. "*Zetermordio!*" Funke called out, a medieval plea for help over the engine's roar. "OK, I will slow down," the pastor promised. "But only if you give me the Bibles."

The Open Doors employee had also told Bambowsky that two Norwegian couriers had just been apprehended by the KGB at a camping site outside Moscow. The pair who had been under surveillance ever since entering the country had been transferring their literary cargo from the secret compartments in their car when the officers seized them and the books. By now, IM Gerd had, of course, penetrated the Bible-smuggling groups to the extent that he could alert his handlers to upcoming clandestine handovers of literature, thus allowing the Stasi and the KGB to observe the activities.

For secret police behind the Iron Curtain, agent provocateurs were a useful tool, used to entice people to do things they wouldn't otherwise have thought of doing. IM Gerd, the natural-born actor, excelled at the art form. Smuggling Bibles to the Soviet Union was one thing, "but shouldn't we also bring Christian magazines?" he asked Erwin Damson one day. Bambowsky had arrived in Korntal to collect yet another load of books from *Licht im Osten*. Having watched Bambowsky's growing success for several years now, Erwin Damson was excited about the offer. He immediately phoned his friend Pastor Helmut Matthies, who edited a conservative Christian weekly, *IDEA Spektrum*.

"We have this pastor from East Germany who's completely trustworthy, and he's volunteered to smuggle Christian magazines," Damson told Matthies. Pastor Matthies was astounded by such good fortune. While East Germans had access to a few left-leaning Christian magazines from West Germany, IDEA Spektrum was out of bounds. And now an East German preacher would smuggle it?

Several days later, Pastor Bambowsky turned up at *IDEA Spektrum*'s office outside Frankfurt am Main. After a warm welcome, Bambowsky surprised Matthies by suggesting they pray together. "I'm an evangelical too," he explained, adding that he belonged to the East German evangelists' association. Bambowsky knew full well that Matthies was a traditional Lutheran pastor accustomed to reciting prayers from a prayer book rather than coming up with his own. But the East German also knew that prayers convince. As the two men sat down to pray, he began extemporizing, invoking the Holy Spirit and putting their collaboration in God's hands.

It worked. "What a devout man," Pastor Matthies thought to himself. It didn't even matter that Bambowsky, with his flamboyant flop of unruly hair, seemed to have nothing in common with most pastors Matthies had ever met. Matthies concluded that Bambowsky's heart was in the right place, and Damson had already told Matthies that he had contacts. Barely able to contain his excitement, Matthies quietly thanked the Lord for answering his prayers.

The two pastors decided to meet monthly. Each time, they agreed, Bambowsky would take fifty copies of *IDEA Spektrum* back with him to East Germany. Because Bambowsky seemed concerned about money, Matthies immediately offered to pay for his expenses. Soon the pastor-journalist even offered the devout Bambowsky a little extra money on the side, from his own savings. "That's the least I can do for a man who is risking his freedom for the spread of the gospel," Matthies told himself.

Several months into the meetings, Bambowsky again came to visit Matthies. As usual, they began their conversation with an extemporized prayer. "If only I could pray like that," Matthies thought to himself, as he often did when praying with Bambowsky. Then the East German delivered important news. "From now on I'd like to take 200 copies of each issue instead of fifty," he announced. Though he was excited about the prospect, Matthies harboured concerns. How on earth would Bambowsky be able

221

to get such an enormous load across the border undetected? The Barkas's secret compartment might be able to fit 800 magazines, he calculated based on similar secret compartments. But he was under no illusion that Bambowsky would travel only for *IDEA Spektrum*.

"How do you do it?" Matthies anxiously asked. Bambowsky deflected. "That's my secret. What's important is that the magazines get to the GDR, isn't it?" It is indeed, Matthies agreed. But he kept pushing. The whole idea seemed too dangerous. "How is it that you can come here every month?" he demanded. He knew that it was very difficult for East Germans to secure travel permits, especially for those who were neither married nor retired. The government correctly assumed that married people with children wouldn't defect but would return to their families. Retirees were, of course, very welcome to leave the country, the burden of their financial support shifting to West Germany.

But Bambowsky was a relatively young, unmarried man. "I have an aunt in West Berlin who is very ill, so I'm allowed to visit her," he told Matthies, using his standard cover story. Matthies was reassured. Bambowsky evidently cared about both persecuted Christians and his dying aunt. And Bambowsky offered further good news: he would deliver the magazines not just to ordinary Christians but to bishops and other church leaders as well. Most bishops in East Germany were wary of subscribing to *IDEA Spektrum* with its conservative leanings. Now they would be able to receive it thanks to Pastor Bambowsky.

Pastor Matthies had been praying for the magazine to reach influential church leaders, and it was becoming reality. When Bambowsky asked him for a list of suggested recipients, Matthies eagerly wrote down as many names as he could think of. But the magazine deliveries were a Church Bureau bait for dissidents. A bishop who was open to receiving *IDEA Spektrum* clearly had a strongly anti-regime mindset and must be monitored more closely.

In July 1977, Bambowsky travelled to Budapest and convened with

Erwin Damson and his wife, who had entered the country by car from Austria. The Damsons were already under surveillance by Hungary's domestic intelligence agency, whose Church Department was coordinating the East German pastor's trip together with the Stasi. This part of the Soviet bloc sister agencies' increasing cooperation was working smoothly.

Damson was having serious problems. *Licht im Osten*'s vans were being stopped so often at Warsaw Pact border crossings that the group had largely given up using its own couriers. It was now relying on Open Doors, which used American students as couriers. It was a better arrangement because Americans faced less harsh consequences than Western Europeans if arrested at a socialist border, Damson told Bambowsky.

Earlier in the year, Damson had himself been detained by customs officials in East Berlin and questioned for several hours. He was convinced that several couriers in East Germany were also being watched by the Stasi, not because anyone had informed on them, he thought, but because they had probably been a bit too chatty about their clandestine work. Damson had good reasons to be anxious, and he assumed Bambowsky might be worried too. But, he assured Bambowsky, "You're not at risk of being found out".

And despite the risks, Damson had concluded that *Licht im Osten* needed new recruits in East Germany. "I'll only recruit people that I have cleared with you," he told Bambowsky. From now on, Bambowsky would vet potential East German couriers on behalf of *Licht im Osten*. Bambowsky adopted an air of concern and assured his friend that he'd do his best. While patiently listening to Damson, inside he was desperate for the meeting to end so he could report the news to Bartnitzek.

It was a good thing he didn't rush to end the meeting, because Damson had more news. *Licht im Osten*, Damson explained, wanted to start having Bambowsky smuggle parts for printing presses. "Get prepared for a Soviet trip in the autumn," he advised. Printing press parts were more difficult to smuggle than books, and they were more valuable. Bambowsky was being promoted. And one more thing, Damson asked: could Bambowsky write, anonymously of course, an article for *Licht im Osten*'s magazine about his impressions from the Soviet Union – persecution of Christians, controls by the authorities, surveillance? Of course he could.

Damson just had one more issue he wanted to discuss. Thanks to increasingly strong anti-Soviet propaganda on American television, Open Doors – *Licht im Osten*'s ally and competitor – was now in excellent financial shape. In just the past several months, networks had broadcast several reports about the Soviet Union's violations of human rights and persecution of Christians, as well as about brave Bible couriers.

Clearly, Open Doors needed the ambitious East German pastor and had money to pay him. But Damson asked Bambowsky to limit his work with Open Doors and intensify his activities for *Licht im Osten*. There was clearly strategy behind the new exciting tasks Bambowsky was being offered. Then Damson delivered a surprise: "Open Doors maintains relations with two contacts in Bonn who are said to have links to intelligence agencies." He didn't want Bambowsky to increase his work for Open Doors, but the two intelligence sources might be useful. Damson volunteered to arrange for Bambowsky to meet them.

After several hours, Damson and Bambowsky bade each other farewell. The Damsons drove to Lake Balaton, a popular holiday destination. Hungarian secret police had already sent its first reports to the Normannenstrasse. After arriving back in Germany, Bambowsky seamlessly reinserted himself into his ecclesiastical duties, preaching at a village church outside Berlin.[111]

Bambowsky's middling pastor career belied an exceptionally ambitious nature. After the Budapest meeting with Erwin Damson, *Licht im Osten*

111   Stefan Pohlke, "Chronik des Kirchspiels zu Dassow 1989–2012", April 2018, http://pix.kirche-mv.de/fileadmin/elkm/KR_Grevesmuehlen/Dassow/Chronik_des_Kirchspiels_zu_Dassow_1898-2012_-_Homepage.pdf (accessed 3 May 2019).

asked him to smuggle Bibles to the Soviet Union – but he declined. Printing presses were a step up from the Scriptures. Book duties were beneath him now that he had been elevated to printing-press courier. And he had no interest in exposing himself to risks just to transport a few Bibles eastward. And, as Bartnitzek noted in his log, Damson supported Bambowsky's stand. Bartnitzek summarized Damson's position: "There are plenty of people who can do such small things. He was aware that Gerd was primed for greater things." Indeed, Damson was planning to give Bambowsky a master list of *Licht im Osten*'s most trusted contacts in the Soviet Union.

The day of 15 October was an important one in Gerd Bambowsky's life. Bambowsky's boyfriend, Knuth Hansen, was ordained pastor in East Germany's small Reformed Church.[112] Lieutenant Bartnitzek noted the upcoming event in his report, without commenting on Bambowsky's sexual orientation. In Western countries, homosexuality was, in 1977, still a matter of curiosity or worse. But no one in the Lutheran Church or the Märkische Volksmission seemed bothered that Bambowsky was gay – or that he had a boyfriend living with him part-time: "don't ask, don't tell" East German-style.

Christianity's ten commandments do not instruct Christians not to betray their friends. Most Christians – most people – simply know that betrayal is wrong. But the Church Bureau worked with many professional Christians who lacked that moral compass or chose to ignore it.

Pastor Gerd Bambowsky was, by all accounts, unbothered by betrayal – of others by him, that is. But he expected others to be loyal to him. Although he had now become Damson's trusted adviser in East Germany and had agreed not to work for Open Doors, he went back to Open Doors anyway. The year 1979 had barely begun when the Dutch group arranged

---

112   Hansen was a Mennonite but appears to have been ordained by the Reformed Church. It's an understandable arrangement given that there were only several hundred Mennonites in the GDR. See Imanuel Baumann, "Deutsche Demokratische Republik (Mennonitengemeinde)", *Mennlex V*, 15 September 2016, http://www.mennlex.de/doku.php?id=loc:deutsche_demokratische_republik (accessed 3 May 2019).

for Bambowsky to carry out a new assignment: the handover of a book delivery bound for the Soviet Union. The Church Bureau was ahead of the Dutch Christians: it quickly turned the rendezvous to its own benefit. Bartnitzek summarized the events: "On 20 January 1979 (early) the IM was informed by telephone that a literature-smuggling vehicle travelling on the transit route from Hirschberg to Drewitz would wait for the IM at 19.5 kilometres (exit Belzig) at 2300 hours. At the appointed time the IM established contact with these couriers. The vehicle was a VW minivan (red on top, white at the bottom, licence plate number [redacted]). The transporters were a Dutch woman of around 25 years who introduced herself as [name redacted]. Furthermore two American citizens, [redacted] around 22 years and [redacted] around 19 years. With the exception of [name redacted] nobody spoke German. The literature was transferred [to Bambowsky's minivan] on a side road around five kilometres from the autobahn (direction Belzig). It was almost exclusively literature in Cyrillic writing, which is earmarked for further transport to the Soviet Union. (The literature will shortly be handed over to the MfS by the IM for the purpose of destruction.)"

In one evening, Bambowsky thus betrayed both his old friend Damson and Open Doors' inexperienced crew. But it didn't seem to trouble him. On the contrary, he was eager for more smuggling work. At the same time, Joachim Wiegand – recently appointed to Department XX/4's top post – was formalizing the Church Bureau's collaboration with the KGB's Church Department. Wiegand and Colonel Romanov of the Fourth Department of the Fifth Directorate of the KGB had already signed an agreement to that effect, and Division XX had also launched an overall cooperation plan with the Fifth Directorate. In addition, Division XX had deepened its cooperation with its sister divisions in Czechoslovakia, Bulgaria, Poland, and Hungary.[113] Information from IM Gerd and other pastor agents would

---

113   Auerbach et al, *Hauptabteilung XX*, p. 25.

now be more efficiently shared between the sister agencies.

Bambowsky's cover story – his real work as a preacher and pastor-in-training – was receding into the background. Although he often turned up for church services, Bambowsky didn't seem very interested in finally being ordained a Lutheran pastor, or in any other ecclesiastical duties. By contrast, the Stasi and smuggling work excited him. IM Gerd wanted to increase his foreign trips.

But how to travel abroad more frequently without arousing suspicion? Pastor Matthies was not alone in wondering how a middle-aged unmarried man could get permission for so many border crossings. Even the most devoted nephew would not subject himself to monthly trips involving travel permit applications.

Bambowsky had a sister in West Berlin, who would clearly be a perfect solution. There was just one complication: the two siblings were not on speaking terms. To get a long-term travel permit from the East German authorities, Bambowsky needed a doctor's certificate stating that his sister was critically ill, but that was clearly not possible given that she was neither ill nor inclined to help him. Bartnitzek, however, was a resourceful handler. After some brainstorming, the officer and the agent decided that the pastor would ask a female friend in West Berlin to get a doctor's certificate identifying her as Bambowsky's sister and stating that she was critically ill. Meanwhile, Bambowsky casually began mentioning his schizophrenic sister in West Berlin to his collaborators.

Bambowsky – who now used another codename – was about to depart for Tallinn and Riga. Another pastor smuggler-cum-agent would travel to Kiev several months later. The man was, not coincidentally, Knuth Hansen – Bambowsky's boyfriend.

Hansen was a useful helper, especially now that he was an ordained pastor. Not only could he smuggle books to the Soviet Union but he was also already receiving book deliveries from Licht im Osten on behalf of

Bambowsky at his new vicarage in Wiesenburg, a town conveniently located just off the transit autobahn between West Germany and West Berlin.[114]

Perhaps Christians are more susceptible to deception by their fellow Christians. Though Bible-smuggling organizations such as Open Doors, *Licht im Osten*, Mission Mobilization, and Campus Crusade for Christ were highly skilled at the cloak-and-dagger operations required to evade surveillance behind the Iron Curtain, they were remarkably naïve in their associations with helpers. By now, much of their work involving East Germany was futile as they had been penetrated by the Stasi.

It was 9.30 p.m. on 1 October 1979. The season-opening performance at East Berlin's famous opera house, the *Staatsoper unter den Linden*, was about to end. East German state media reported that the evening featured both international singers and guests as well as East German retirees, who *Neues Deutschland* boasted were newly flush thanks to pension increases.[115]

Taking advantage of the international activity around the opera house, an American courier steered his Volkswagen station wagon to a parking area behind the building, where Bambowsky was awaiting him. Together, they drove their respective vehicles to a dark side street behind the Ostbahnhof. The Ostbahnhof was one of East Berlin's two main train stations, conveniently located only some 200 metres from the Wall. The two men climbed out of their cars and the American quickly handed Bambowsky three suitcases containing books and cassette tapes. He also passed the pastor a letter in English. Bambowsky put the letter in his back pocket. As usual, Bambowsky took the books to several depots around the country. But he gave the letter to Bartnitzek, who promptly determined that

---

114   Because West Berlin was disconnected from the rest of West Germany, West Germans could travel between West Berlin and the rest of West Germany using one of the four autobahns. However, they needed special permission to leave the autobahn and enter the GDR. That made autobahn resting areas preferred meeting places for smugglers.
115   "Archiv der Ausgaben von 1946–1990: Glanzvoller Auftakt der XXIII. Berliner Festtage", *Neues Deutschland*, 1 October 1979, https://www.nd-archiv.de/artikel/447975. glanzvoller-auftakt-der-xxiii-berliner-festtage.html (accessed 3 May 2019).

the writer operated another book depot in East Berlin.

Although he revelled in his thriving undercover career, Bambowsky finally had to attend to his duties as a Lutheran seminarian. Miraculously, he passed his final exams. On 10 October, Gerd Bambowsky was ordained by Bishop Albrecht Schönherr in Lehnin, an hour south-west of Berlin. Was it a merely coincidence that Bambowsky had chosen to be ordained in a church near the transit autobahn between West Germany and West Berlin? Whatever the case, Bishop Schönherr gave Bambowsky a one-year assistant pastor position at the church in Blankenfelde, an East Berlin suburb.

And so, in December 1979, Pastor Richard Schröder welcomed a new permanent house guest to his vicarage in Blankenfelde. Bambowsky would have an office in the house and live in a room on the second floor during the week, commuting to his East Berlin apartment on weekends, except when he had liturgical duties. Schröder, an opposition-leaning cleric then also teaching at the Sprachenkonvikt, was the sort of clergyman the Stasi needed to monitor. Soon after Bambowsky's arrival in Blankenfelde, Schröder concluded that he had a split personality. Consequences didn't matter to Bambowsky; the only thing that counted was the performance. Three decades later, Schröder realized that Bambowsky shared this characteristic with another former pastor colleague of his: Aleksander Radler.

But even Schröder was oblivious to the gregarious Bambowsky's true nature. Then again, Schröder had long ago decided that he would not try to figure out whether friends and acquaintances worked for the Stasi. Were he to suspect everyone, he'd become paranoid, he had concluded. "Oh well, he's from an actor family; he's bound to behave differently," Schröder told himself after meeting his new colleague. And Schröder didn't object to Hansen staying at the vicarage.

An anomaly did, however, strike Schröder: Bambowsky's Barkas: how could a freshly ordained pastor drive a car that was only available for hard currency? Very soon Schröder began steering clear of Bambowsky. He simply didn't like him. "A slimy man, very difficult. He was not a straight shooter," Schröder describes Bambowsky when I come to visit him. But Bambowsky had an undeniable talent for preaching: "Rhetorically, as speeches, his sermons were good," Schröder explains. "For him a church service was like a stage play." The retired pastor still lives in Blankenfelde, only a few streets down from the vicarage from which Bambowsky operated. Fittingly for a man who went on to a career as a theology professor and Social Democratic politician after East Germany's collapse, every wall in Schröder's house is lined with bulging bookcases. (In the bathroom, there are postcards poking fun at communism.)

Since Bambowsky seemed bored by Blankenfelde's family-oriented lifestyle, Schröder didn't make anything of his new colleague's frequent absences. Pastor Schröder's wife, though, began to worry about what would happen if Bambowsky was given Blankenfelde's assistant position permanently. She didn't like him one bit. But far from everyone in Blankenfelde disliked Bambowsky. The rookie pastor had, in fact, quickly established a fan base within the congregation.

The year 1980 had barely begun when Bambowsky shared news of another breakthrough with Lieutenant Bartnitzek. Knuth Hansen, he reported, had been elected leader of East Germany's Mennonite Church. The post was less imposing than it sounds: the Mennonites were a tiny denomination with only several hundred members. Still, despite being newly ordained, Hansen clearly enjoyed a position of trust within the community.[116] Meeting in Berlin on 9 January, Bambowsky and Bartnitzek agreed that Bambowsky would infiltrate Hansen into his own smuggling network and prepare him for courier trips to the Soviet Union.

Bambowsky had been busy delivering copies of *IDEA Spektrum* to East German clergy as well. "The IM established contact with all bishops in the

116   Hansen served as the pastor of a Mennonite congregation in East Berlin. Tim Huber, "Germans mark 25 years since fall of Berlin Wall", *Mennonite World Review*, 17 November 2014, http://mennoworld.org/2014/11/17/news/germans-mark-25-years-since-fall-of-berlin-wall/ (accessed 3 May 2019).

GDR as well as leaders of church educational institutions in other influential middle cadres," Bartnitzek logged.

Now for the litmus test: which of the church leaders had accepted the magazine and which ones had turned it down? "The director of the preacher seminary in Wittenberg [Hans-Jürgen Schulz] declined to receive this magazine. He expressed that it's a politically reactionary magazine and as a Christian and a GDR citizen he can't in good conscience distribute such magazines", IM Gerd's file reports.

Several bishops, though, had enthusiastically accepted copies of *IDEA Spektrum*. "Bishops Hempel, Krusche, Wollstadt, Natho very happily received the magazine", Bartnitzek noted. Department XX/4 would increase its monitoring of them.

Neither IM Gerd nor pastor-editor Helmut Matthies knew that two of the bishops on Matthies's list, Ingo Braecklein and Horst Gienke, were themselves Stasi agents, and that Schulz, too, had Church Bureau dealings. As with so many other intelligence agencies, participants unknowingly manoeuvred around one other.

There was just one more thing. "My job is really a burden," Bambowsky told Bartnitzek, who had long ago morphed into Bambowsky's personal adviser. "It's very hard having to drive 35 kilometres each way." Bambowsky wanted a new job. He had already applied for the assistant pastor job in the town of Neuenhagen, closer to his home in East Berlin, where Hansen was now working as well.

"I've settled too well in Blankenfelde. The parish leadership wants to keep me forever," IM Gerd had disingenuously told one of his handlers at another meeting. Richard Schröder, however, wanted Bambowsky to leave sooner rather than later.

Bartnitzek gave his agent several points that might help Bambowsky make a good impression on the pastor in Neuenhagen, Dietmar Linke. But Bambowsky "was not informed about the operational treatment of Linke",

Bartnitzek noted in his file. The Stasi already had Linke, a well-known regime critic, under surveillance. Planting IM Gerd as his assistant seemed an extraordinarily good move.

Indeed, why waste time? With Bartnitzek next to him, Bambowsky called Pastor Linke and made an appointment for a longer conversation. Oh, and speaking of phones, Bambowsky asked his handler, "Can you help me get a second telephone line and wall outlet?" A second telephone line: many East Germans still didn't even have one line. But Bambowsky didn't consider himself an ordinary East German.

Meanwhile, the American couriers kept up their deliveries to Bambowsky. Bartnitzek diligently noted the details of recent deliveries: 12,000 books; 80 books and 108 cassette tapes; 370 books, 400 tracts, 120 prayer booklets, 100 slides about Israel, and *IDEA Spektrum* magazines.

In order not to arouse suspicion, Bambowsky had to deliver some contents to their intended recipients. But he still brought many of the books to Department XX/4. In Korntal, Erwin Damson was getting concerned. "Where are all the books ending up?" he asked his co-workers. No one could figure it out. Worse still, several of *Licht im Osten*'s vehicles had gone missing. Damson knew they had crossed over to East Germany. Where were they? When Damson queried Bambowsky about it, the pastor swore he had no idea.

By now, Damson had realized that Bambowsky was gay. Although, at a personal level, he was not entirely comfortable with Bambowsky's homosexuality, Damson was primarily concerned about security: was Bambowsky exposing himself to blackmail? What would happen if the Stasi pressured him into working for them? Surely the Stasi had found out about the preacher's sexual orientation, Damson reasoned. But he didn't tell Bambowsky about his concerns.

When Lieutenant Bartnitzek and IM Gerd met again, the officer suggested a new track. Distributing *IDEA Spektrum* in order to identify reactionaries behind the Iron Curtain was fine, but how about influencing the content?

"We need to use the church magazine *IDEA* for operational purposes," he explained.[117] The two men agreed that IM Gerd would feed Matthies articles that served the Stasi's interests. West German church leaders critical of the German Democratic Republic would, as a result, change their opinions, Bartnitzek predicted.

It was now 1980, and Bambowsky was one of the most prolific middlemen in an underground movement that delivered 900,000 Bibles behind the Iron Curtain each year.[118] Bartnitzek described one delivery by an Open Doors courier: "He transported around 2,000 books and textiles from Holland via the FRG [West Germany] to West Berlin. He had stored around 1,000 books in the conspiratorial compartments built into the car and the rest in suitcases in the trunk. On his entry he left the books in the suitcases with Mrs [redacted]. He brought the 1,000 books from the compartment to the Capital of the GDR [East Germany's official name for East Berlin] and left them at the home of IM 'Gerd'. At the same time, he brought textiles (shirts and sweaters) to a value of around DM400."

The Christian smuggling was booming, with Gerd Bambowsky as an operational pillar. As a result, Christians in the West were becoming even more generous in donating to the Bible-smuggling groups. In February 1981, the UPI newswire reported that, in the previous year, the three largest Bible-smuggling organizations had raised $21 million.[119] In reality, much of the good-hearted Christians' hard work was in vain – or worse, was causing harm to the intended recipients.

On a winter day, I meet with Helmut Matthies in Berlin to talk about

---

117   "This way we will conduct offensive subversive measures against a number of clerical powers," Bartnitzek noted.

118   Donald Gould, "A Groundling's Notebook: Biblelark", *New Scientist*, 22 February 1979. View *New Scientist* archive at: https://books.google.co.uk, p. 590 (accessed 3 May 2019).

119   David E. Anderson, "Dispute arises over Bible smuggling into USSR", *Sarasota Journal*, 27 February 1981, p. 12. For *Sarasota Journal* archive, visit https://news.google.com/newspapers (accessed 3 May 2019).

the pastor colleague who betrayed him. Even though decades have passed since their underground collaboration, Matthies is a vivid repository of stories involving Bambowsky. It's easy to see why: unlike the many pastor agents who merely eavesdropped, Bambowsky used his personality. As the Church Bureau had quickly determined, he could be put to productive use as an agent provocateur, enticing Westerners to engage in smuggling operations they hadn't previously thought of. And, because of his strong personality, his victims have extremely clear memories of him.

Despite his phenomenally productive collaboration with Bambowsky, by 1981 Matthies had the gnawing feeling that something wasn't quite right. One day that year, he couldn't contain his curiosity any longer. Although he had asked Bambowsky many times where the magazines went after Matthies handed them over, the East German had always deflected. This time, Matthies told himself, he would insist. When Bambowsky arrived for yet another magazine-collection visit, Matthies – trying to sound casual – blurted out, "Show me where you bring the magazines". Bambowsky could see no way out. "OK," he responded, "meet me in Dahlem and I'll show you."[120]

Dahlem was a neighbourhood within the American sector of Berlin that also housed US armed forces.[121] Bambowsky collected Matthies at the S-Bahn and then, to Matthies' horror, drove directly to the US military base. As the two men approached the guard post, Matthies became stiff with fear. Would he be questioned? Arrested? He said a desperate prayer. But he needn't have worried. Bambowsky flashed a badge, and the guard waved the men through with a smile.

---

120   Because Gerd Bambowsky's file for this period is missing, I have not been able to verify Matthies' account of the trip. However, the other information provided by Matthies is confirmed by Bambowsky's file.

121   Following World War II, the Allies divided Germany into four occupation zones. The British, French, and American zones subsequently became West Germany, while the Soviet occupation zone became East Germany. The same arrangement was made in Berlin, where the three Western zones became West Berlin and the Soviet zone East Berlin.

Once inside the barracks, the two Germans were ecstatically greeted by several American soldiers in uniform. The soldiers told the startled Matthies that they were Baptists and proceeded to extemporize prayers, with intermittent exclamations of "Hallelujah!" When Bambowsky handed the soldiers the *IDEA Spektrum* magazines, Matthies was further perplexed: did the US troops smuggle the magazines to East Germany? How on earth did Bambowsky know them? How could he enter the US base without a vehicle inspection? What exactly was the ID card he had shown the guard? Bambowsky left the boxes of *IDEA Spektrum* with the soldiers and, without incident, the two men took their leave.

Still, Matthies couldn't shake off his fear. The soldiers could just be a ruse. What if the magazines remained at the base and never made it to East Germany? Had he known that Bambowsky was friendly with the US Army chaplain, he would have been reassured. But in this drama, Pastor Matthies was a pawn on the chessboard. So were the chaplain and the soldiers. And Bambowsky was playing them all.

The confused Matthies again worked up his courage. "Show me where the soldiers bring the magazines," he said. "That's going to be really tricky; we might get caught," Bambowsky replied with feigned anxiety. Matthies insisted. As a journalist, he was dying to find out – and, as a pastor, he trusted that the Lord would protect him. "I'm not married, I'm a West German, what can happen?" he reassured himself. Not surprisingly, West German Bible smugglers often contemplated what might happen to them if they were caught smuggling goods behind the Iron Curtain. They faced fewer risks than citizens of communist states, for certain, but it was dangerous, nonetheless. "Just show me, I'd simply like to know," Matthies told Bambowsky.

Bambowsky relented. The men agreed to meet on the East German side of Friedrichstrasse station. Bambowsky arrived in his Barkas and Matthies got in. Not unreasonably, Matthies expected to be taken to a shed or barn.

Instead, Bambowsky drove to an area far outside the city centre. He took so many small roads that Matthies soon lost his bearings. The scenery along the roads was lovely, but the only thing the West German cared about was whether he had now left East Berlin; he thought his entry permit didn't allow him to leave the city. His heart pounding, he kept drawing up scenarios of what might happen if they were discovered. "Don't worry, we're fine," Bambowsky reassured him. He finally stopped the car and the men walked to a shed on the verge of collapse. "Here you are; this is where the soldiers bring *IDEA*," he announced. Matthies' heart sank. He had expected a shed, but not one in such poor shape. Now he hesitated to even enter. "What if it falls on top of me?" he said, mostly to himself. Bambowsky dismissed his concerns: "Don't worry; it's all a disguise."

Bambowsky unlocked the shed – and Matthies found himself entering what looked like a modern reading room. For a moment, he thought it was an apparition. But there it was in front of him, a brightly lit and freshly painted room, covered by wall-to-wall bookcases holding every conceivable Western publication including *IDEA Spektrum*. Matthies was speechless.

Suddenly, Bambowsky opened the front door and Matthies spotted a police car drive past. "Oh no, we're about to be discovered! We have to get you out of here!" Bambowsky whispered. He locked the shed behind them and they hurried to the car. "I'll take you back to Friedrichstrasse so you can get back to West Berlin," Bambowsky said. He sped back to central Berlin, again using small country roads. In the passenger seat, Matthies fervently prayed that he'd avoid arrest and that the Barkas wouldn't crash.

When they reached Friedrichstrasse, Matthies hurried through the border control and got on the S-Bahn. It had been a close call and a perplexing one. How could US soldiers smuggle Christian literature in collaboration with an East German pastor? But it seemed to be an effective system. Matthies knew that at least some bishops had received *IDEA Spektrum*.

Back in his office, Matthies finally managed to calm his nerves. And soon

Bambowsky was back to collect another load of magazines. Over coffee, he delivered a surprise. "I will bring *IDEA Spektrum* to Moscow, Leningrad and the Baltic states," Bambowsky announced. Matthies had feared bad news, but instead, Bambowsky was now saying that he'd smuggle the magazines not just to East Germany but to the Soviet Union as well – in fact, he had already begun doing so. "Fantastic," Matthies thought to himself. "Since quite a few people in the Soviet Union speak German, this will strengthen them."

As if reading his fellow pastor's mind, Bambowsky reached into his bag and proffered thank-you postcards from Christians in Kiev and Moscow. "Thank you for the gifts", the postcards said. Bambowsky told Matthies that he'd met with Baptist leaders and that they had given him the postcards to hand to Matthies. Matthies couldn't help but be moved, and a bit proud too. Who would have thought that his small magazine would be read within an atheist superpower?

"And now, about the money," Bambowsky continued. Matthies suspected what was coming. Bambowsky liked the Deutschmark thank-yous from *IDEA Spektrum*, *Licht im Osten*, and the other groups. Now that he was doing more work, Bambowsky argued, it would be appropriate to pay him more. Matthies immediately agreed. Of course Bambowsky should be adequately compensated for his additional efforts, especially since they were already so successful.

Erwin Damson at *Licht im Osten*, too, had already experienced his courier's materialistic side. At each meeting, Bambowsky brought up remuneration; a number of times, he had even taken up an impromptu collection at *Licht im Osten*'s office. "He's unbelievably greedy," Damson told his wife.

On 8 February 1986, Pastor Gerd Bambowsky received the Merit Order of the National People's Army, in silver, in recognition of his "outstanding achievements in the Ministry for State Security". In his commendation,

Minister for State Security Erich Mielke wrote: "For many years of faithful fulfilment of duties, particular achievements, initiative and high operational readiness in solving special tasks to strengthen and secure our socialist fatherland."

CHAPTER 15

LOSING MOTIVATION

By the late seventies, Wiegand had been promoted to Department XX/4's top officer for the "operational area" and gained a law degree at the MfS School in Potsdam. In Stasi parlance, the operational area was the foreign countries where the Firm operated. For most Stasi departments, that primarily meant West Germany.

But since East German Christians had a much wider international network than most East Germans, it meant large international operations for Wiegand. Take Manfred Stolpe, the top layman in the Berlin–Brandenburg diocese. IM Sekretär helped not just Department XX/4 but, by extension, East Germany's government. Wiegand gives me an example. "Before Chancellor [Helmut] Schmidt's visit to the GDR [in 1981], Stolpe travelled to see him. When he came back, he told us the issues that Schmidt was planning to bring up with Honecker. I wrote it all down and it went to the Minister [Mielke] and Honecker. The man had better information than the HVA!"

Wiegand is not exaggerating Stolpe's value. The West German government sometimes used Stolpe as a messenger for important communications with East Berlin. Chancellor Schmidt's visit to East Germany in 1981 was extraordinarily tricky. The East German government had pre-empted negotiations by announcing that each West German visitor would now have to exchange DM25 per day, up from a daily exchange amount of DM13. Thanks to Stolpe, the East German government knew how West Germany's chancellor would respond. Stolpe's particular skill was, of course, that he seamlessly blended official dealings with the Stasi – which were unavoidable for many church leaders – with undercover work for the Firm.

Wiegand and I talk about pastor agents' motivation for spying: those who did it for career reasons, those who needed a sense of belonging, those who believed in socialism. But the one unifying reason so many pastors were willing to work for the Stasi, Wiegand says, was that like other East Germans, they presumed the German Democratic Republic would last. "Until 1989, nobody believed that the Wall would come down so soon," he points out. "Everybody thought things would go on much, much longer. And so you'll work together with those people [the Stasi] and help your church." Help your church – perhaps. But many, perhaps most, pastor agents primarily wanted to help themselves. Wiegand acknowledges as much: "It was a mix of helping the church and helping yourself. Every church had a partner church [in West Germany] that sent them medications, typewriters, clothes, cars, anything you could ask for." Wiegand and his colleagues could easily have stopped the deliveries. "Of course the clergymen didn't want that to end either and that's why they made a small deal with us," he explains.

In 1979, Franz Sgraja retired from the Church Bureau's leadership and was succeeded by Wiegand. But although Wiegand was excited about his elevation, he sensed that East Germany was less stable than it appeared. As he knew from the Church Bureau's agents and from official news reports, Czechoslovakia's Charter 77 could at any moment spill over to East Germany. But as director, he would at least be able to perfect his soft-glove approach.

"I wanted us to do things more cleverly," he explains during one of our meetings. "No arrests. If you arrest someone, you have to release him again. That becomes a big deal. And arrest a clergyman, that's just something you don't do."

Can't arrest a clergyman? Of course you can, if you want to. The other Warsaw Pact countries' secret police agencies were still doing so in full force. On 1 November that year, the KGB had arrested Gleb Yakunin, an Orthodox priest. His crime: to have written a petition pleading with Christians abroad to support their Soviet brethren. Father Yakunin was sentenced to five years in a penal camp, followed by expulsion from the Soviet Union. Some secret police agencies were even murdering pastors. In October 1984, three officers from Poland's secret police the Służba Bezpieczeństwa kidnapped Jerzy Popiełuszko, a Roman Catholic priest who supported the growing opposition movement. The officers beat him up, tied a rock to his foot and threw him into a river to drown. But it was a pyrrhic victory for the Służba Bezpieczeństwa: Father Popiełuszko's death and funeral became global news, further strengthening Poland's democracy activists.

Wiegand remained certain that charming rebellious clergymen was more effective. "I wanted to win them over, wanted them to support the state," he says. He doesn't deny, though, that there were more than a few tough cases. No charm, no flattery and no gifts could make a pastor like Rainer Eppelmann more compliant, though the Church Bureau even sent several women to him, with the mission of turning pastoral conversations into affairs.[122] The Stasi even planned to cause a car accident involving Eppelmann.[123]

Wiegand introduced other changes too. No longer could the Church Bureau reveal its agents' real names to other Stasi departments. "Of course [other MfS officials] got angry," he says. "But I can't be cultivating somebody for several years and then give his real name to just anybody." Eventually

---

122   Gieseke, *Mielke-Konzern*, p. 189.
123   Gieseke, *Mielke-Konzern*, p. 185.

Wiegand won the battle by appealing to one of Minister Mielke's deputies. And although it named part of his plan, Wiegand's insistence was later to protect many pastor agents from being unmasked.

Wiegand also decided that the Church Bureau's recruitment files would remain active not for six months but seven years. He tells me why: "The MfS procedure says, 'I want to recruit Schmidt'. You establish a File Schmidt. According to the procedure, within half a year I have to decide whether File Schmidt remains active or goes to the archive. Then you write a recruitment proposal." In Wiegand's opinion, six months was simply too little time to cultivate an agent. It had to be an unrushed procedure, or otherwise the attempt might needlessly fail. "Six months, that's just not possible," he explains. "With a clergyman, you can't tell within six months whether it will work or not. Sometimes it took seven years to recruit them. The MfS had its procedures, but I had mine."

Joachim Wiegand's new procedures didn't much concern Aleksander Radler in his Swedish outpost, where his assignment was intelligence-gathering rather than recruitment of new agents. Radler was now a firmly established presence at church events. His colleagues often invited the Radlers to their homes too, and they enjoyed meeting the East German theologians he sometimes brought to Lund. "I have so much darkness within me," he sometimes told friends, but they made nothing of it.

Wiegand's colleagues in Frankfurt an der Oder had nurtured great hopes for Radler, in whom they saw potential for another Stolpe – only better, thanks to the doors a Reverend title opens. But, with Radler, the Stasi had now hit the barrier that every intelligence agency worries about when recruiting an agent who spies for reasons other than ideology. Someone like Jürgen Kapiske was driven by his love of East Germany and a desire for revenge against his better-born peers. That meant certain disadvantages for the Church Bureau, as ideologically committed agents are often strong-headed and reluctant to follow orders. By contrast, an agent like Radler typically showed great enthusiasm and commitment as long as it brought excitement or advantages. But when a mercenary agent gets bored, the quality of his work deteriorates. For the last several years, IM Thomas – Radler – had delivered increasingly low-value intelligence. Despite being a free and prosperous country, Sweden clearly held less and less appeal to him. Radler wanted to return to East Germany.

By 1985, Radler had lobbied East German theology professors, the education ministry, and the Stasi so hard for a professorship in the GDR that the Stasi felt compelled to convene a meeting. At 3 p.m. on 16 May, IM Thomas entered a conspiratorial apartment to meet with Ditmar Heydel, the Stasi officer who was so expertly handling Jürgen Kapiske. It was not by coincidence that Heydel had been chosen for the meeting. As far as the Stasi was concerned, Radler was becoming tricky and time-consuming. But Heydel couldn't be too harsh with him either: like any other agent, Radler might then turn his back on the Firm and reveal his secrets. Heydel was relieved when undercover officers who were posted near the apartment radioed him reporting that IM Thomas had been observing intelligence protocol as he approached the safe house. Before approaching the door, he had made sure that no one was watching. That was a good sign.

Heydel was gearing up for a long meeting. He offered IM Thomas coffee and cake and inquired about Ulla and the girls. If IM Thomas felt guilty for misleading his wife about his work – in fact, about his entire identity – he didn't reveal it. Heydel then steered the conversation towards IM Thomas's antagonizing efforts to get an academic post in East Germany. He levelled with Radler: "The decision-makers in the church and the theology departments are not that interested in giving you a job."

Radler, usually talkative, was speechless. Hadn't colleagues said they would support his application? Apparently they have merely been polite. The reality that Heydel was gently trying to explain to IM Thomas was that there were plenty of theologians in East Germany, and that not even the

MfS could give Radler the career boost he so desperately wanted. "Can't I just move back to the GDR anyway?" the agent asked. The 1968 Jena episode – nearly twenty years in the past – should be history by now. The six students he dispatched to jail by giving their letters to the Stasi had been released to West Germany long ago.[124] The risk that they would unmask Radler as a Stasi spy was minimal.

Yes, Heydel said, it would be fine for IM Thomas to return. "But that doesn't mean you'll get a position at a university," he cautioned. In fact, Radler's job prospects were dismal. "I can't tell you this strongly enough," Heydel said. "Even the church is unlikely to hire you." The Stasi had tried. Six years previously it had mounted a major effort to facilitate his return, discreetly lobbying universities to take him. But each university had declined the offer.

The careerist semi-orphan had betrayed his friendships for the benefit of the Stasi. Wolfgang Clifford Aleksander Radler had assumed that providing intelligence would ensure a good academic career – but now, not even the church wanted him. Listening to Heydel, he barely managed to respond: "Of course I'm very disappointed. But I'm grateful for your efforts." It was a lovely spring day; outside children were playing in the sunset. But Radler wasn't paying attention. His world had fallen to pieces.

"I know it's not much consolation, but there are a couple of options," Heydel added. He explained that Radler could remain in Sweden ("the operational area" in the official terminology), where he could either work as a pastor or remain in his academic career. Alternatively, the MfS could help Radler get a position with an international church organization abroad.

---

124   The West German government regularly paid East Germany to release East Germans jailed in their own country for political offences; for East Berlin, the trade provided important access to hard currency. Until the collapse of the GDR, West Germany bought out a total of 33,755 political prisoners. "So wurden DDR-Häftlinge freigekauft", *DW*, 7 August 2012, https://www.dw.com/de/so-wurden-ddr-h%C3%A4ftlinge-freigekauft/a-16149420 (accessed 21 May 2019).

Heydel mentioned the Lutheran World Federation in Geneva.

"I'll think about it," the dejected Radler said. He hadn't thought he'd stay in Sweden for seventeen years, and now he was facing the prospect of remaining there even longer. Others would risk their lives for such an opportunity, but Radler was despondent. Geneva didn't appeal to him either. It was 9 p.m. now. Six hours earlier, he had entered the safe house thinking he'd be rewarded for twenty years of Stasi duty. Heydel tried to cheer him up, but to no avail. Observing the protocol of undercover meetings, Radler headed out into the evening.

On 17 May, Radler returned to Lund. As usual, his colleagues showed sympathy for the dutiful son who so often visited his mother in East Germany. And Radler was still well-liked at the university. Every now and then, he even helped colleagues who specialized in German theology. This spring, he had promised to help a doctoral student prepare for his PhD viva, a public event to be conducted in German. Playing the professor who would examine the doctoral student, Radler – speaking in German – asked every question the visiting examiner might conceivably pose.

On the day of the viva, Radler strode up the medieval staircase to the imposing lecture hall where the public examination was to be held, taking a seat next to the doctoral candidate's family. Wearing the collar and black cassock of a Church of Sweden pastor, the doctoral candidate took his place in the podium below the visiting West German examiner to defend his thesis on the mystic thinker Johann Arndt. The doctoral student was my father. He passed.

Though they shared an interest in German theology, it was perhaps no coincidence that Radler had befriended my father. In its 1981 register of agents who were active abroad and their respective assignments, Division XX listed IM Thomas's assignment as "reconnaissance of reactionary clergy and educational institutions in the NSA", using the German acronym for non-socialist countries – in other words, the West.[125] My father, a well-known conservative pastor, clearly counted as a reactionary.

Following his successful viva, my father returned to ministry and we moved to the countryside. In the early hours of 28 February 1986, I was awakened by a phone call from my grandmother. "Palme has been killed," she said. I immediately suspected that she had misunderstood. Who would want to kill the prime minister? Besides, no politicians were ever assassinated in Sweden. But my grandmother insisted that I turn on the radio. She was right: the radio was repeating the shocking news of Olof Palme's death over and over. An assailant had shot him as he was walking home from the cinema with his wife. Palme hadn't been accompanied by bodyguards – this was Sweden, after all.

The murder shook the Swedish public. Several months later, the police had still arrested no suspects and its investigation seemed rudderless. It was pursuing leads in South Africa, leads connected to Iran and Iraq, leads to far-right Swedish police officers, leads pointing to a mistress whose father was a KGB agent in London. Or could Palme have been killed as a result of his vocal efforts to keep Sweden outside both NATO and the Warsaw Pact?

With the assassin still at large, fear took a grip on Sweden. Hans Holmér, the Stockholm police chief running the investigation, gave press conference after press conference, looking drained but offering no new clues. Was he incompetent? In cahoots with a murder conspiracy? All over the country, people were unsettled.

In May 1986, preparations were underway in Lund for the centuries-old ceremony where the university's successful doctoral candidates receive their diplomas and top hats. The ceremony, which is held in Latin, always takes place in the cathedral. As every year, the Swedish Army positioned its historic cannon outside the cathedral, ready to salute the new doctors.

---

125   Radler was still being run by Division XX's office in Frankfurt an der Oder, not the Church Bureau's central office in Berlin.

The doctoral candidates had practised their part of the ceremony. The university's protocol staff had arranged the procession order for the new PhDs and the ceremonial marshals – university officials and scholars – accompanying them. Radler was the theology department's marshal. The undercover agent now represented the Swedish establishment.

At the ceremony, Radler processed into the cathedral, surrounded by many of Sweden's, and the world's, best academics. He smiled to himself.

But soon it was back to intelligence duties again. On 28 August, IM Thomas delivered news to the Stasi about the Swedish church in Berlin. The Church of Sweden newspaper had reported that the Swedish congregation in Berlin was about to appoint a new rector and that some twenty people had applied. IM Thomas conveyed the news, adding that one of the top candidates was rumoured to be Sam Dahlgren, European secretary at the Lutheran World Federation.

Although the election of a new rector for the Swedish congregation in West Berlin might potentially have interested Division XX, it didn't need a spy in Sweden in order to find out what the Church of Sweden newspaper was reporting. What it did need was steady information about Dahlgren, the rumoured top candidate, who happened to be an expert on the relations between the church and the state in East Germany. If appointed, he would be the Church of Sweden's public face in Berlin. Even though it would have been easy enough to find out where Dahlgren stood on matters of East Germany and the church, IM Thomas delivered no valuable insights.

On 29 October, IM Thomas again took the train from Malmö to East Berlin and onwards to Frankfurt an der Oder, where an officer was expecting him in a conspiratorial apartment. If Radler was apprehensive about meeting here again, one year after his fateful conversation with Heydel, he hid it well. Over the years, Radler's cheerful face had revealed none of his inner turmoil, never showed the strain of his multiple identities.

The Stasi had sent IM Thomas to Sweden with great effort in the clearly explained expectation that he would deliver exclusive intelligence on the thinking of the Swedish establishment. The assassination of Olof Palme had been a perfect opportunity for IM Thomas to prove his worth – indeed, he could have added useful insights to what the HVA's agents were reporting. But, to Division XX's disappointment, IM Thomas had failed to add any new information on the high-profile murder investigation. Had IM Thomas developed qualms about his second identity? Whatever the case, he still wanted the Stasi to support his career ambitions.

Despite the disappointing intelligence, this turned out to be a routine meeting. Heinig didn't upbraid IM Thomas. That was good, because Radler had had a fateful several months on the personal front. In August, he had become a father for the third time when an extramarital affair produced a son.

Friends in Lund were pitying the kind Ulla. Had they known that Radler's frequent trips to see his mother in East Germany were, in fact, often to various cities around Europe on behalf of the Stasi, they would have felt even more sorry for Ulla, who was unwittingly playing a bit part in the standoff between the communist bloc and the West.

Meanwhile, Radler was getting increasingly despondent about his academic career in Sweden. He'd long got by on his charm and undeniable intelligence, but he was simply not managing to get a professorship. This made him even more desperate to secure a post in East Germany. Despite Lieutenant Heydel's warnings, he released another cascade of letters to sundry contacts.

And he still sent occasional news to Frankfurt an der Oder. On 9 June 1987, he reported that a friend ("very active in the church"), who was also a senior police officer, believed that far-right elements in the Swedish police had killed Olof Palme. "This is not an individual opinion, but one that he says is shared by other police officers," IM Thomas cabled.

In his Swedish academic capacity, Radler regularly travelled to East

Germany as well, taking Swedish students to locations associated with Martin Luther. One day, he turned up in Leipzig, where his former university acquaintance Christoph Kähler was now a pastor. As Radler knew, Kähler had remained critical of the government. But, as during their student days, Kähler sensed that something wasn't right. "He came with a group of Swedish students," he tells me. "Of course I wanted to tell them interesting things, but I knew it was a trap."

Radler was also using the trips to lobby for himself. So it was that one Sunday morning, a visitor unexpectedly turned up at Michael Beintker's door. It was Radler, whom Beintker had never met. "Bengt Hägglund said I should meet you," he told the surprised Beintker. Hägglund, a respected theology professor at Lund, was unaware of Radler's plans, but Radler knew that using the professor's name would give him credibility. As predicted, Beintker invited Radler in for coffee and a professional connection was established. This, Radler hoped, would bring him another step closer to a professorship in East Germany.

CHAPTER 16

A CRUCIAL FOREIGN MISSION

Jürgen Kapiske could still back out. Just as the Church Bureau didn't punish pastors who refused to become informants, and there was no punishment for pastors who failed to deliver useful information or decided to quit. "Nothing happened if you told the Stasi you didn't want to work for them," Christoph Demke points out. As bishop of the Church Province of Saxony, Demke told his pastors to let him know about any recruitment attempts by the Stasi. Though some pastors did tell him, Demke realized that others had not only spoken to Wiegand's men but signed up to assist them as well. It never dawned on him, though, that his right-hand man Detlef Hammer might be a Stasi officer.

Kapiske didn't back out. In fact, he liked Lieutenant Heydel. "He was quiet and thoughtful," Kapiske tells me in his study. It's a bitterly cold day. We make tea in his kitchen, unchanged since East German times. Nostalgia or lack of money? I can't tell. But the kitchen is extremely tidy, as is Kapiske's study, whose wall-to-wall bookcase features books about East Germany and contemporary history. There are several books about Dietrich Bonhoeffer, too, a pastor Kapiske admires.

We talk about Kapiske's time as a newly ordained pastor in Gross Neuendorf. Despite the inner and outer complications that come with maintaining dual identities, Kapiske was still convinced that he was doing a good thing for his country. From his rural outpost, he had managed to make inroads into Charter 77, establishing contact with several members and planning a trip Prague.[126] Though he was genuinely interested in the network and its efforts to bring attention to Czechoslovakia's repression of dissent, he also knew that the Stasi was eager to learn more about the Charter members' activities; above all, of course, whether they were helping East Germans develop a similar initiative.

In the Normannenstrasse, the Church Bureau quickly relayed news of Kapiske's contacts to their colleagues across Division XX. Clearly impressed with Kapiske's results, Division XX decided that the pastor would, from now on, operate on behalf of the entire Division, not just the Church Bureau. IM Walter "will continue to penetrate the network of clerical underground powers in the GDR, the CSSR [Czechoslovakia], and the NSA [non-socialist countries] under the cover of working for the church press", Major Eberhard Böttcher explained in a department-wide memo. The Stasi also shared Kapiske's reports with its Warsaw Pact sister agencies.

Kapiske wasted no time. He swiftly arranged another get-together with his Charter 77-connected pastor friend, whom we will call Hans Albrecht. Albrecht agreed to show him the Charter itself as well as a secret report by three Charter signatories including Havel.

After making a quick phone call, the pastor disappeared. Several minutes later, he reappeared with the documents. "The great thing that's happening in the CSSR is that regime critics are gathering under one roof," he confided. Soon he'd go back to Czechoslovakia to see how he could further assist

---

126   Charter 77 was a petition signed by over 240 Czechoslovaks, asking the government to recognize basic human rights.

his friends, he explained. He also wanted to determine how their activities could be copied back home in East Germany. Kapiske tried to memorize the highlights of the explosive documents. In his subsequent report to Heydel, he explained that "the report details the arrest and interrogation of individual Charter 77 signatories; the search of [signatories'] apartments and confiscation of books and manuscripts". The pastor–journalist had established how the Czech dissidents were trying to communicate their fate to a Western audience.

Major Böttcher advised IM Walter to follow the trail and, in April 1977, Kapiske travelled to Prague in his capacity as a church journalist. The trip was a journalism-and-Stasi mission. But on a personal level, Kapiske was also curious about what was happening in the country that had blossomed during the Prague Spring. "It was a mix of personal and professional," he tells me.

I ask Kapiske about the account of his Czechoslovak efforts in his Stasi file. He gives me a somewhat different version of his Charter 77 infiltration than the one described in the file. "Since I was already in touch with a Czech pastor I thought, 'let's see where it takes you and what they're all about'. I told them that I already knew Milan Machovec and that I wanted to meet a few other people. That's how I met Milan Balabán as well." Machovec was a prominent Marxist philosopher, known for inviting Christian thinkers to his seminars at Prague's famous Charles University. He had been fired by the government for his non-conformist views and was barely making a living as an organist in a Catholic church. But he had an international following and had signed Charter 77. Balabán, a Lutheran theologian, had likewise signed the Charter.

Perhaps Kapiske isn't remembering the details of his Charter mission, or perhaps he wants to minimize it. But even if he wanted to refresh his memory, he's stymied. Paradoxically, he can't access his Stasi file.

According to the file, thanks to his pastor acquaintance Kapiske quickly managed to arrange meetings with Charter 77 signatories. One evening, he got together with two Charter supporters at a Prague café. The café was noisy and off the beaten track, offering the veteran activists a degree of security. Familiar as they were with government surveillance, they would meet only in locations where they could communicate without being overheard or recorded.

At the café, the activists revealed their worries: the Czech church leadership was cracking down on Charter 77 signatories and supporters. Christians and moderate communists now needed to work together to form a civil rights movement, they suggested. They also divulged that Charter 77 would not have been published without Western support. Hans-Peter Riese – a West German correspondent and a friend of Charter co-founder Pavel Kohout – had delivered the open appeal to several Western newspapers including the *New York Times*, Italy's *Corriere della Sera* and *The Times* of London. As Kapiske knew, the papers had printed it on 7 January.

During their four and a half hours at the café, IM Walter tapped into a powder-keg of information. As Pastor Jürgen Kapiske, he had gathered information most ordinary agents would never be able to access.

Even though he had once again betrayed the confidence of a friend, Pastor Albrecht, Kapiske's conscience was clear. "The church is a power factor in this Cold War," he told himself. "It's not an innocent bystander, just as it was not an innocent bystander in the Third Reich." He did regret hurting some of his colleagues and acquaintances, but the church? Not at all.

After returning to Gross Neuendorf, Kapiske learned that he wouldn't be staying there much longer. Lieutenant Heydel had come through for him, or perhaps it was just a coincidence. Either way, just over a year after being ordained, the reluctant pastor landed a job as deputy editor of the *Mecklenburgische Kirchenzeitung* in Schwerin, the newspaper of East Germany's northernmost diocese. Individuals connected to the Stasi had pushed his candidacy. "The combat task in preparation of the 30th anniversary of the GDR has been accomplished," noted now-Major Heydel in his report, using the regime's militaristic vocabulary. "IM Walter's future deployment opens wide possibilities of penetrating enemy powers' conspiracy that is working against the real-existing socialism through political clericalism." The Stasi, in other words, wanted IM Walter to find out how Western countries were using East German Lutherans for their political purposes.

Kapiske had barely arrived in his new job when the Stasi tried to recruit a fellow pastor in the area. Instead of calling the number the Stasi officer had given him, the pastor reported the episode to his bishop, Heinrich Rathke. Rathke then feistily called the number himself and complained about the recruitment pitch, hung up and proceeded to warn all his parishes of Stasi informants in their midst. Would anyone think of Kapiske?

Nobody. In fact, soon afterward Kapiske was appointed Rathke's personal secretary. Heydel had provided him with a Minox miniature camera, along with a container for secret documents, and had taught him how to use it. "There will be higher demands on conspiracy," noted Heydel after handing his agent the camera.

Kapiske's new church position was important to the Stasi. Rathke, a Bavarian, had been serving in an East German parish when the Berlin Wall came up and found himself stuck behind the Iron Curtain. But he'd gone on to become one of East Germany's bravest regime critics – he was the Heinrich Rathke who had, as a young pastor, so resolutely turned down two Stasi recruiters. As a young pastor, he had also chased the police car carrying a local farmer who had been arrested for protesting against forced collectivization. Rathke was promptly sent to jail himself. As bishop, after finding out about one pastor's upcoming meeting with his Stasi handler, he instead turned up at the meeting himself, declaring the relationship over. He spoke out against military lessons in schools and the criminal prosecution of pacifist teenagers. His own children were already paying the price for his outspoken stance: they had been barred from attending university.

Rathke held another important position, too, leading the East German Lutherans' cooperation with the Russian Orthodox Church. Wiegand's staff classed him as "hostile-negative". Though Rathke could hardly know it, some 100 agents from the Church Bureau and other MfS departments kept him and his family under surveillance. And Rathke certainly had no idea that his personal secretary was one of them.

Kapiske was proving himself a highly talented journalist. Soon he was appointed editor of the newspaper of Church Province of Saxony, where Detlef Hammer was already keeping the Church Bureau *au courant*. In East Germany, church newspapers played a crucial role. With government-run media only disseminating regime propaganda, many people turned to church newspapers for real news. And the Church Province of Saxony's newspaper was the most important one. With church newspapers, the Stasi often resorted to issuing commands, threatening to ban publication if editors didn't comply. But it was not a smooth method.[127] Now the Firm had its own man in the Magdeburg editor's seat.

Kapiske impressed his colleagues as a good journalist, though he struck them as a bit shy. "He does spend a whole lot of time in front of the computer," Martin Kramer, a senior pastor based at the diocesan headquarters, often thought to himself. Kramer and other diocesan staff saw plenty of the pastor–journalist, but Kramer didn't reflect any further on Kapiske's industrious typing. One thing, however, struck him as odd: when it was Kapiske's turn to lead the office's daily morning service, he never offered a meditation like the other pastors did, instead reading a prayer from a book. "What sort of pastor wouldn't give a meditation?" Kramer asked himself. "Is he too busy? Does he have nothing to say about the Bible readings?" But Kramer kept his concerns to himself.

On 19 July 1980, the Olympic Games were inaugurated in Moscow.

---

127   Rossberg and Richter, *Das Kreuz mit dem Kreuz*, p. 47.

It was, however, a rather subdued affair. The United States boycotted the Games, and in protest over the Soviet Union's invasion of Afghanistan, so did another sixty-four countries – nearly half of the countries qualified to participate. As usual, East Germany did well, winning 121 medals. The Games had barely ended when workers at the Lenin Shipyard in the Polish city of Gdansk shocked the world by successfully organizing a strike. The shipyard workers were protesting against the government's decision to raise food prices once again – and, to everyone's surprise, they forced the government to change course.

The workers gave themselves the name Solidarity and chose an electrician named Lech Walesa to be their chairman. Soon, Solidarity had become a force the government couldn't control. Sensing trouble, East Berlin imposed a visa requirement on Poles who had, until then, been able to enter East Germany freely. Soon Poland's own government under General Wojciech Jaruzelski imposed martial law.

But not even martial law could quell Solidarity. On the contrary, Walesa and his fellow workers were winning even more support among workers. Crucially, the by now immensely popular Pope John Paul II supported the protesting workers. Although no other trade unionists behind the Iron Curtain were as bold as Solidarity, dissent was rapidly growing. Alarmed Soviet leaders considered an invasion of Poland to prop up Jaruzelski and to set an example to its other vassal states. In the end, they decided it would be counterproductive.

In November 1982, former KGB boss Yuri Andropov succeeded hard-line Soviet leader Leonid Brezhnev, who had died in office. Andropov introduced modest reforms, removing corrupt party officials and allowing the publication of statistics that revealed the Soviet economy was stagnating. But he adopted a hawkish foreign policy. Four months into Andropov's reign, Ronald Reagan branded the Soviet Union an "evil empire".

Elsewhere in the Ministry for State Security, another officer had, years earlier, perfected the subtle art of espionage, with spectacular results. Markus Wolf, the son of a Jewish communist doctor and playwright, had grown up in Moscow after his family fled persecution in Nazi Germany. In 1945, the Soviet Communist Party dispatched the 29-year-old to its occupation zone, and he soon found himself in charge of East Germany's new foreign intelligence agency, the HVA. Wolf, trained as an air force engineer, had no background in espionage. But he was dashing, intellectual, and charming. From a hopeless starting position *vis-à-vis* West Germany, which had inherited much of Nazi Germany's intelligence apparatus, Wolf soon turned the HVA into a formidable espionage operation, known for its creativity and its agents' unswerving loyalty. When HVA agents serving abroad clandestinely visited East Germany, Wolf hosted dinner parties for them at his country house.

By the seventies, General Wolf held Western adversaries in fear with his clever schemes. One of them involved love, real and fake. Noticing that secretaries in West German intelligence agencies and other government offices received little respect, yet had access to the same confidential information as their bosses did, he had dispatched undercover HVA officers who charmed the secretaries, became their lovers, and convinced them to hand over secret information. If the woman insisted on marriage, the HVA officer went along with that too. The scheme worked: thirty-six secretaries are known to have fallen for Wolf's Romeos.[128]

But even though the HVA scored success after success, Wolf himself had remained invisible. Desperate Western intelligence agencies had labelled him "The Man without a Face", a moniker that stuck even after Swedish intelligence managed to snap a photo of him during a visit to Stockholm in 1978. Markus Wolf is said to have served as inspiration for Karla, the mysterious and powerful communist spymaster in John Le Carré's spy thrillers.

---

128   Elisabeth Pfister, *Unternehmen Romeo: Die Liebeskommandos der Stasi* (Berlin: Aufbau Taschenbuch-Verlag), 1999, p. 29.

Spying for Wolf's HVA meant belonging to the elite. Department XX/4 and the Stasi's other domestic units were, by and large, effective in gathering information but, because their agents spied on fellow citizens, their work had a dirty reputation. IM Walter was a mere pastor spy, but his infiltration of Charter 77 hadn't escaped the HVA's attention.

By the early eighties, Kapiske was working away at the diocesan newspaper in Magdeburg. For the time being, the Czechoslovak authorities had managed to quell Charter 77. Czechoslovak dissidents who had gone into exile were experiencing rather different events: in 1984, Havel's school friend Miloš Forman – the Academy Award-winning director of *One Flew Over the Cuckoo's Nest* – released the film *Amadeus*, which won eight Oscars. Havel himself was working in a brewery, having only been released from prison in 1983.

A long time had gone by without any Church Bureau assignments abroad for IM Walter. Then, in the summer of 1984, the Lutheran Church suddenly decided to send Kapiske to Budapest. The Lutheran World Federation would hold its global conference there, the first time behind the Iron Curtain. The conference would feature a daily newspaper, written in English but with one page each in German and Hungarian. Kapiske was just the man for the job. "I was told I would be doing the German page," he tells me. "The whole thing lasted about a month. Every day, we produced the paper and proofread it. We worked until late at night." When the Lutheran World Federation held its next conference, in 1990, the Iron Curtain was no more.

Although Kapiske didn't realize it, the newspaper assignment was a test. The MfS had apparently arranged his invitation, and together with the HVA the Church Bureau was testing his suitability for long-term international assignments. "They wanted to check whether I could work independently, how I got along with people from other countries, was I accepted by other people, could I speak English at least at a level where I can talk to the boss?"

Kapiske tells me. Fortunately, not only was he able to converse with the boss, the American journalist Herb David, he also got along well with him. "He was a very quiet man," Kapiske recalls. Together, the team produced a quality newspaper with a highly professional feel. HVA officers were watching, and they liked what they saw.

Aleksander Radler was having less success. Requesting career advantages in exchange for services to the Stasi clearly seemed like an excellent idea to men like Radler and Krügel. But did it occur to them that the appointment of a less qualified person would immediately raise red flags among their colleagues? And did the pastor agents realize that if every Church Bureau agent requested, say, a professorship, every East German theology department would be infested by the Stasi? That would hardly be a healthy environment for the country's pastors-in-training. Of course, it didn't really matter to the agents-cum-academics. What mattered to them was seemingly only the progress of their careers, not the future of the church.

Around the same time that he delivered the disappointing news to IM Thomas, Heydel had alarming news of a different kind for IM Walter. The Soviets had told East Germany's leaders that there was a concrete risk of war in Europe, and that the war would take place in East Germany. In such a situation East Germany's many pastors and church groups with close links to the West would become a loose cannon. Heydel instructed IM Walter to find out if pastors were making preparations to support prospective Western invaders.

Though he didn't mind assignments in East Germany, Kapiske had enjoyed his visits to Hungary and Czechoslovakia, and he enthusiastically welcomed every prospect of foreign travel. He kept an eye on everything, from the political opinions of Western officials, clerics, and journalists to the details of news organizations' radio equipment. And, like any good spy, he effortlessly engaged new acquaintances in conversations and self-revelation. One Swiss journalist turned out to be a reserve army officer, telling Kapiske over a glass of wine how the Swiss military viewed the Warsaw Pact. Another man, a pastor from Switzerland, turned out to be a Czechoslovak who had simply remained abroad after the Prague Spring. The spokesman for the UN in Geneva, a former assistant to West Germany's minister for development, was still on the West German government's payroll, Kapiske reported to Heydel.

IM Walter supplied details of UN officials' careers, addresses, homes, furniture, cars, and families. And he possessed a keen eye for inconsistencies in people's lifestyle. After several visits to Geneva, he told Heydel about the get-togethers hosted by a friendly Lutheran World Federation secretary. Widowed with two young children, the secretary nonetheless put on lavish receptions for church trip participants at her home. "It's highly likely that she gets funds from somewhere, but it's not clear from which side or for what purpose," he observed. Was she working for an intelligence agency?

From 1978, the Stasi had paid IM Walter a monthly stipend of 250 marks, about a quarter of the average East German's monthly income. By now, IM Walter was effortlessly communicating with Heydel through safe house addresses and phone numbers, and made sure he was not being watched while travelling to their meetings in various cities. The Stasi also reimbursed his expenses. "I'm doing what's good for the GDR," he kept telling himself. He never asked for gifts. Once, though, the Church Bureau helped him get a new car tyre, an item surprisingly hard to come by in East Germany.

And Kapiske still thought that the church was destabilizing the German Democratic Republic. In fact, he felt that the Lutheran Church on both sides of the German border was playing a strategic Cold War role, insisting as it did that it was one and the same church. The church kept pushing for a united Germany and assigned the highest political importance to the matter, Kapiske informed Heydel.

Now dissent was beginning to bubble under East Germany's steely surface too. While the country didn't have a Solidarity or a Charter 77, it had Lutheran peace prayer meetings. By the mid-eighties, the meetings were beginning to both proliferate. And, as Joachim Wiegand and his officers knew well, "peace prayers" meant not peace but unrest.

In 1985, with Charter 77 emboldened by the reform efforts of new Soviet leader Mikhail Gorbachev, the Church Bureau again sent IM Walter to Prague. This time, his mission was to uncover tensions and disagreements within the group. The HVA had its own spies, of course, but IM Walter had excellent access. On 29 May, he took the morning train from Dresden, which would deliver him to the Czechoslovak capital some four hours later.

After booking himself into Hotel Solidaritat, Kapiske boarded a tram to see his old Charter 77 acquaintance Milan Balabán. The Lutheran pastor and Old Testament scholar had been forced out by the government and was now working as a labourer. In the Balabán household, unexpected visitors could mean heartbreak. "What brings you here?" asked Balabán's wife, surprised to see Kapiske at the door. Did she sense that something was wrong? If Kapiske was nervous, he didn't show it. He easily chatted away, inquired about the family, and filled Mrs Balabán in on East German news. Almost immediately (within twenty minutes, he told Heydel), he had convinced her of his good intentions and she had invited him back for morning coffee with her husband the following day.

Would Balabán trust Kapiske? Even though Charter 77 members were under heavy surveillance by Czech secret police, they were still managing to communicate with Western contacts. If Kapiske could uncover these communication channels, and find out whether the leadership was fracturing, he'd score a victory for the Stasi and its allies.

Over coffee, the conversation proceeded haltingly at first, but after a while Balabán began to relax. Had his wife known what was transpiring, she might have thought twice about serving Moravian vodka with the strong coffee. Kapiske asked the Czechoslovak cleric about theological matters and inquired about Charter 77. Four hours later, Kapiske left the apartment, his head crammed with details about Charter 77. Back at the hotel, he quickly wrote down his notes and concealed the sheets in the container given to him.

As IM Walter knew, an agent's most valuable asset is his ability to inspire trust. A trusting contact will introduce you to others, and if you gain their confidence, too, your access will snowball. Conversely, once one source harbours suspicions about you, you risk losing a whole group. Jürgen Kapiske engendered trust because he was so quiet, so serious; an entirely improbable intelligence agent.

Balabán's trust opened doors. The following afternoon, another Charter 77 signatory invited Kapiske to her home. "I came without a bag," he subsequently reported to the Church Bureau. Bringing a bag would have aroused suspicion. After half an hour or so, other leading Charter members turned up. With caution acquired during many years of underground activism, the hostess and her visitors proceeded to communicate in a most elaborate fashion: they exchanged questions and answers written on pieces of paper, occasionally adding whispered comments. Every few minutes, the hostess disappeared to the bathroom, where she shredded the pieces of paper and flushed them down the toilet.

The guests couldn't linger. A married couple among them had to get back to their home in a small town far from Prague. A court, sentencing them for their Charter 77 activism, had ordered them to register daily with the police office there. With a large yield of information again committed to his head, Kapiske bade the hostess farewell and embarked on a two-hour journey to his next destination.

It was already late at night when he rang the doorbell of yet another Charter 77 supporter. "Do we know each other?" the startled dissident asked as he answered the door. But when Kapiske mentioned their joint acquaintance to the East German pastor, the cautious dissident readily invited Kapiske into his home. The two men chatted for a while, but Kapiske didn't want to appear too curious. "Well, it's already late; I should be on my way," he said after a while.

The two men agreed to meet when Kapiske returned in the summer; then they'd take a long walk in the park so they could speak freely. Back at the hotel, an exhausted IM Walter jotted down his mental notes from the day's meetings and went to bed. The next morning he took the train back to Dresden.

Back at his office in Magdeburg, Kapiske sat down and typed. No wonder Pastor Kramer always saw him typing. Then again, a journalist types for a living. "The [Charter 77] spokespersons are in charge of preparing papers that would get considerable public attention," IM Walter informed Heydel, who had by now been promoted to lieutenant-colonel. "They're also in charge of reproducing and distributing the papers to Western publications." For security reasons, the spokespersons' tasks – including delivering information to Western diplomats and journalists – were clearly defined and carried out by them only, without the other members being given the details, Kapiske explained.

The responsibility – not to mention the surveillance – put the spokespeople under immense pressure. Kapiske reported that a former spokeswoman, who had handled most of Charter 77's important contacts, was close to a mental breakdown.

But despite the constant harassment, Charter 77 members were cleverly managing to run seminars which, by now, functioned almost as an alternative university. Indeed, the seminars had become a destination for opposition-minded Czechoslovaks far beyond Charter 77. But Kapiske had spotted a potential weakness in this growing alliance: discord among the Charter's Catholic, Protestant, and Marxist members. Some Catholics and Protestants squabbled over religious matters, while some of the Marxists suspected the Catholics of wanting too strong a voice. It was a conflict that could be exploited.

IM Walter had also discovered the secret behind Charter 77's successful hiding of Western books and magazines. At an agreed time and date, members gathered at a specified apartment, bringing their reading materials with them. Within a matter of minutes, they traded the goods among themselves and quickly departed. Because the apartment might be bugged, not a word was said throughout the exchange procedure. IM Walter reported that the Charter 77 activists were, in fact, extremely skilled in communicating without speaking, conducting even complex conversations in writing. In order to identify agents provocateurs, the activists added previously agreed-on letters to their missives. If a message, for example, contained the letter I in a particular place, they knew it was real. If not, they knew it was a trap by the secret police. "Forward immediately," Heydel scribbled on IM Walter's report.

The hard-working agent delivered further disturbing news from Czechoslovakia as well: "A number of activities have the aim to stem its increasing isolation at home and achieve a wider effect. That's why [Charter 77] is trying to position itself in international matters (ecological questions, peace, the so-called German matter). One gets the impression that Charter 77 wants to ingratiate itself with certain influential groups in the West." Peace and the environment: what's not to like? This was a blueprint that East Germany's own dissidents could easily copy – as could democracy activists around the Warsaw Pact.

Indeed, sensing that environmental and peace activism could turn into anti-regime activism, in 1982, the East German government had banned its citizens from wearing badges with the motto "Swords to Ploughshares". And in 1983 – the 500th anniversary of Luther's birth – the Church Bureau had been stocked up from twenty-four to thirty-two officers at headquarters. They were told to put their "absolute focus" on the environmental movement. The instructions from the Stasi leadership were clear:

Political-operative defence measures are to be offensively developed so that hostile-negative forces – regardless of the reason (peace movement, independent of the government, environmental protection, human rights, etc.) cannot be formed and organized. Counterrevolutionary activities

following the example in the People's Republic of Poland must
be prevented at the earliest stages.[129]

Despite its large brief, Department XX/4 still had a minuscule staff. Even in the critical year of 1989, only around 120 officers belonged to the Church Bureau.

IM Walter was unaware that the Church Bureau was now sharing his reports with the HVA. With Kapiske able to infiltrate the celebrated Charter 77 so smoothly, HVA began sensing great potential in the pastor as a full-time foreign agent.

But despite IM Walter's success in Czechoslovakia, Heydel didn't give him another assignment there, nor any other foreign missions. IM Walter was baffled by this sudden rejection. But when I ask him about it, he has an explanation: "Heydel apparently wanted to keep me. Afterwards, I found out that he had risen through the ranks thanks to me." There it is again, the bond between case officer and agent. If the relationship works well, an agent is rarely transferred from one handler to another: the risk the bond won't be equally strong is too great. And an officer who has spent years cultivating and training an agent naturally wants to keep him.

Back in the Normannenstrasse, Wiegand had recently solved a dilemma involving the invaluable agent Wolfgang Schnur. Schnur had grown unhappy with his handler, and Wiegand knew that simply assigning him to another officer would not improve matters. He was now running Schnur himself. As Wiegand had predicted, that made Schnur feel more important and had brightened his mood.

---

129   Auerbach, *Hauptabteilung XX*, p. 98.

CHAPTER 17

CHURCHES SPREADING OPPOSITION

In a prison near Halle, Katrin Eigenfeld was hearing strange rumours about Detlef Hammer. The Christian youth worker was in jail for anti-government subversion. From her fellow inmates, she had learned that there was something strange about her brother's friend Hammer. As soon as she was released she went to see her brother, Gerhard Gabriel. "There's something about Detlef that's not right," she said. But Gabriel, now a pastor, dismissed her fears. "Katrin, you're seeing ghosts," he reassured her. "What's supposed to be wrong?" Though he didn't tell her so, he was convinced that prison had made her a bit crazy. How could Katrin ever think that his friend Detlef would be hiding something?

By now, church lawyer Hammer was a prosperous man. With assistance from the Stasi, he had managed to buy a spacious house in Magdeburg, renovation making it more deluxe still; it even featured a small swimming pool. None of his colleagues at diocesan headquarters had a swimming pool.

In fact, not even the leader of the SED in Magdeburg had one. Hammer had also begun collecting art, and regularly gave friends cash and loans.[130] When people inquired about his wealth, he said his father had given him money. That was a lie: Hammer financially supported his parents. So where was the money coming from?

Eigenfeld was not the only person getting suspicious. At Halle's Stasi office, Hammer's handlers were increasingly concerned about their agent's wealth. They knew how much they were paying him, of course, and knew his church salary, but he seemed to be living far beyond these means. In November 1985, the officers decided to investigate. They asked the local banks for information about accounts belonging to Hammer and his wife, Silke. The banks reported balances totalling 295,800 marks – a fortune. The Church Bureau had no idea that Hammer had also opened bank accounts in West Germany.

In addition to his church salary, Hammer was receiving a monthly Stasi officer salary of 2,100 marks, but even that wouldn't have allowed him to amass such a large amount of money.[131] Hammer had always been good at making financial gain out of his engagements: even as a student he had made sure the Stasi compensated him for espionage outings. But not all of this money had come from the Stasi. Had their undercover officer been recruited by West German intelligence?

Despite strenuous efforts, the officers failed to trace the funds. Given the lack of evidence, the Church Bureau decided not to confront Hammer. Besides, it needed him. As instructed by the Church Bureau, Hammer had stayed in touch with Gerhard Gabriel and Wolf Krötke. Every now and then, he met up with Gabriel and the two men relived their student days. Gabriel wasn't just any pastor, coming as he did from a long line of opposition-leaning clerics. As a result, he was usually very cautious about his activities.

130   Schultze, *Spionage gegen eine Kirchenleitung*, p. 37.
131   Schultze, *Spionage gegen eine Kirchenleitung*, p. 35.

In his village alone, several Stasi agents were watching him. But even now he never turned turn down a drink with his friend Detlef.

Krötke, for his part, was delighted to help his old protégé, and now there were practical ways in which he could do so. Hammer had told him that he sometimes received deliveries of books and office equipment – including personal computers, a novelty – from West German sister churches. These deliveries had to be handled with the utmost care, but Krötke was a discreet man. Every so often, Detlef Hammer turned up at Krötke's apartment with new deliveries, which the two men quickly transferred from Hammer's car into Krötke's car boot. Sometimes they were even helped by a man who presented himself as a Swedish diplomat. As instructed by Hammer, Krötke then drove the cargo to a secret depot. The missions were time-consuming, but Krötke was delighted to assist Hammer's efforts on behalf of the church.

One day, when Hammer asked Krötke about his jail sentence out of the blue, no alarm bells went off either. Krötke had never mentioned his conviction to the students in Halle; in fact, he never spoke about it. And political convictions such as his were not indexed in any sort of publicly accessible registry. It was odd that Hammer would inquire about a sentence he couldn't know about. But it didn't enter Krötke's mind that his friend may have illicit contacts. Still, he was puzzled. "That's very strange; how do you know about it?" he said. Hammer quickly caught himself: "Oh, it's just in a file at the consistory."[132] Krötke was relieved. "Well, I suppose they get the information somehow," he thought to himself, and the two men chatted amiably about his time in jail.

But, by the late eighties, the Church Bureau's agent recruitment was stalling. In 1987, it was cultivating sixty-one potential new IMs. According to its own calculations, it needed seventeen new agents, but by the end of the year, despite approaching so many potential new agents it had only

---

132   Consistory, *Konsistorium*, is the official name of a German regional church's head office.

managed to recruit eleven. "The activities defaming the MfS have increased and have become more effective with the public. That is having negative effects. As a result, some contacts could not be continued and/or expanded", the department noted.[133] Pastors who may otherwise have decided it made career sense to work for the Stasi seemed to be sensing that it was no longer a wise step.

East German opposition activists were, for their part, intensifying their activities. A growing number of groups were meeting in churches and parish houses to – at least officially – discuss human rights and environmental issues, and they were adding new participants at a disturbing rate. In the Zion Church in East Berlin, activists had even created an environment library.

At MfS headquarters, concern was growing. Department XX/5 was responsible for "securing travel" – in other words, travel permits and monitoring of East Germans' foreign trips. The department even had officers monitoring Soviet bloc vacation spots popular with East Germans.[134] In December 1986, one of Department XX/5's group heads had concluded, "The adversaries are relentless… They are creating hostile structures in the GDR through peace workshops, the peace decade, and human rights seminars", adding that the number of citizen appeals had more than doubled in the past year.[135]

The government would embarrass itself by arresting Christians gathering in support of trees and lakes. Paradoxically, the growing unrest in the GDR was making IM Thomas – Aleksander Radler – even more useful. The voices of East German dissidents were being amplified by supporters in countries such as Sweden.

---

133   Der Bundesbeauftragte für die Unterlagen des Staatssicherheitsdienstes der ehemaligen DDR (Hg.): Hauptverwaltung A (HVA), *Aufgaben, Strukturen, Quellen. (MfS-Handbuch)*, Berlin, 2013, p. 99, http://www.nbn-resolving.org/urn:nbn:de:0292-97839421303496 (accessed 21 May 2019).
134   BStU, *MfS-Handbuch*, p. 109.
135   BStU, *MfS-Handbuch*, p. 119.

Meanwhile, the Stasi and the HVA were negotiating a rare transfer. It concerned IM Walter. The two agencies had decided that Jürgen Kapiske would leave the Church Bureau for a post as a foreign agent. Being moved to the HVA was a gigantic leap. The vast majority of Stasi agents remained part-time informants. But, with his infiltration of Charter 77, his good use of his journalist cover, and his fruitful collaboration with international Lutherans, the soft-spoken Kapiske had made a stellar impression on the HVA.

A fortuitous opportunity arose: the Lutherans had a job opening that suited Kapiske. A representative from the Lutheran World Federation flew in from Geneva to interview Kapiske in East Berlin and soon afterwards offered him the job as editor-in-chief for the Information Service for Lutheran Minority Churches in Europe, the Lutherans' Budapest-based news service. Around the same time, Heydel informed him of his impending transfer to the HVA.

"It felt completely surreal," Kapiske tells me. He says the moment reminded him of what he had told Heydel about Richard Sorge in 1972: that he admired the German journalist who worked as a Soviet spy during World War II. "Now I'm entering the very same waters," Kapiske thought to himself. As we sit in his study, he reflects on the moment when he was told he'd become a fully-fledged foreign intelligence agent. "I was not unhappy; I was very excited although I wasn't sure what they were expecting from me and where I was heading," he says.

Was it a divine coincidence that the Lutherans offered Kapiske a job just as the HVA wanted to send him abroad? Perhaps intelligence agencies gave the Lutherans a slight nudge? "I don't know who spoke about it first," Kapiske says. "Perhaps the HVA or the KGB had their fingers in it." IM Walter met with Heydel, who told him the name of his new handler: Hans-Dieter Schlippes, an HVA agent who had previously served undercover in West Germany. This meeting, Heydel tells IM Walter, would be their last: an agent is not supposed to maintain contact with a previous handler. Though Kapiske was excited about his elevation, having to part with Heydel filled him with sadness. For fifteen years now, Heydel had been his closest confidante. Kapiske received a new cover name from the HVA. The transfer was complete.

But suddenly there were complications: the Hungarian authorities were refusing to let Kapiske work in their country. Kapiske was baffled: was it something to do with his moderate support of environmental groups in the Magdeburg region? If so, why would that pose a threat to Hungary? Kapiske was told that he would instead be moving to Vienna, as would the Information Service for Lutheran Minority Churches. Although the Hungarians' refusal irked him, Vienna held an undeniable appeal: a fortuitous turn of events.

As we sit in Kapiske's study, he explains: "That's where the whole mirror thing begins. You're between two mirrors and you don't know what's real and what's not. It could be that the Hungarian authorities were nudged by others to block me, that it was actually a measure in my favour. The security agencies may have said, 'let's do it this way to make him more credible.' Vienna was at any rate more useful for the HVA."

That's an understatement. Why would the HVA need a pastor spy in Hungary, a fellow socialist country where the Church Bureau could dispatch its own pastors on regular visits? Vienna was a different matter altogether. It was the capital of Western-aligned Austria, which neighboured several Warsaw Pact states and hosted the headquarters of key international organizations including OPEC, the international energy agency IAEA, UN agencies, and the OSCE, which monitored security in Europe. Not surprisingly, Vienna was also home to more spies than any other European city.

In 1988, the Kapiske family – which now included a young son – packed up their apartment in Magdeburg and relocated to Vienna. Adjusting to the capitalist West was more challenging than they had expected. Even though they had – like most East Germans – regularly watched West German television and were familiar with the Western lifestyle, it was difficult to acclimatize. The West was so materialistic and people had such different ways of interacting, they felt. That also made it difficult to make new friends.

Fortunately, the HVA wasn't expecting Kapiske to deliver immediate results. Lie low for a year, observe, don't do anything offensive, get integrated, Schlippes had instructed him. That's how intelligence agencies run sleeper agents, who live as ordinary residents in another country: they can "sleep" – seemingly do nothing – for several months or even years before being activated.

Getting a place in the East German embassy's school in Vienna for young Master Kapiske also proved difficult: not surprisingly for a school run by the East German government, its staff didn't much like pastors. And unfortunately, Kapiske Sr couldn't reveal his HVA role to the school. "It was a totally crazy set-up," he tells me. "You really belong to the system and also feel that way, but at the same time you have to keep a distance."

Kapiske also had to find his feet in his new job. The Information Service for Lutheran Minority Churches had to be set up with all the resources a news agency needs: computers, page design software, distribution systems – and, of course, journalists and freelancers. "We invited the existing correspondents to Vienna and looked at where we needed to add correspondents, what our official line would be, where we should increase reporting," Kapiske remembers. But he also found time to join an international Lutheran delegation travelling to visit Protestants in the southern Soviet republics of Kazakhstan and Tajikistan.

Around the same time, IM Thomas – Aleksander Radler – had an appointment with Archbishop Bertil Werkström at the palatial archbishop's office in Uppsala, Sweden. The head of the Church of Sweden was an avowed friend of the GDR. But what he told IM Thomas was alarming. "W. is of the opinion that Swedish Christians should show solidarity with the [environmental activist] group in the Zion Church in order to courageously show that one can oppose a dictatorship," IM Thomas reported to his handlers. Apparently, Werkström now supported the regime's foes. Was the Church of Sweden even planning to intervene publicly on behalf of the environmental and human rights groups meeting in church buildings across East Germany?

As East German dissidents grew more outspoken, the Church Bureau's concern about the support they were receiving from Western European state churches also increased. The Church of Sweden supporting East German dissidents was akin to the Swedish government doing so. In one report, IM Thomas relayed a conversation he had just had with Sven Lindegård, the bishop of the southern diocese of Växjö. "He is very well informed and receives his information via Gienke," IM Thomas reported, referring to the bishop of Greifswald (who was also a Stasi IM). "This information doesn't just concern general issues but also internal information about the life of former state secretary Gysi." Klaus Gysi had recently retired from his post as the powerful State Secretary for Church Affairs. "Gienke doesn't think Löffler [Gysi's successor] is as intelligent as Gysi, but that he's a person who is interested in a good relationship with the church." Thus the Stasi learned, via IM Thomas and an unsuspecting Swedish bishop, what a key East German cleric thought of his country's new top church official.

By now, Wiegand was taking an interest in IM Thomas's assignments. Any opportunity to steer church opinion in a pro-East Berlin direction had to be used, even if it was an academic research project in the West German city of Göttingen about Warsaw Pact churches. "After consulting with Comrade Colonel Wiegand, there is large interest on the part of the MfS in the IM participating in the study on eastern European churches", Major Heinig noted. Wiegand wanted IM Thomas to influence the study in a "loyal/realistic" direction and saw further opportunities for the pastor-agent to establish promising contacts with Western academics involved with "East research", Heinig noted. Heinig used quotation marks for "East research". The countries behind the Iron Curtain never referred to themselves as "the East".

As instructed, IM Thomas did attempt to steer the Göttingen conference in a "loyal/realistic" direction. At the Normannenstrasse, however, Wiegand

GOD'S SPIES

was secretly fighting a growing and disheartening feeling that steering theological conferences in a socialist direction would achieve little for the survival of the German Democratic Republic – and that neither would more agent recruitment and church infiltration.

By the end of 1988, the Lutherans were busy planning their annual *Kirchentag* gathering, to be held in Rostock the following year. With discontent bubbling underneath the German Democratic Republic's orderly surface, the Stasi was on even higher alert than usual. Imagine the embarrassment if West German media showed East German Christians carrying banners demanding free and fair elections. Fortunately, Lieutenant Hartmut Kullik and his fellow Rostock-based officers had been watching the pastor leading the *Kirchentag* planning and had a good feeling about him. Even though his grown children had left for West Germany, the pastor seemed to hold no hostility towards the government.

"The [*Kirchentag*] wanted to use the Platz der Jugend [Youth Square] for their final event," Wiegand tells me. "I told Kullik to go and talk to the pastor. I said, 'ask the pastor to promise that there will be no political statements at the event.'"

But this year, the Church Bureau had a new headache. A recently established movement called *Kirche von unten* (Church from Below) was growing fast, and many members were planning to go to Rostock for the *Kirchentag*. Because *Kirche von unten* was a new movement, the Church Bureau had not yet penetrated it, and its agent line-up of bishops, pastors, and professors would at any rate have had poor prospects of infiltrating this grassroots organization. "If [the pastor] can guarantee that *Kirche von unten* won't dominate the *Kirchentag*, he'll be allowed use the Platz der Jugend", Wiegand instructed Kullik, who relayed the request.

OK, no *Kirche von unten*, the pastor promised. Wiegand was pleased. "Over the years, and especially at the [*Kirchentag*], he had showed that he was sensible," he tells me, referring to the pastor. Especially considering how hard it was becoming to find cooperative pastors, this was a very promising development. The Church Bureau established a prospect file. The pastor's name was Joachim Gauck.

A couple of times in that first Vienna year, Kapiske returned to East Germany. There was to be absolutely no contact with the Church Bureau, he had been instructed. But he couldn't resist and, on one of the visits, he rang Heydel. A phone call can't do any harm, he told himself. "Maybe it was devotion," he ponders as we discuss the calls. It had been a model officer-agent relationship.

In Lund, Sweden, the crocuses were filling the lawns in front of the university library in the spring of 1989 and, as every year, the sight brightened the mood of the harried scholars. Aleksander Radler, meanwhile, had even more reason to rejoice. His nearly two decades-long lobbying campaign for a professorship in East Germany had finally reaped its rewards. The University of Jena, where he had spent that fateful year as a student, had offered him a visiting professorship in systematic theology. The appointment had been "operationally supported by Department XX/4 and has been the IM's wish for many years", Heinig noted in Radler's file. Despite its harsh message to IM Thomas four years previously, the Stasi had continued to intervene on his behalf. Intelligence agencies don't leave their agents hanging.

It was agreed that despite temporarily moving to Jena, IM Thomas would keep up his work for the Firm abroad. Heinig listed IM Thomas's assignments, set in close collaboration with Wiegand:

•   Elaboration of regime information, developments in the Swedish Church, ecumenical relations between the Swedish churches and the GDR churches.

•   Reconnaissance of plans, intentions and methods of enemy forces in the operational area during the preparation of the Study on East European churches

Enemy forces in the operational area were Western European academics critical of East Germany. IM Thomas earned a crucial new assignment too:

- Elaboration of information on the planned launch of an anti-terror department at the United Nations in Vienna. (Information required by the HVA)

Heinig specified that IM Thomas was expected to uncover who worked at the new UN anti-terror department and how the department collaborated with intelligence services and other government agencies. Strangely, the mighty HVA needed the assistance of Reverend Dr Aleksander Radler. But his Vienna-based colleague Jürgen Kapiske was not told.

On 10 March 1989, Radler travelled from Lund in to Jena. The stint there, he felt certain, would open the door for a permanent post and a permanent return to the country he professed to love. In conversations with Heinig and the other officers, he had always professed more affection to the German Democratic Republic than to any person. What could possibly go wrong now?

Jürgen Kapiske, meanwhile, was making good journalistic progress in Vienna, and the Kapiskes had made several close friends. As planned, Schlippes issued regular instructions. Now he came to visit his agent. The two men convened with all the precautions of professional spies, ensuring that neither was under surveillance. Kapiske was excited: now he'd finally launch his HVA career. Instead, Schlippes delivered a surprise: "We're cancelling this operation," he announced. Kapiske's HVA career was over before it had even begun. He was confused and disappointed. "Maybe they have a selection process where beginners like me are removed if they don't bring any value," he told himself.

But he soon learned that the move had nothing to do with his competence level. The HVA had simply decided to dissolve its fledgling international church operations in Vienna. Kapiske began entertaining a new fear: was the intelligence agency possibly preparing for the end of the German Democratic Republic? He was, of course, well aware that protests were growing at home. But did the HVA know something else, something that was not public knowledge?

"I was devastated," he recalls as we sit in his study. "You meet a lot of people [in the Church Bureau and the HVA], and most were good people. On the personal level, we got along. But my primary interest was to keep this small country alive. Realizing that it was over was very bitter."

Officially, though, all was well. Kapiske was simply a church journalist and carried on his work at the news agency as if nothing had happened. The magazine went out each week; a professionally produced publication that the Lutherans could be proud of. Kapiske also introduced a novel addition: news via fax. It allowed the news to be distributed much faster. And with several Warsaw Pact countries tentatively liberalizing their churches' freedom, and Yugoslavia beginning to crumble, there was much to report.

CHAPTER **18**

EAST GERMANY ON ITS KNEES

June 1989: Each year the heads of several secret police church divisions convened to exchange news and ideas; this time they were meeting in Budapest. The comrade from Cuba had arrived, as had his counterparts from the Soviet Union, Poland, and Bulgaria. Comrade Wiegand, too, had travelled to the Hungarian capital. Over the years, he had tried to convince his Soviet colleagues that a friendly attitude towards Christians was more effective than penal camps. And although Wiegand enjoyed the Soviets' respect – the result of several successful joint operations – his words had fallen on deaf ears. The KGB persisted in its brutal treatment of Christians.

It was an intimate gathering in Budapest; the men knew one another well. As their discussions got underway, Wiegand again lobbied for a soft-glove approach. But he was harbouring a secret: a fear that the method no longer worked, or indeed any other method of keeping people content with communist government. In fact, he had come to the conclusion that the game was over for the German Democratic Republic. But the communist leadership was obstinate. One recent Christmas season, Minister Erich

Mielke had proposed banning a church-organized parade. "I'm not a traitor, but you can't support such a regime," Wiegand thought. "All this talk about the GDR in a hundred years' time, of course it's all nonsense." These were dangerous feelings to entertain.

When visiting East Germany, Jürgen Kapiske heard similar sentiments among Wiegand's colleagues. "There was dissatisfaction within the MfS and the HVA," he remembers. "People [at the Church Bureau] had very open conversations, perhaps because they had the inner freedom to discuss such things. They often discussed the GDR's financial situation. They knew that it would be no walk in the park even if the GDR survived." But Stasi officers must absolutely not express such doubts in public. More than ever, their efforts were critical to the nation's survival.

In June 1989, the Stasi was on edge. Division XX – the main directorate to which the Church Bureau belonged – now had a total of 470 staff including thirty-five undercover officers, as well as its IMs.[136] But the officers were at a loss: how to quiet citizens who were willing to say publicly they wanted a different government? The peace prayer services presented a dilemma to Wiegand. "Let them do peace," he explains his approach. "I was in favour of peace too; it's not as if I like war." So how could he intervene against peace prayers?

By now, not just Division XX but entire governments – in East Germany, of course, but also in Hungary, Czechoslovakia, Austria, and West Germany – were struggling to cope with the rapidly unfolding events. Tens of thousands of East Germans were trying to reach the West via Hungary and Czechoslovakia; some 6,000 others had already ensconced themselves in West Germany's embassy in Prague. For years, defecting East Germans had taken refuge there. It was an inconvenient way of escaping from East Germany: you couldn't bring any belongings, and it involved a long wait. Most returned home after receiving a promise from East Berlin that they

---

136   Auerbach et al, *Hauptabteilung XX*, p. 36.

would be able to legally emigrate to West Germany.[137] But this summer, East Germans were apparently throwing all caution to the wind. Sanitary conditions in the compound of the mid-sized embassy were getting desperate.

Other East Germans had fled to the West German embassies in Budapest and Warsaw. All were refusing to leave. East Berlin wanted to stem the exodus and limit its international humiliation; the West German government was concerned about safety at its embassies and the well-being of the refugees.

In East Germany, the peace prayer services were igniting. At Leipzig's large St Nicholas Church, the Monday peace services were now so popular that the congregation spilled out onto the street. If it banned the peace services, the Stasi would create an international PR debacle; the German Democratic Republic would be ridiculed. Let's co-opt the services and send the message that the government supports peace, Wiegand suggested to the Interior Ministry's church department. But the government refused to talk to protesters. Department XX/4's pastor agents could only try to steer peace prayers in a less radical direction.

At the Budapest meeting for church department heads, Wiegand was suddenly told that a Hungarian minister wanted to see him. "Why would he want to see me?" Wiegand wondered as he approached the minister's office. It's against protocol for a minister to discuss policy issues with a mere department head from another country. As Wiegand stepped in, the minister delivered an explosive message: "When you return home, go to Comrade Mielke and tell him that we're opening the borders [to Austria]," he told the stunned Wiegand. "We can't contain it anymore! With immediate effect we will stop controls at the border, we'll end the literature ban, we'll

---

137   "30 September 1989 – Die Prager Botschaftsflüchtlinge", *Bundeszentrale für politische Bildung*, 29 September 2009, http://www.bpb.de/politik/hintergrund-aktuell/69294/prag-30-september-1989-29-09-2009, (accessed 3 May 2019).

allow newspapers and magazines, and there will be no more action against opposition activists."

Wiegand was taken aback. The political ground was beginning to shift beneath him and East Germany. Though the Hungarian government had previously said a border opening was imminent, he was now in a highly precarious spot. The minister had asked him to pass the message along to Erich Mielke, but Mielke led the entire ministry and didn't interact with department heads. What to do? Wiegand wrote the message down. When he returned to East Berlin he shared it with a colleague.

That raised the next question: what to do with the memo? Wiegand decided to speak to Colonel General Rudi Mittig, Mielke's long-time deputy. General Mittig was more approachable than the stern Mielke and had, for years, allowed Wiegand to come to him directly. With trepidation, Wiegand made his way to Mittig's office. "Should I give the memo to Mielke?" he asked. Mittig advised against it: "That's dangerous. What you've written there is negative, there's no optimism any more. That's an atmosphere of decline. He'll accuse you of being a defeatist. I don't know what will happen to you." Still, the message from Hungary had be delivered, or Mielke might find out that his own ministry had withheld vital communication from him. Mittig had an idea. "I'll just give Comrade Mielke the memo with your name removed," he said. To this day, Wiegand doesn't know if Mielke ever read his memo.

If Mielke did read the message from Hungary, he took no action. Several months earlier, in February, the Hungarian government had, in fact, told the East German government that it intended to open the border to Austria. But the Hungarians' crucial announcement had elicited no reaction in East Berlin. In truth, not even the fierce Mielke could have stopped the exodus of his countrymen to Prague and Budapest. By now, too many East Germans were escaping. It left the Hungarian and Czechoslovak governments in a tough spot. In desperation, the Hungarians had found in Wiegand a messenger of last resort.

On 27 June, Hungary's foreign minister "Guyla Horn" and Austria's foreign minister Alois Mock jointly cut a hole in the fence separating the two countries. East Germans could now freely make their way to West Germany via Hungary and Austria: a roundabout journey, yes, but an entirely legal one. The next day, *Neues Deutschland* stayed silent on the dramatic developments, its top story instead carrying the headline "Erich Honecker arrives in Moscow for working visit".[138] Another front-page story reported that East Germany's delegation had participated in the final ceremony of a youth festival in Pyongyang, North Korea. *Neues Deutschland* editors also considered a disarmament conference in East Berlin and East German reactions on a ceasefire agreement in Angola more newsworthy than the opening of the Hungarian border.

Hungary had quietly begun opening the fence several weeks previously, dispatching soldiers to cut large openings in the fence adjacent to border crossings. Before that, East Germans had been escaping across unfenced wooded areas. In addition to wanting to resolve an international crisis, the Hungarians had a practical reason for opening the fence. It was old and rusty and needed to replaced, but the Soviets – who, as a part of sealing their satellite states off from the West, had paid for the fence in the sixties – were refusing to finance a new one.[139] And why should the Hungarians pay? The only people escaping across the border to Austria were East Germans. Hungarians could freely travel to Austria. But in East Berlin, the Politburo still refused to believe that the Hungarian border guards would actually let all the fleeing East Germans cross.

At the Church Bureau, Wiegand assembled his officers and relayed the Hungarian message. Hearing the news, Major Hans Baethge, the head of

---

138   "Archiv der Ausgaben von 1946–1990: Erich Honecker zu Arbeitxbesuch in Moskau eingetroffen", *Neues Deutschland*, 28 June 1989, http://www.nd-archiv.de/ausgabe/1989-06-28 (accessed 3 May 2019).
139   "Als sich der 'Eiserne Vorhang' öffnete", *MDR*, 6 October 2014, https://www.mdr.de/damals/archiv/artikel88334.html (accessed 3 May 2019).

the Catholic Church unit, immediately began shredding his files. "You're not allowed to do that," Wiegand reprimanded him. "It's absolutely not OK." Files were the Stasi's currency. The vast system of informant reports and files containing everything from operational details to psychological evaluations of citizens under surveillance was the arterial system in the body that was the Stasi. "Jochen," sighed the officer, using Wiegand's nickname, "it's just not going to work. We've really got no chance any more."

For Colonel Joachim Wiegand, this was the moment when he realized that the German Democratic Republic was over. "At that point it makes no sense to resist," he tells me.

As summer of 1989 turned into autumn, East Germans were escaping in ever larger numbers. On 11 September, Hungary abandoned efforts to police its Swiss-cheese fence and completely opened the border.[140] Within three days, an estimated 15,000 East Germans had crossed the border to Austria. At West Germany's embassy in Budapest, meanwhile, 180 East Germans were still camping out in the compound. The West German foreign ministry ordered the embassy temporarily closed.

In Czechoslovakia, more chaos was unfolding. The East Germans who had ensconced themselves at the West German embassy in Prague were refusing to leave. Conditions were now so dire that East Berlin had no choice but to negotiate with Bonn. On Saturday 30 September, West German foreign minister Hans-Dietrich Genscher emerged on the embassy's balcony. The refugees had grown edgy and were wary of reprisals initiated by East Berlin. Was the minister about to tell them they'd be sent back to East Germany? He began: "Dear compatriots, we have come to tell you that today your departure..."[141] The rest of the sentence was drowned out by the crowd's ecstatic cheering; the word "compatriots" had signalled to them

---

140   "Als sich der 'Eiserne Vorhang' öffnete", *MDR*.
141   "Genscher spricht den berühmten Halbsatz, Prager Botschaft, 1989", *Frankfurter Allgemeine Zeitung*, http://www.faz.net/aktuell/politik/prager-botschaft-1989-genscher-spricht-den-beruehmten-halbsatz-13176162.html (accessed 3 May 2019).

that they were free. Soon the refugees were leaving for West Germany on specially arranged trains. In its next edition, *Neues Deutschland* ignored the event, leading instead with headlines that the People's Republic of China had celebrated its fortieth anniversary and that 2,000 kilometres of East German railways had been electrified in the past eight years.[142]

A week later, on 7 October, the German Democratic Republic celebrated its own fortieth anniversary. The government had proceeded with its grandiose celebration plans; Soviet leader Mikhail Gorbachev arrived in East Berlin; there were to be concerts and military parades. Stasi agents received awards; IM Gerd was given the Battle Order for Merits to the People and the Fatherland. The anniversary was an achievement for the young country. But the celebration seemed anti-climactic.

In the Normannenstrasse, the Stasi officers had grasped what was in the making. Most were frantically shredding their files. They knew it was against the rules, but they also knew that their country with its rules, protocols, propaganda, and pervasive web of spies, was in its death throes.

Logically, they first shredded files currently in use. The archived files – former IMs and current IMs' older files – would have to wait. But now the Stasi's proud culture of meticulous over-reporting and file-keeping was coming back to haunt the officers. There were millions of pages, and they knew that time was running out. Emboldened citizens might arrive any time, demanding to see their files.

142   "Archiv der Ausgaben von 1946–1990: Ausgabe vom 02.10.1989", *Neues Deutschland,* 2 October 1989, http://www.nd-archiv.de/ausgabe/1989-10-02 (accessed 3 May 2019).

CHAPTER 19

THE BERLIN WALL COLLAPSES

Summer 1989. East Germany's Lutherans were finalizing their plans for their annual *Kirchentag*.[143] But the third one had long been planned to take place in Leipzig – and the opening event, on 6 July 1989, was fast approaching. Some participants worried there would be clashes with the police. The Stasi was on high alert. Leipzig was the country's most rebellious city; many of its churches had for years been hosting activist groups, and now, of course, the weekly peace prayers had the regime on the back foot.

The Church Bureau and other Stasi departments made meticulous preparations. Given the volatility of the situation, Wiegand got personally involved. His Leipzig staff had already received intelligence that some 200 church-affiliated activists were planning a protest march on the final day of the *Kirchentag*. They were planning to demonstrate against Politburo member Egon Krenz's support of the Chinese government's massacre of

---

143   "Aufkleber: 'Was ist der Mensch, daß du seiner gedenkst' vom Kongress und Kirchentag 1989 in Leipzig", *Runde Ecke Leipzig*, July 1989, http://www.runde-ecke-leipzig.de/sammlung/index.php?inv=15793 (accessed 3 May 2019).

students in Tianamen Square in June. "They acted to restore order," Krenz had said about the massacre, where soldiers had shot and killed several hundred pro-democracy protesters. The Chinese government had been roundly criticized around the world. East Germany's authorities would look silly if it banned a protest march by Christians supporting the Chinese victims – or, worse still, arrested the protesters. That would result in protests; pastors would pray for those arrested from the pulpit; Western media would report.

The authorities decided they couldn't ban the conference either, but they only granted permission on the condition that the Lutherans promised to keep opposition groups away. The organizers promised; the *Kirchentag* proceeded smoothly.

With the *Kirchentag* nearly over, the protesters were still planning to march, but the Church Bureau had an additional tool at its disposal: it could deploy its pastor agents to steer events, not merely report intelligence. Ahead of the conference, Wiegand travelled to Leipzig. The trickiest part was the planned protest march, which was now going to criticize election fraud. Wolfgang Schnur, the trusted IM, had tried to avert the march, but to no avail. "We arranged for two of our pastors to walk at the very front of the protest march, and for them to lead the march not into the city centre, as planned, but to a church," he tells me. "I had told the head of the Leipzig police to make sure there were no police officers near the protesters, just traffic police." There were to be no damaging press images of citizens confronted by police.

Like clockwork, the two IM pastors led the protesters to St Peter's Church. One of the IM pastors addressed the assembled crowd: "We've had an excellent *Kirchentag*, and now that it's ending, you want to riot? Be sensible. Put your banners away and go home." The protesters went home. But some participants later remembered the march differently: the police had forced them to gather in St Peter's Church.[144]

Even though one march had successfully been averted, peace prayer services and protest marches were now proliferating even faster. In recent months the protestors had grown alarmingly fearless. The Politburo seemed paralyzed, unprepared for dissent after years of hounded acquiescence by most citizens. Since the politicians had no idea of how to address the growing unrest, the task of keeping the country under control fell to the Stasi.

On 9 October 1989, following the peace prayer service at St Nicholas's Church, tens of thousands of Leipzigers began to march through the city. For several weeks, following the Monday peace prayer services brave Leipzigers had marched from St Nicholas to the central square, the Augustusplatz. But on this day, 9 October, the size of the crowd was unprecedented, far beyond the capabilities of Stasi monitoring. At 5 p.m., the protesters – lacking a permit and defying the police – began marching. "We are the people", they chanted, a pointed reference to the German Democratic Republic, which labelled itself a people's republic but whose leadership seemed to lack interest in its citizens.

Nobody had any idea what might happen next. Police officers dispatched to the march didn't know whether they would be ordered to intervene or to stand back. Would the government call in the country's armed forces, the National People's Army?

In the Normannenstrasse, Wiegand received a call from one of his officers in Leipzig. "There are 70,000 people marching through the city! Tell the people in Berlin, don't shoot for God's sake!" the officer shouted. Wiegand was an intelligence officer, not a police chief and besides, he was in Berlin. "How am I supposed to do that?" he asked his officer. "Try!" the officer yelled. As he had done after his Budapest trip, Wiegand turned to Rudi Mittig, whom he reached by phone. Stasi officers in Leipzig were at

---

144   "Aufkleber: 'Was ist der Mensch'", *Runde Ecke Leipzig*.

a loss, Wiegand told the general. "A worker can't shoot another worker," Wiegand ventured.

Suddenly, at 6 p.m., the city's official public announcement system transmitted a dramatic appeal. Conductor Kurt Masur, two leading dissidents, and the city's top SED officials jointly appealed to the protesters and the security forces not to use violence. The march ended without altercation, and without a single shot having been fired.

"On this evening the fear crossed sides," Rainer Eppelmann tells me. "Until then, the government had all the tools required to suppress the counter-revolution. After that evening, the governing people were the fearful ones." He continues: "If they had rolled us flat or jailed us, no chancellor of the Federal Republic of Germany would even have lent them one million Deutschmarks." He's referring to West Germany's loans to East Germany, which were by now keeping East Germany alive.

Now espionage was meaningless. Even Wiegand began shredding files. Among the documents he destroyed first were several years from Schnur's file.

I'm back at Wiegand's apartment. We're talking about those summer and autumn months of 1989. "The concept of socialism didn't work," he reflects. "If it had worked, it would have been good. But the way things were going here, the whole thing had failed. Then they said, 'MfS, you take care of it, prevent the people from leaving.' When everybody is leaving, the state can't continue operating."

But in October 1989, despite the demonstrators' victory in Leipzig, the East German leadership refused to acknowledge the seriousness of the situation. On 10 October, *Neues Deutschland* had as its main news that Erich Honecker had received a Chinese delegation.[145] The next day, there

---

[145] "Archiv der Ausgaben von 1946–1990: Ausgabe vom 10.10.1989", *Neues Deutschland*, 10 October 1989, http://www.nd-archiv.de/ausgabe/1989-10-10 (accessed 3 May 2019).

was nothing to be read about the Leipzig mass demonstration either. *Neues Deutschland* instead led with a story on "youth brigades" mastering new technology at a carpet factory and warned of the United States' attitude towards chemical weapons.[146] The following Monday, the Leipzigers were out again, in even larger numbers. Their fellow citizens in other cities were demonstrating too. The following week they were out on the streets again. And the week after that. "We are the people," they shouted again. Many even ventured "we are one people". They were calling for reunification.

On 9 November 1989, the East German government's spokesman, Günther Schabowski, was giving an international press conference in East Berlin. Responding to a reporter's question, he volunteered that East Germans would be permitted to freely cross over to West Berlin "immediately". Schabowski was improvising: he hadn't consulted with his government colleagues or the security services. Recognizing world history in the making, all international news outlets immediately made Schabowski's announcement their top story. Delirious East Germans rushed to the Wall, where border guards simply let them pass and withheld fire. Soon scores of East Germans were climbing on top of the Wall, an act that only a few hours previously would have resulted in them being shot. The Berlin Wall had fallen.

---

146   "Archiv der Ausgaben von 1946–1990: Ausgabe vom 11.10.1989", *Neues Deutschland*, 11 October 1989, http://www.nd-archiv.de/ausgabe/1989-10-11 (accessed 3 May 2019).

CHAPTER 20

DESTROYING THE EVIDENCE

On 10 November 1989, *Neues Deutschland* reported on Schabowski's press conference in small story with the headline, "GDR government spokesman comments on new travel rules".[147] Any remaining East Germans who had relied on *Neues Deutschland* for their news had long since given up. The German Democratic Republic would not survive.

At the Normannenstrasse, officers began leaving in droves, trying to find work elsewhere while they had a chance. Minister Erich Mielke alone seemed oblivious to the imminent end of his Agency. "But I love everyone," he insisted on 13 November to the assembled members of the Volkskammer, East Germany's parliament. The ordinarily docile parliamentarians were incredulous. The East German Politburo had just forced Erich Honecker, the country's leader, to resign. And amidst the extraordinary turmoil,

---

147   "Archiv der Ausgaben von 1946–1990: DDR-Regierungssprecher zu neuen Reiseregelungen", *Neues Deutschland,* 10 November 1989, https://www.nd-archiv.de/artikel/1966348.ddr-regierungssprecher-zu-neuen-reiseregelungen.html (accessed 3 May 2019).

Mielke believed the Stasi could survive.

He was mistaken. On 17 November, Hans Modrow – Honecker's hastily elected successor and a reformist SED official – announced that the Ministry for State Security would be dissolved and succeeded by a new agency, the Agency for National Security (AfNS). Modrow dispatched Mielke into retirement and appointed MfS Lieutenant General Wolfgang Schwanitz head of the renamed agency. Schwanitz took immediate action, instructing his officers to destroy their files.[148]

Speaking to his Church Bureau staff on 2 December, Wiegand remained defiant: "I have always advocated fighting the powers in the Christian denominations who abuse their denominations. That's how I view the enemy, and that remains my conviction." However, he saw opportunity as well: the SED should revise its hostile stand towards Christians, he proposed, as many Christians wanted a "socialist GDR".[149]

For decades, the Stasi had operated a well-organized destruction system where large machines pulped files that were too sensitive or no longer needed. But now there was simply too much paper for the machines to process, especially at the furious speed at which the officers needed to dispose of the compromising material. Within days, officers were resorting to simply ripping up their files. Wiegand, too, was shredding. "The last two to three years of my files are gone," he tells me. Hans Baethge, the Department XX/4 officer in charge of the Catholic Church, had little to worry about, since he had begun shredding as soon Wiegand returned from Budapest.

Despite the chaos engulfing every institution in their country, the public had grasped what was happening in the Stasi's offices. In the early morning of 4 December, a doctor in the south-western city of Erfurt saw thick black

148   Der Bundesbeauftragte für die Unterlagen, *"Stasi raus – es ist aus!" Stasi am Ende – die letzten Tage der DDR-Geheimpolizei* , Berlin: BStU, 2015, p. 17, https://www. bstu.de/assets/bstu/de/Publikationen/dh_13_stasi-raus-es-ist-aus_barrierefrei.pdf (accessed 19 May 2019).
149   Auerbach et al, *Hauptabteilung XX*, p. 102.

smoke emerging from the chimney of the local Stasi office. She called a friend, Almuth Falcke, whose husband, a local assistant bishop named Heino Falcke, had long been under Stasi surveillance. The Falckes sped to the Stasi office and parked their car so it blocked the building's entrance. Within minutes they had been joined by other residents. Soon some 4,000 people had gathered in front of the building. Together they forced their way into the office and demanded access to the files.

The same day, sensing that the Stasi's other regional offices were about to be stormed as well, Schwanitz ordered his officers to cease the shredding and pulping.[150] "I have ordered that the extinction and removal of Agency documents must immediately stop", he wrote in a telegram to all AfNS offices. Schwanitz explained that he was responding to appeals by representatives of the democracy movement led by Wolfgang Schnur. As the general knew, Schnur had been one of the Church Bureau's top agents. But the lawyer-cum-star agent had now quickly switched sides; with the Stasi no longer useful to him, he was presenting himself as a democracy activist.

On 7 December, Modrow's government condemned "the unjustified collection of information by the former Ministry for State Security" and prohibited future collection. The AFNS would, in other words, only administer the Stasi's old files. There would be no more surveillance of innocent citizens.

On 13 December, Schwanitz ordered all regional Stasi offices – now AfNS offices – closed. Two days later, Wiegand was instructed to dissolve Division XX, to which Department XX/4 belonged; more senior officers had already left the division or were not available. He wasn't exactly sure how one dissolved a Stasi division, but he began by speaking to the around 400 remaining staff members. He shook hands with everyone. "This is it, you can do anything you like but don't do anything stupid, and relinquish

---

150   BstU, *"Stasi raus – es ist aus!"*, p. 33.

your weapons," he told them. Some of the agents called him crazy, shouting out, "We have to defend the country!" In the end, Wiegand claimed every gun. And he instructed the officers: "You must not betray your IMs or give them to the Russians." The German Democratic Republic and the Soviet Union were fellow socialist countries, but who knew how the Soviets might use Stasi agents? There it was again: keep your promise. Wiegand gave the staff one final instruction: "No resistance". ("It would have been futile," he tells me.)

That afternoon, a large group of angry citizens stormed the Normannenstrasse. From a window, Wiegand saw them gather outside the headquarters, chanting anti-Stasi slogans. Suddenly, they were forcing their way inside. Fortunately for Wiegand, they didn't reach his office, but he heard them smash china in a nearby kitchen. "I heard them shout, 'They ate like pigs!'" he recalls. The well-mannered officer is clearly offended by the accusation. Elsewhere, the protesters smashed officers' desks and pulled out files from the cabinets.

After several hours, the crowd retreated. Soon, members of the Citizens' Committee – a self-appointed group of democracy activists – arrived. They had already prevented local Stasi offices from shredding their files, and now they wanted command of the headquarters. "They introduced themselves and said, 'we're dissolving everything'," Wiegand recalls. "I told them how I viewed matters and said that we would make sure there was no resistance and no funny business by the MfS staff. Then a police officer arrived as well. It was the three of us, the police officer, the man from the Citizens' Committee, and me. That's how Division XX was dissolved."

As 1989 turned to 1990, the turmoil around the country increased. With the Berlin Wall gone, would East Germany survive? More and more demonstrators were shouting "we are one people". Wiegand now faced an enormous task. In dissolving Division XX, he had to conduct a complete inventory of its belongings: its safe houses, cars, office equipment, weapons

– and its files. In a memo to the country's new leader Modrow on 14 December, Schwanitz had relayed the enormity of the task involving the Stasi's files: "Written materials from the past forty years have been stored in hard-to-determine quantities (several thousand tons)."[151]

But officers had been efficient: according to Wiegand, when he began compiling the inventory on 15 January, some 70 per cent of Division XX's files had been destroyed. Like him, most officers had shredded their active files first, as they contained current operations. Some officers had managed to shred older files as well. We will thus never find written details of much of the Stasi's final years. So it is that, after 1980, there are no entries in Gerd Bambowsky's file. The previous years' records show weekly meetings between Bambowsky and his handlers, as well as his actions between the meetings. And Bambowsky clearly kept up his work, since he was awarded a medal for it on the German Democratic Republic's final anniversary in 1989. As for the foreign intelligence agency, the HVA, it kept shredding and pulping until June 1990.

"I'll show you," Wiegand says and walks over to his bookcase. Then, seconds later, with irritation in his voice: "I used to have such good order." He can't find the book he's looking for. But moments later, he locates the volume: the inventory of Division XX as of 31 March 1990, the Stasi's last day of existence. That day was also Wiegand's final day on the job: he and most of his colleagues had been dismissed. The next day, the colonel drove to his allotment and tended to the vegetables.

Wiegand's inventory volume is an extraordinary documentation of Stasi operations. Among other things, as it closed shop, Division XX had 4,820 parcels in its possession. What were the contents of those parcels? Wiegand didn't open them. "And," I ask him, "where did the weapons go?" "I gave them to Peter-Michael Diestel," he says. In March 1990 Diestel, a young co-founder of the new Christian Social Party of Germany, had just been

---

151 BstU, *"Stasi raus – es ist aus!"*, p. 91.

appointed East Germany's interior minister. That's how the mighty Stasi ended, or at least its Division XX, including the Church Bureau: Wiegand presented its handguns to a young Christian Democrat.

ANXIOUSLY WAITING PASTOR SPIES

In his home in Vienna on 9 November 1989, Jürgen Kapiske watched the Berlin Wall fall. "I watched the news but I couldn't comprehend it all," he tells me. "It was so over the top. But I had to come to terms with it. My colleagues [at the news service] all congratulated me and said things like, 'You're free!'"

Free? That might have been true for many East Germans, but for Kapiske and his fellow agents the commanding feeling was now fear. Would they be unmasked? Although they had been assured that their identity would never be revealed, the MfS hadn't factored in a sudden collapse of the entire country.

He remembers his final conversation with his HVA handler, Hans-Dieter Schlippes: "He told me that everything would be destroyed. Afterwards, when he was back in Berlin, he told me that it had been destroyed, though he also told me that he couldn't be certain that it had been destroyed everywhere. And early on, he had told me that when you're with the HVA, there's always a risk of being unmasked."

Still, with Schlippes having destroyed everything, Kapiske was probably fine. But he worried about his beloved East Germany. He realized that the Berlin Wall events would end with Germany being reunited, and that frightened him. "It would be much better if the GDR remained a small country," he thought.

The year 1990 arrived. Kapiske kept up his editor duties. In its first issue of 1990, *World Encounter* – the Evangelical Lutheran Church USA's quarterly magazine – published a feature story entitled "Where is Home? Soviet Lutherans in Central Asia". Author: Reverend Jürgen Kapiske. The piece was the result of his October trip with an international group of Lutherans. He reported that Central Asian Soviets appreciated the USSR's improved religious freedom but were fretting that the old Stalinist times may reappear. The American Lutherans clearly had no idea they were publishing an article by an HVA agent.

Wolfgang Schnur, meanwhile, was now fully inhabiting his anti-regime persona. In the autumn of 1989, he and several other opposition activists including Rainer Eppelmann and Christoph Kähler had founded the new party, *Demokratischer Aufbruch*. Now, in early 1990, Schnur was the party's chairman and needed to hire a press spokesperson. He settled on the daughter of a left-leaning pastor friend he had known for many years. Her name was Angela Merkel, née Kasner.

If Detlef Hammer laughed a bit nervously when the Berlin Wall fell, nobody at the diocesan headquarters in Magdeburg noticed it. But like Schnur, Kapiske, Radler, and other agents, Hammer was now enduring a gruelling wait. Would the Citizens' Committee – there was now one in Magdeburg too – that was preventing the Stasi from shredding its files come across his file too? Was there even a risk of the German Democratic Republic collapsing? In that case he would be found out, that he knew for sure.

But the Stasi's well-planned insertion of undercover officers had paid off. When the Magdeburg Citizens' Committee appointed church liaisons to assist in evaluating the Stasi files, it chose Hammer to represent the Lutheran Church.[152] As news spread across the country of how far the Stasi managed to infiltrate Lutherans, Hammer fanned the flames by pointing to outrageous cases he had seen in the Stasi files during his work with the Citizens' Committee. Nobody would suspect him now, he calculated.

It was an excellent deflection strategy. And although Katrin Eigenfeld kept bringing up what she'd heard in jail, nobody paid her much attention. On the contrary, Hammer's church career was accelerating. On 3 May 1990, he was appointed president of the mighty Church Province of Saxony. He was only forty years old. Hearing the news at his vicarage outside Berlin, Gerhard Gabriel was thrilled: "Our Detlef has been appointed President of the Consistory, and on top of that the youngest-ever President," he told his wife. Wolf Krötke, too, was overjoyed.

Hammer himself was, however, less excited. "I was actually planning to leave the service of the church after sixteen years," he told the diocese's newspaper in an interview after his appointment. "But now I am prepared to take on this position. That's because the church administration worries me. It's not only bloated, it also doesn't correspond to our church structures." [153] Talk about administrative structures seemed a strange answer for an outsider who had just reached the pinnacle of church power. In the same interview, Hammer praised his wife, telling the church journalist that without "my wife I would not be able to live and work like this".[154]

But Silke Hammer was barely figuring in her husband's life anymore. And the real reason for Hammer's desire to leave the church's employ had nothing to do with Silke. Hammer knew it was only a matter of time before

---

152   Schultze, *Spionage gegen eine Kirchenleitung*, p. 60.

153   Schultze, *Spionage gegen eine Kirchenleitung*, p. 60.

154   Schultze, *Spionage gegen eine Kirchenleitung* , p. 61.

his double life would be exposed and, when that happened, he would lose his job along with his reputation.

While being interviewed during the selection process for the post, Hammer had told the hiring committee that his marriage was on the rocks. That, he knew, was a red flag in the church. With rare exceptions, a pastor or high-ranking lay official who divorced risked losing his job. But to Hammer's surprise, the committee's members were supportive: "Brother Hammer, we will carry that burden with you," they told him. His scheme had failed. Instead of being fired, he was promoted.

Soon Detlef Hammer informed Bishop Demke that he wanted to resign. To his friend Gerhard Gabriel he said that his marriage was beyond repair and that, as a result, he would have to step down. But Gabriel had heard of the hiring committee's unusually supportive stance. "Why, then, does he want to leave?" Gabriel asked himself. Another high-ranking diocesan official, Hammer's friend Marion Staude, had already abruptly resigned. Gabriel was puzzled. So was Bishop Demke.

In August, Hammer left his wife and their spacious home and moved to a small apartment in Magdeburg. At the diocesan headquarters, news spread that he was now dating Staude. Ordinarily, the church wanted its staff members to be married or single; cohabitation was frowned upon. But Bishop Demke was an understanding man: who was he to judge the domestic arrangements of a valued staff member? Demke's wife, however, had long been uneasy about Staude. "Just listen to her," she had told her husband long ago. "She uses expressions that you church people just don't use." But the bishop felt that language habits were not a strong enough indication to take action against an employee. And what could he have done, anyway? Fire her because she didn't sound "churchy"? Besides, now she had resigned on her own volition.

With German reunification approaching, a West German government official made an appointment to see Wiegand. "Had Department XX/4 recruited Joachim Gauck Rostock pastor?" he wanted to know. "No,"

Wiegand responded. "But we were intending to." On 3 October 1990, the day of Germany's reunification, the pastor was appointed director of the new Stasi archive, the Federal Commissioner for the Records of the State Security Service of the former German Democratic Republic.[155] In 2012, he became President of Germany.

For Wolf Krötke, as for all East Germans, 1990 had already been a turbulent year. But 2 October was an especially momentous day for the long-suffering cleric – and not just because the two Germanies would reunite the following day. In a grand ceremony at the *Französische Friedrichstadtkirche*, the French Church in central Berlin, he received the Karl Barth Prize, a prestigious theological award. After the ceremony a nervous-looking Detlef Hammer made his way to Krötke. "I'm getting divorced," he announced. "Can we talk?" That was major news, but hardly a suitable topic for a busy reception. "Detlef, this is not a good time," Krötke said. "All these people here want to talk to me. I'll call you and we can decide a time to meet." As promised, a couple of days later Krötke called Hammer. But Hammer was busy and said he would call back.

Back in Magdeburg, Bishop Demke was relieved that Hammer had made no further mention of resigning. How would he run the diocese without his right-hand man? But on 17 February 1991, Hammer suddenly handed in his notice, asking to be relieved of his duties by 31 March. He cited "changes in my personal living situation" as the reason.[156] In the end, Hammer, remained in his post several days past that date. On 2 April, his forty-first birthday, his diocesan colleagues threw a big party for him. Like Bishop Demke, they were genuinely sorry to lose him. And who would fill the corridors with laughter now? At the birthday party, Hammer seemed a bit uneasy and complained of

---

155   Geschichte des Stasi-Unterlagen-Archivs, Der Bundesbeauftragte für die Unterlagen des Staatssicherheitsdienstes der ehemaligen Deutschen Demokratischen Republik, https://www.bstu.bund.de/DE/BundesbeauftragterUndBehoerde/Chronik_der_Behoerde/_node.html (accessed 3 May 2019).

156   Schultze, *Spionage gegen eine Kirchenleitung*, p. 63.

pains in his big toe. He went to the doctor. It's a case of gout, the doctor said, and prescribed medication.

In the evening, Hammer hosted a birthday party at his apartment for several close friends. Thanks to the medication, he was his jovial self again. His daughters were there, too, as was Marion Staude. And the medication didn't stop Hammer from enjoying his beloved whisky. The last guest left after midnight. Hammer himself would be picked up by his diocesan driver at 7.30 a.m. the next morning. It would be a short night, but Hammer still got by on little sleep.

Just before 7.30 a.m., the driver arrived. He saw lights on in Hammer's apartment, but when he rang the doorbell, nobody answered. He tried again. After several more attempts, the driver left. At the diocesan offices, he informed the personnel chief. That afternoon, police officers went to Hammer's apartment. When he still didn't open the door, they forced it open. He was dead.

"There are no indications of an unnatural death," a pathologist concluded after examining the body. Detlef Hammer had had the good fortune of passing away before his Stasi career was discovered.

Dead within hours of a lively birthday celebration: Bishop Demke was mystified. "Pains in your toe one day, and the next day you're dead? I suppose that's possible," he told himself. Gerhard Gabriel and Wolf Krötke, too, were taken aback. But then again, one hears of fatal heart attacks even among young people.

The popular Detlef Hammer was soon put to rest in a large funeral arranged by the diocese. But when listening to Bishop Demke's sermon, something struck Gabriel as odd. The sermon seemed so detached, not at all the warm testimony Gabriel had expected. What had happened? Did the bishop know something that he, Gabriel, did not? In the congregation Wolf Krötke, too, was racking his brains. What had Hammer been trying to tell him that day in the French Church? Why had he, Krötke, not taken a moment to listen? Why had

Hammer never called him back? Maybe Hammer had really wanted to tell him something other than news of his divorce.

Around the same time, Jürgen Kapiske's contract with the Lutheran newswire ended as planned and he returned to his old job in Magdeburg. He was struggling with himself: should he tell the church his secret? If so, when would be a good time? He resolved he would have the talk – but inevitably the appropriate moment failed to materialize. One day, he read in the newspaper that his diocesan president Detlef Hammer, had in fact been an undercover Stasi officer. Kapiske, of course, knew that Hammer had died, but now the magazine reported that there were doubts as to whether he was actually dead. His family hadn't been allowed to see his dead body, and he had swiftly been cremated.

When the Berlin Wall fell, Hammer had a fortune of some 1 million Deutschmarks. Hammer's brother, Dietrich, was now suggesting that he may have fled abroad. Detlef did, after all, have a large life insurance, and he did enjoy the company of women. Dietrich thought Detlef might be living in Tunisia.[157]

One day in 1992, a Swiss TV crew suddenly turned up at Jürgen Kapiske's office. Its producer had been tipped off by a Viennese friend of Kapiske's. The journalist had also found IM Walter's Department XX/4 file – it was intact. Hans-Dieter Schlippes had destroyed Kapiske's HVA file, but since Kapiske no longer had a case officer at Department XX/4, no one had shredded his file there. Speaking to the TV team, Kapiske initially denied everything: "My training fell into place," he tells me. "I had learned to deny everything. All your good intentions vanish. It was also a bit of defiance." Kapiske had planned to make his admission on his own terms, but now he was on the defensive. Soon the documentary was aired on Swiss television. Had Kapiske told his church superiors earlier, they might have looked the other way, as they did with most

---

157   "Kirche: Schmerzen im Zeh", *Spiegel*, 30 January 1995, p. 54, http://www.spiegel.de/spiegel/print/d-9158647.html (accessed 3 May 2019).

other pastor agents. But under media scrutiny, their hand was forced. Kapiske was tried by a church disciplinary court. Although he tried to explain his motivation for working with the Stasi and the HVA, he sensed that the judges were unsympathetic. The court ordered Kapiske defrocked. Soon afterwards Hans-Dieter Schlippes got in touch, confessing that at the time of Kapiske's transfer to the HVA he should have collected Kapiske's file from the Church Bureau for subsequent destruction. He had forgotten.

Meanwhile, Manfred Stolpe – formerly IM Sekretär – had launched a political career in the Social Democratic Party and quickly been appointed to the party's board. Despite rumours circulating about his Stasi activities, in 1990 he won the first democratic election in the state of Brandenburg and became its prime minister.

Around the same time that Kapiske and Hammer were unmasked, a Berlin pastor named Dietmar Linke was researching the Stasi. Linke was the vicar with whom Gerd Bambowsky had wanted to work – a move enthusiastically supported by the Church Bureau. Then, in 1993, Linke uncovered several references to Aleksander Radler in Stasi files. Confronted with the allegations, Radler vehemently denied them. But people were beginning to wonder. Radler was so unusual – what with his life in Sweden – that his case attracted particular interest.

Since the fall of East Germany, Radler had advanced from his position as a lecturer at the University of Lund and guest professor in Jena to full professor at the University of Halle. Rather ironically, he was now occupying the chair in theological ethics. Soon after Germany's reunification, Michael Beintker – whom Radler had strategically befriended in the eighties – had been appointed dean of the Halle theology department; he had hired Radler for the post. Radler had been a strong candidate, especially since he had spent most of his career away from the Stasi-infested world of East German theology.

But the rumours from Linke's research kept circulating. They even reached me in nearby Jena. One day I was having lunch in the university canteen. A friend stopped at my table. "Didn't you say you knew Aleksander Radler?" she asked. "Yes, why do you ask?" I responded. "Well, he's been accused of working for the Stasi," she reported. "But he says it's not true, and my father is defending him." My friend's father was later discovered to have reported for the Church Bureau. Meanwhile, Radler's Swedish pastor friends were calling him to ask about the allegations. Their calls were not accusatory; they just wanted to understand. If he had spied, it wouldn't be that surprising, given how many pastors had done so. And all over Germany, pastors were placing similar calls to their fellow pastors. But Radler denied any links to the Stasi.

Helmut Matthies – the editor of *IDEA Spektrum* – had been told of a West German arrest warrant against Gerd Bambowsky. A couple of days before Christmas 1995, he travelled to Berlin and made his way to Bambowsky's apartment. He rang the bell. Knuth Hansen opened the door. "May I speak to Gerd?" Matthies asked. "I'm afraid he can't come to the door; he's taking a bath," Hansen responded. "OK, I'll wait," said Matthies and sat down on the stairs outside the apartment.

After an hour, Matthies again rang the doorbell. To his surprise, Bambowsky opened the door. "Don't worry," Matthies reassured him. "I just want to know why you did it." Bambowsky invited Matthies to the living room. "My church salary was too low," he volunteered. Matthies was appalled: a pastor should consider the salary before deciding to get ordained. But then again, over the years, he had noticed Bambowsky's taste for the good life. "Gerd," he countered, "you had your pastor salary, you got money from Open Doors, from *Licht im Osten*, from *IDEA*. Now we learn you were paid by the Stasi and the KGB too. You were wealthier than any bishop in the GDR!"

Bambowsky tried another approach. "As a homosexual there were disadvantages I had to live with, and this was a way of balancing them," he said. "I don't believe you," Matthies responded. East Germany, he insisted, was much more liberal on gay issues than West Germany. Bambowsky offered a final explanation. "Communism was a better system," he argued. Matthies gave up. During many recent sleepless nights, he had come to the conclusion that the shed tour with Bambowsky had been fake. The cop outside wasn't an officer on random patrol but an officer sent there with perfect timing to make the tour even more realistic, he now realized. But what else about Bambowsky had been fake? The American soldiers? Matthies couldn't figure it out.

Erwin Damson of *Licht im Osten* also called Bambowsky. They met at a Berlin train station. After some awkward small talk, Damson asked the same question. "You were on one side; I was on the other side," the flamboyant pastor retorted and walked off.

IM Gerd disappeared from Matthies's life as suddenly as he had appeared. "Perhaps he really spied out of conviction," Matthies reflects as we sit in his office. "But what's clear is that he caused enormous damage. People were jailed. And the worst part is that because of him, tens of thousands of Russian New Testaments were destroyed."

No one knows exactly how many Bibles and other Christian books were diverted by Bambowsky; according to some calculations, the number reached several hundred thousand. At any rate, the number of Bibles dispatched towards the Soviet Union didn't match the number that was eventually delivered, and the Bibles stored with the Stasi in Berlin didn't make up for the difference. Large numbers of books had clearly been destroyed – books that had painstakingly been paid for through gifts by generous Christians.

Bambowsky's commitment to communism – or at least to communism interspersed with Western consumer products – may indeed have been genuine. Several years after East Germany's collapse, he was still active in the SED's successor party, the Party of Democratic Socialism (PDS), running for local office and heading a Christian group within the party.[158]

By 1994, Aleksander Radler had decided that his position as professor of theological ethics in Halle was untenable. He resigned and returned to the Church of Sweden, to the Diocese of Luleå in the north. With the diocese

---

158   *Partei des Demokratischen Sozialismus*, Party of Democratic Socialism.

opting not investigate Pastor Linke's findings, Radler was appointed rector of a rural parish.

He was lucky: the talk about his Stasi links quickly died down. There had been no further discoveries, and as Radler had correctly calculated, Sweden's far north is a world away from the former East Germany. But in Frankfurt an der Oder, the Gauck Agency was hard at work. Among the many sacks of shreds abandoned by frantic Stasi officers, Gauck Agency workers had discovered a surprising amount linked to IM Thomas. Reconstruction specialists began piecing them together; a painstaking and time-consuming process. By 2012, they had reconstructed a remarkable 1,500 pages from IM Thomas's file – with many more in process.

The Gauck Agency made a small announcement about its findings. Swedish newspapers, ordinarily rather indifferent to church matters, jumped on the story. Even a British tabloid, the *Daily Mail*, reported on the Swedish pastor who had spied for the Stasi: "Swedish pastor secretly worked for East German Stasi for quarter of a century – betraying students who trusted him", it reported.[159] But Radler denounced the allegations as "ludicrous". If he had indeed been a Stasi agent, he asked a reporter for the Swedish tabloid *Expressen*, "When would I have had time to study?" "Were you a spy?" the reporter asked. "No, 150 per cent," Radler responded. He denied even knowing the Jena students who went to jail.[160]

Given the extremely serious allegations against its pastor and the attendant publicity, the Diocese of Luleå was compelled to act. It engaged a Stasi expert, Professor Helmut Müller-Enbergs, to investigate whether IM Thomas was in fact Aleksander Radler. After combing through the hundreds

159   Emma Clark, "Swedish pastor secretly worked East German Stasi quarter of a century–betraying students who trusted him", *Daily Mail*, 26 July 2012, http://www. dailymail.co.uk/news/article-2179491/Swedish-pastor-secretly-worked-East-German-Stasi-quarter-century–betraying-students-trusted-him.html (accessed 3 May 2019).
160   "Dokument: Svenska prästen var Stasi-agent", *Expressen*, 14 April 2012, https://www.expressen.se/nyheter/expressen-avslojar/dokument-svenska-prasten-var-stasi-agent/ (accessed 3 May 2019).

of restored pages, in the summer of 2012, Müller-Enbergs delivered his findings. Radler, Müller-Enbergs declared, was indeed IM Thomas. Radler resigned. That September, the Church of Sweden defrocked him.

But in an almost surreal epilogue, ex-pastor Radler was allowed to remain in the vicarage. His appointed successor was none other than his second wife, who had been his academic assistant at the University of Jena. When East Germany collapsed, Radler had managed to leap from his visiting professorship in Jena to a post as professor at the seminary in Naumburg. From there, he had catapulted himself to the much more prestigious Halle post.

When Radler was unmasked as the cunning IM Thomas, Michael Beintker was shocked. Like many East Germans with anti-government leanings, he had prided himself in a finely tuned radar for Stasi agents and had, of course, accurately identified Siegfried Krügel. But the thought had never occurred to him that Radler might work for the Stasi.

I'm again sitting with Jürgen Kapiske in his study. He pulls out his address book and looks up Schlippes, his HVA handler. Schlippes's address is there, as is his phone number. "But he moved house some time ago," Kapiske says. "He disappeared. I think his firm in Berlin went bankrupt." Kapiske has Ditmar Heydel's address and phone number too. The Church Bureau officer and his agent have remained in touch. Kapiske has often urged Heydel to write down his memories; he has even promised to publish the book. After being sacked and defrocked by the Church, Kapiske started a small publishing house. But Heydel has declined to write down his memories. Like most other Stasi officers, he probably feels he will be misunderstood by a public unwilling to grant men like him any sympathy.

In his soft-spoken way, Kapiske has come to terms with the price he has to pay for his double life. "It wasn't the end of the world that everything came out in the open," he says. "What was bad was that everything came out in such an exaggerated way. Naturally people wanted to judge me."

After his defrocking his marriage broke up, too.

Kapiske isn't angry; he doesn't try to hide his actions. But other pastor agents are not as sanguine about their fate. To this day, the vast majority of them have refused to talk about their Stasi past, or have flatly denied it.

Was losing one's reputation and ordination too large a price to pay? I ask. Kapiske reflects, as he often has, on his motivations and their consequences. The point was helping to build a sensible country in a part of the world where people had experienced a ravaging war, Kapiske reasons. But he allows that employing a vast network of agents was misguided: "Of course we made many mistakes. A lot of things happened that were not good and had bad consequences. But what the GDR was trying to do was not fundamentally wrong."

He expresses no regrets over his conflicting existences as a pastor and a Stasi agent in the German Democratic Republic. "It didn't hurt me," he says. "But perhaps my interaction with the government should have been taking place in the open. In the public arena, I might have been able to contribute to the survival of the GDR." He thinks that, instead of working for the Stasi, he should have assumed a public role, as a party functionary, perhaps, or a state newspaper editor. "Unfortunately I'm not a public sort of person," he sighs.

Today the former pastor is still digesting the short life of the German Democratic Republic and his part in it. "What was the point of it all? I keep asking myself that, and will for the rest of my life," he says. His publishing company, which he runs out of his house, is part of that rehabilitation process. "I wanted to collect the memories and experiences of the people who were involved," he explains. "There are so many people with stories to tell." Like Ditmar Heydel, many refuse to speak, correctly surmising that the public is predisposed against them. Kapiske himself doesn't feel objective enough to write his memoirs. As I get ready to head out into the cold, to the train station where Kapiske wrote his pro-Dubček slogan back in 1968, he says, referring to his failure to write down his memories: "But that's not the end of the world. Now you will write them down, and you have the necessary distance."

If Radler is writing his memoirs, he's not telling anyone. If I could have met him, I would have asked him what I asked Kapiske: what was the point of your espionage? Kapiske wanted East Germany to survive. But like Siegfried Krügel, Aleksander Radler seems to mostly have spied for personal gain. And like Gerd Bambowsky, he seems to have relished the thrill and the Stasi recognition.

Radler didn't even get the recognition. Although Colonel Wiegand effortlessly recalls details of every agent and operation I ask about, with Radler he draws a blank. "Aleksander Radler? That name doesn't ring a bell," he says. Though Radler was run from the branch office in Frankfurt an der Oder, Wiegand signed off on several of his assignments. And as a pastor spy permanently based in Sweden, Radler was unique. But his intelligence work was apparently so lacklustre that Wiegand can't even recall his name.

In 2000, Siegfried Krügel died in Leipzig where, after seven years in Halle, he had managed to become a professor at the university in 1977. The Church Bureau had come through for him. When the peace prayer services in Leipzig turned into mass protests against the government, he had little to fear: he had retired from academia several years previously. But in the end, his Faustian bargain with the Stasi achieved little. There are almost no references to his academic oeuvre.

CHAPTER 22

GOD'S SPIES:
WHAT WAS THE POINT?

I have again come to visit Wiegand. With so many brutalist tower blocks impossible to tell apart, Gerda has correctly surmised that even though her husband has again given me directions I may get lost. As I hurry through the maze of grey buildings on a chilly morning, she's waiting for me on the pavement. She grabs my arm and we walk over to the Wiegands' nondescript building.

Wiegand has coffee and cake waiting, but first I return a book he lent me on my previous visit. "You kept your promise," he says. Keeping one's promises is important to Joachim Wiegand. As in our previous conversations, I again try to make him identify churchmen who worked for the Church Bureau and have not yet been unmasked. But, as during our previous conversations, he refuses to comment on anyone unless I have evidence. "I promised them I'd never reveal their names," he explains. Those people include at least two undercover Stasi officers who made careers in the Lutheran Church. In revealing identities, Wiegand could make news and destroy reputations. If he sold the stories to tabloids, he would get easy money too. But no. "I made a promise, I have a moral obligation towards them," he repeats.

Not a few have tried to get Wiegand to name names. After East Germany's collapse, two West German intelligence officers came to see him. They knew that as head of Department XX/4, Wiegand submitted an annual budget. (Being a good socialist, he calls it a financial plan.) It included estimated expenses for IMs – their stipends, rewards, and reimbursements. Wiegand explains how it worked: "I signed for the money, which was then passed on to our officers and IMs as needed." When the West German officers came to interview Wiegand ("interrogate," he says), they asked where the money went.

Wiegand recounts what happened next. "I'm not going to tell you," he told the officers. "Our IMs got it." The West Germans wouldn't let him off so lightly. "Tell us the names of the IMs or we'll start a criminal investigation against you, since you received the money. Perhaps you pocketed the money yourself." West German authorities had little interest in East German pastors who spied for Department XX/4; that was not their jurisdiction. But they were very interested in West Germans who did so. Wiegand refused to identify anyone.

On Wiegand's bookshelf, I spot a volume printed for a small audience. It's a *Festschrift*, an essay-collection that academics often publish in honour of a fellow academic's birthday. Wiegand is most certainly not an academic. But for his eightieth birthday, in 2012, a number of his colleagues arranged a *Festschrift* for him. It was published by Jürgen Kapiske's publishing house. Several of Wiegand's former Church Bureau colleagues including his old boss Franz Sgraja wrote essays, as did agents including Rosemarie Müller-Streisand. Members of Wiegand's family contributed, too.

Wiegand pours me coffee and I ask about the end of East Germany. The colonel doesn't seem to miss the country, which turned out so differently from what he hoped for when he left his life as a war-weary farmhand to join the Firm. But he seems troubled by the question of where communism went wrong. "The idea [of communism] was good, but it was poorly executed," he says. Does his conscience trouble him as he reflects on his long career with the Stasi? Some might argue that he was simply doing a job necessary for the survival of his country. But others might describe Wiegand as an evil operator, a man who preyed on people's basest instincts, fears, and weaknesses. Wiegand remains firm: he tells me he has nothing to apologize for.

I ask if he remains in contact with his pastor agents. Ever discreet, he refuses to say. "But I do know that some of them pray for me," he adds. Later, it emerges that even though he doesn't regularly meet with them, he remains on friendly terms with several of them. Kapiske, of course, published his *Festschrift*, and Hanfried Müller (formerly IM Hans Meier) kept sending Wiegand his academic journal, the *Weissenseer Blätter*, until it ceased publication. Once, as Wiegand was locking his car in central Berlin, someone tapped him on the shoulder: Paul Dissemond, the Roman Catholic priest. It was a friendly encounter.

Wiegand remains in close touch, though, with his former officers. They meet at least once a year for organized outings to a city in Germany's east; have lunch together and enjoy the local highlights, perhaps a canal tour or a castle visit. Recently, they met in Dresden and visited the Frauenkirche, the church bombed by the Allies and magnificently restored in 2005. Those tasked with defeating the Church paying their respects to the famous Frauenkirche: there's plenty of irony in it, but Wiegand mentions it matter-of-factly.

At those gatherings, the officers don't reminisce much about the German Democratic Republic, Wiegand tells me; they share news about their health and about current politics. In between their larger outings, some officers keep in touch by phone, and half a dozen of them in Berlin meet up for beers every few months. These days, the officers convene for funerals too. Recently, Wiegand saw Hans Baethge, his Catholic Church department head, at a birthday party. Baethge brought up Wiegand's message from the Hungarian minister. If more Stasi officers had been as rebellious as Baethge in June 1989 and defied rules by shredding their files, the world would know a lot less about the infamous agency. From the perspective of future historians, it's fortuitous that Stasi officers followed rules.

Aged fifty-eight when East Germany collapsed, Wiegand was too young to retire. But like his former colleagues, he also carried a stigma that essentially made him unemployable. "My colleagues and I all had difficulties after the so-called Wende," he tells me, displaying the unhappiness many East German socialists feel over the turn their country has taken.[161] Writing to Modrow in December 1989, AfNS director Schwanitz had voiced similar concerns: "The dismissal of thousands of staff members and their integration into the civilian sector is turning out to be extraordinarily complicated. Partly there are also substantial personal problems, including discrimination going as far as death threats."[162] On 11 January 1990, the AfNS had 28,495 employees; 6,427 staff members had been dismissed in the previous ten days.[163]

In the end, the private sector proved surprisingly welcoming to former Stasi officers. "Even if I said, I'm such-and-such, in Berlin it was no problem, I always managed to cobble something together," Wiegand tells me. He got a job in real estate. So did many of the Church Bureau's other officers. Kapiske's HVA handler Hans-Dieter Schlippes set up a real estate firm with none other than Kapiske's Department XX/4 case officer, Ditmar Heydel. In the early nineties, real estate was booming as the majority of East Germans

---

161   *Die Wende*, the change, is the term used in German for East Germany's collapse.
162   BstU, *"Stasi raus – es ist aus!"*, p. 116.
163   BstU, *"Stasi raus – es ist aus!"*, p. 116.

got the opportunity to choose their own homes.

Selling real estate was far from his intended career, but Wiegand has been able to make a living and vacation abroad. He and Gerda don't travel any more, he says; "We've already been everywhere." It upsets him, though, that he – like other Stasi officers and high-ranking East German officials – receives a substantially smaller pension than his years of service would entitle him to: he refers to it as a 'penalty pension'..

Some Church Bureau officers have fared much worse. Wiegand describes one of them as "a good man, he studied philosophy in Leningrad [now St Petersburg], is extremely intelligent, speaks fluent Russian and speaks English. But Jahn [Roland Jahn, an East German dissident who now heads the Gauck Agency] is hunting him. The only thing he can do is drive a taxi." One might argue that a man who spent his life working for the Stasi deserves to be hunted.

Though most Church Bureau officers have never revealed the names of their agents, many agents have nonetheless been unmasked, as victims requested their files from the Gauck Agency and correctly identified the friends and acquaintances reporting on them. Once names were named, church leaders were put in an awkward position. How should the church react to the steady stream of pastors identified as Stasi agents? The Lutheran Church, of course, faced the biggest challenge. Jürgen Kapiske was expeditiously defrocked, as was Gerd Bambowsky. But they were exceptions. Perhaps taking the spirit of Christian forgiveness too far – and neglecting to stand up for the agents' victims – most Lutheran dioceses only defrocked a few pastors each. Some clerics were suspended. Most agents, though, were allowed to remain in their posts, ministering to parishioners often well aware of their shameful past.

Wiegand hands me the report issued by one of the dioceses: seventy-one pastor agents identified, only one sentenced by the church. Seventy were thus blessed by the church, Wiegand argues. "Why weren't more pastors defrocked?" I ask Friedemann Stengel, the chronicler of East German

Lutherans' dark secrets. "The church was probably concerned about losing a large number of pastors," he says. "And the proportion of IMs rose in parallel with the hierarchy." In other words, many bishops were Stasi agents and should have been dismissed along with ordinary pastor agents. That would have caused the church acute embarrassment.

But the church also faced extreme challenges in separating its good pastors from the bad ones: with so many files shredded, church officials often had no way of knowing how many pastors had actually served the Stasi. Lucky ones just didn't have any trace of their activity. "Already then the church knew that the files of particularly active IMs had been destroyed," Stengel says. "With no evidence available, the church protected the suspected perpetrator. In some cases, such shredded files have been found and pasted together. But in some cases, the files are gone." Stengel calls the Lutheran Church's lenient approach to its Stasi sinners "embarrassing – or in the best-case scenario naïve". Punishments were rarely meted out equally. While Kapiske was defrocked, Berlin assistant bishop Günter Krusche – a former professor at the Sprachenkonvikt and a member of the World Council of Churches' central committee, who had spied for the Stasi for two decades – was quietly awarded early retirement. The church even let him remain in his WCC post.[164]

Former agents quickly figured out that it was better to keep quiet and hope for the best. Christoph Demke, the bishop of the Church Province Saxony, discovered that he had been monitored not just by Detlef Hammer but by several of his pastors as well – and by his driver. In 1990, he issued an appeal to his pastors to come forward if they had worked for the Stasi. But no one responded. "That really pains me," Demke tells me. Indeed, only one pastor IM has confessed without being confronted by evidence. He was dismissed.

As a young theology student in Halle in the early 1990s, Friedemann

---

164   Axel Springer, "EKD vor neuer Debatte um Stasi-Verstrickungen", *Die Welt*, 15 May 1997, https://www.welt.de/print-welt/article637292/EKD-vor-neuer-Debatte-um-Stasi-Verstrickungen.html (accessed 3 May 2019).

Stengel found himself in the small minority supporting the university's decision to remove Traugott Holtz, a theology professor who had informed on his students. Holtz – Prof. IM Baum – argued, perhaps with some logic, that he had simply tried to educate the Stasi officers and that his talks with the officers benefitted his students and the university. To collaborate or not to collaborate: a matter of personal ethics. But today, former collaborator-pastors, their victims, and younger pastors are all having to coexist within the same dwindling church.

For many years, Aleksander Radler thought he had got away with his Stasi activities. For many months, so did Heinrich Fink, a Lutheran pastor and theology professor. On 6 December 1989, Wiegand had instructed Klaus Rossberg to destroy Fink's file. But the shreds never made it to the pulpification machine. When, in 1991, rumours began to circulate that Humboldt University's newly appointed rector had worked for the Stasi, Wolf Krötke went to see his old friend, Fink. "Can you swear on your ordination vows that you were not an IM?" he asked. Fink swore. But at the Gauck Agency, the puzzle masters were beginning to match and paste shredded files. Acting more decisively than the church, in 1991 the city of Berlin fired Fink from the Humboldt.

Helmut Matthies can't understand why Pastor Gerd Bambowsky, who so deviously helped persecute Christians, wasn't immediately defrocked. "The church took a long time to reach its decision, and meanwhile he was allowed to perform weddings, baptize people, bury people," he says. "The church never expressed any remorse. It behaved in a very embarrassing way. The church always complains when a politician or businessman makes a mistake, but this man…"

Wiegand offers an explanation that resembles Friedemann Stengel's analysis: It would have been too embarrassing for the church to acknowledge the number of agents. Besides, Wiegand says, the agents didn't actually cause the church a great deal of harm.

That claim can be disputed. A career destroyed as the result of a fellow pastor's Stasi reports, a friendship in ruins? The Church Bureau didn't send Christians to penal camps or psychiatric wards, but these things constitute damage, too.

To this day, no court in reunited Germany has managed to convict the Church Bureau's officers of any crimes. A number of them, including Wiegand, are still fighting for their full pensions to be reinstated. A sympathetic outsider might argue that Stasi officers simply served under a state that happened to be undemocratic, morally corrupt even. If we were in their place, would we choose to work for the secret police? Many of us probably would, while a select few may be brave enough to dissent. Until we have been in that situation, who are we to judge?

After the Stasi was dissolved, Wiegand was debriefed several times by West German counter-intelligence, his former adversary. "These people told me, 'if I had been in your situation I would have done the same thing. I did it in the West, you did in the East,'" he recalls. During the Cold War, US intelligence, too, played a dirty game, arranging for several democratically elected leaders with anti-American views to be sidelined or worse. West German agents spied on East German politicians and other leaders: that was their job. But there's also the not-so-slight difference that such intelligence work didn't involve snooping on mere churchgoers or democracy activists.

Former pastor spies either deny their Stasi past or struggle with the guilt over betraying friends and family. But intelligence was the Church Bureau officers' official work. "I can look at myself in the mirror," Wiegand says. "I haven't betrayed anyone." He's at peace with himself. He did his best for communism, but it wasn't meant to survive. Still, he sometimes marvels at the opportunities East Germany provided: "I'm just a simple village boy. I left school because my mother said we needed to earn money. Frankly speaking, we had nothing to eat. And this little village boy got to speak with bishops, even a cardinal."

The mystery is: given the enormous amount of information the Stasi had collected, how could East Germany collapse so swiftly? And given that the church played a leading role in the country's fall, why did the Church Bureau not foresee what was about to happen? What was the point of all the snooping? "The IMs would tell us their honest opinion about what was going wrong in the GDR," Wiegand explains. "We knew exactly what [ordinary] people were thinking, what wasn't working. But the politics failed." And by 1989, there was little point in knowing what people were thinking. What the people wanted was so different from the government's idea of East Germany that there was little hope of reconciling the two positions. From the founding of the German Democratic Republic in in 1949 onwards, its citizens were simply never consulted.

Gerda invites me to stay for lunch and serves a hearty sausage soup. We talk about current politics, including the rise of Germany's AfD protest party.[165] Gerda then reminisces about her own childhood on the northern German island of Rügen, where she attended church every Sunday.

When I ask her husband about Jürgen Kapiske, Gerda looks nonplussed. "He was an IM," I tell her. "Well, I just didn't know those people," she says. "My husband got to know them but he just never told me about them. When he came home after meeting someone in the evenings, I'd ask, 'everything OK?' and he'd say, 'yes, everything OK.'" Halfway through our sausage soup I happen to mention Gerd Bambowsky. Since Gerda doesn't know him either, Joachim summarizes. "Was he a good person?" she asks. "Well, who is a good person?" he replies.

Despite a devout upbringing, Gerda Wiegand no longer believes in God. If God exists, she asks, why do all these bad things happen in the world? This fundamental paradox has occupied philosophers and theologians throughout the centuries. In the fifth century, St Augustine of Hippo – today considered one of Christianity's most important thinkers – grappled

---

165   *Alternative für Deutschland*, Alternative for Germany.

with the question. Thirteen centuries later, philosopher Gottfried Leibniz gave the paradox the name – theodicy – by which it is still known. Gerda Wiegand, a bookkeeper by trade, is unfamiliar with theodicy, but she has abandoned her faith in a God who doesn't prevent evil. "How can I be a Christian when priests abuse children?" she asks. I tell her I agree that it's tragic and baffling.

But Joachim interjects. "These priests who abuse children are just tumours," he says. "You can't dismiss the whole church on account of them." Then he adds: "You can't blame God for the bad things that people do." Colonel Wiegand, the man whose mission was to undermine the church, is defending it. I think back to something he told me in an earlier conversation: "I never condemned religion," he said. "I remain an atheist through and through. I accept the church and appreciate some of its teachings, but I'm an atheist."

"These priests are just tumours": in one simple sentence Wiegand has expressed what Hans-Georg Fritzsche, the theodicy expert and Stasi agent IM Fritz, needed several scholarly volumes to address. Wiegand has met more than his fair share of debased and opportunist clerics, the kind who could make the most devout Christian question the virtues of religion. Yet somehow he's not cynical about the Christian faith.

As March 1990 was drawing to a close, there was another category of items in Department XX/4 possession: Bibles. "We had 30,000 Bibles in the basement," Wiegand explains. So that's where they were. What to do with them now that the Stasi was closing shop? Wiegand could destroy them as planned. But somehow it felt wrong. "I said, 'we're sending them to Russia,'" he recalls. "We packed them in boxes, loaded them on trucks and brought them to the train to Moscow. You can't throw 30,000 Bibles away." Why, I wonder, did Wiegand not put the Bibles in the bin? Why did he go so far as to send them to the Soviet Union's still-persecuted Christians?

Leaving the Wiegands' apartment – "Come back soon!" Gerda calls down the stairwell – I reflect on Wiegand's defence of God and the church. I think about the Bible transport to Moscow, the *Festschrift*, and his many friendships, about his question as to who is a good person. In my research, I've encountered many pastors who sold out their friends, who sold their souls to the Stasi. They're broken people now. And Wiegand and his colleagues, to be sure, exploited their weaknesses.

For someone who, for so long, operated in a world of cynicism, betrayal, greed, careerism, Colonel Joachim Wiegand displays – at least in retrospect – something of the Christian spirit so conspicuously lacking among God's spies. He did his job well, he treated his friends and family well and still does. But what was the point of his efforts? What was the point of the Church Bureau? I reflect on my visits to Jürgen Kapiske. Each time, both the nearby church and the parish office have been closed. That's what the Stasi wanted to achieve. Rather paradoxically, reunification has done a good job of it.

INDEX

ADN (East Germany's official news agency) 143
Agentur für Nationale Sicherheit (AfNS, Agency for National Security) 291–92, 313
autobahn 203, 218, 226, 228, 2329

Baethge, Hans 282–83, 291, 313
Balabán, Milan 252, 261–62
Bambowsky Gerd
    awards 284, 294
    bible smuggling 157–66, 168–76, 180–86, 213–38
    rewards for spying 186, 191, 193–94, 309
    uncovering 304–05, 314, 316
Bartnitzek, Gerhardt 168–69, 173, 175, 180–84, 215–19, 223, 225–28, 230–33
Beintker, Michael 118–19, 249, 303, 307
Berlin Wall 42, 67, 90, 97, 184, 254, 285–89, 293, 296–97, 302
    Günther Schabowski, press conference (9 November 1989) 289
Bible Society, UK 168, 170–71
Bibles and other religious books, smuggling of 108–11, 118, 156–76, 180–86, 206, 213–38
Biermann, Wolf 117–18
Blankenfelde, East Berlin 229–31
Blümel, Erich 48–49, 54–61, 63, 118, 190, 192
Böttcher, Eberhard 251–52
Braecklein, Ingo 231
Brohed, Ingmar 150–51
Brüsewitz, Oskar 177–80, 184, 207
BStU (*Der Bundesbeauftragte für die Unterlagen des Staatssicherheitsdienstes der ehemaligen Deutschen Demokratischen Republik*, Federal Commissioner for the Records of the State Security Service of the former German Democratic Republic) 79, 100, 300, 306, 314, 316
Bundesnachrichtendienst (BND) 36–37, 39, 44, 185, 188
Butter, Willi 38

Campus Crusade for Christ 163, 183–84, 214, 228
Carter, Jimmy 207–09

Catholic Church 37, 40, 43, 80, 82–83, 85, 156, 199, 215, 241, 252, 263, 283, 291, 312, 313

Charter 77 186, 209–11, 240, 251–53, 258, 260–65, 270

Church Bureau, see Department XX/4

Church of Sweden 112, 141, 149–51, 245–47, 272–73, 305–07

Church Province of Saxony 35, 50, 91, 130, 133, 135, 137, 250, 255, 298, 315

CIA 45, 76, 102, 186

Conspiratorial apartment 47, 49, 51–52, 55, 62–63, 94, 99, 110, 127, 181, 187, 194, 233, 243, 247

CSCE, see OSCE

Czechoslovakia

    Charter 77 186, 209–11, 240, 251–53, 260–65, 270

    country 28, 30, 105, 111, 166, 218, 259, 261

    pastors 252, 259, 260, 261

    politics and dissent 30, 55, 96, 115–17, 141, 143, 154, 167, 210, 226, 251, 279, 281, 283

    Prague Spring 115–17, 147, 211, 252, 260

    smuggling of literature 166–67, 185

Damson, Erwin 157–58, 162–63, 175, 181, 184–86, 217, 220–21, 223–26, 232, 237, 305

Demke, Christoph 91, 130–31, 140, 250, 299–301, 315

Department V/IV 37

Department XX/4

    bible (and literature) smuggling 108–09, 156–76, 180–82, 184–85, 213–38

    Brüsewitz, Oskar 178–79

    Butter, Willi 38

    dissolution 282, 291–92, 294–95, 302–304, 311–21

    Division XX 42, 251, 279

    escapees 98, 103

    establishing 43

    intelligence 57–58, 60–61, 79–80, 84, 88, 103, 107, 143, 153–54, 166, 198, 255, 265, 267

    international assignments 209, 257–60, 270–72, 277

    Jesus People, USA 204

    music 61–62, 117

    Jugendweihe (secular confirmation) 83–84

    Kirche von unten (Church from Below) 274

    Kirchentag, 274, 285–96

    Lutherans 40, 45, 66, 77, 80, 83–84, 90, 124, 130, 154–55

Normannenstrasse, *see* Normannenstrasse

pastor spies 38, 47–65, 68, 81, 137, 159, 195, 196, 213, 216, 231–34, 239, 258, 280, 299, 311

publications 76

recruitment 71–91, 137, 207, 242; 250, 254, 267

rewards 53, 54, 59, 118, 126–27, 187–95, 211, 219, 241, 259–60, 309

Sgraja, Franz 38, 125, 135, 153, 164–65, 185, 215, 219, 240, 311

Soviet cooperation 164, 169–70, 226

theology course 42

travel permits 50, 152

Wiegand, Joachim 44–45, 56, 78–79, 136, 179, 226, 239–40, 310–11, 313

Diepold, Jürgen 93–112

Dissemond, Paul 82–83, 85, 312

Division XII 171

Division XX

Department XX/4, *see* Department XX/4

dissolution 292–95

establishing 42–43

foreign cooperation 164, 176, 209-10, 226

foreign intelligence 103, 112, 144

intelligence 245

Swedish Church 247

Dutschke, Rudi 116

East Germany

escapees 42–43, 64, 88, 92–113, 188, 281

travel permits 49–50, 123, 125, 152, 162, 188–89, 195, 227, 269

Eigenfeld, Katrin 266–67, 298

Eppelmann, Rainer 69, 89, 138, 241, 288, 297

Falcke, Heino 292

Fink, Heinrich 316

Frankfurt an der Oder 93–94, 143–44, 148, 198, 217, 242, 247–48, 306, 309

Freie Deutsche Jugend (FDJ) 67, 69, 193

Friedrichstrasse Station (Berlin) 111, 172, 213, 235, 236

Fritzsche, Hans-Georg 70, 72–73, 87–88, 94, 142, 151, 319

Frunder, Henning 109–11

Gabriel, Gerhard 129–31, 135–36, 266–67, 298–01

Gauck Agency, *see* BStU

Gauck, Joachim, 79, 275, 299
Geneva 74, 138, 153, 245, 260, 270
Genex 120, 180
German Democratic Republic (GDR)
Gienke, Horst 231, 273
Gnadau 205–06
Gorbachev, Mikhail 261, 284
Gustav-Adolf-Werk 161–63, 165–69, 174–75

Halle 85–86, 90, 118–20, 123, 126, 128–31, 133, 135–36, 191, 266, 267–68, 303, 305, 307, 309, 315
Hammer, Detlef
    death and unmasking 301–03
    recruitment 128–31
    student 128–33
    Diocesan lawyer 133–40, 178–79, 191, 250, 255, 266–68, 297–302, 315
Genscher, Hans-Dietrich 283

Hansen, Knuth 162, 225, 227, 229–31, 304
Hathaway, David 166–67
Havel, Václav 209–10, 251, 258
Heydel, Ditmar 196–212, 243–48, 250–54, 259–65, 270–71, 275, 307–08, 313
Holtz, Traugott 123, 316
Honecker, Erich 85, 178, 189, 239, 282, 288, 290–91
Humboldt University 59, 70, 72–73, 84, 93, 95, 99, 101, 110, 197, 201–02, 316
Hungary 64, 105, 116, 148, 223, 226, 259, 271, 279, 281–83
HVA (*Hauptverwaltung A*, East Germany's foreign intelligence agency) 103, 152, 210, 239, 248, 257–59, 261, 265, 270–72, 276–77, 279, 294, 296–97, 302–03, 307, 313
HWG (*Person mit häufig wechselndem Geschlechtspartner*, person with frequently changing sexual partner; Stasi term) 81–82, 201

Jehovah's Witnesses 40, 76, 101
Jena 106–12, 149, 151, 161, 244, 275–76, 303, 306–07
Jugendweihe (East German secular confirmation) 80, 84, 86
Juristische Hochschule Potsdam (Potsdam College of Jurisprudence), *see* MfS-Schule (MfS School)

Kähler, Christoph 106, 249, 297
Kapiske, Jürgen

early years 117
spying for the Stasi 196–212, 242–43, 250–65
fall of Berlin Wall and aftermath 296–97, 302–03, 307–09, 311–20, 320
foreign agent 270–78, 279
Karl Marx University (Leipzig) 68, 120, 122
Karlshorst Soviet military headquarters 146
Kasernierte Volkspolizei (Barracked People's Police) 29
Kasner, Horst 67, 77, 82
Kauer, Walther 98
KGB
    agents 154, 189, 215, 246
    Andropov, Yuri 256
    cooperation with foreign agencies 85, 161–66, 169–70, 176, 182, 186,
        209–10, 215–16, 218, 220, 226, 270, 278, 304
    Jehovah's Witnesses 76
    literature smuggling 163–65, 174
    pastors 39–40, 241
    World Council of Churches 153–54
Kienberg, Paul 176, 181
Kiev 182, 227, 237
Kirchentag, annual Lutheran gathering 274, 285–86
Koletzki, Erwin 32
Korntal 156–57, 163, 186, 217, 220, 232
Krötke, Wolf
    Evangelische Studentengemeinde 130
    Hammer, Detlef 268, 298, 300–01
    pastor teacher 131–33, 135, 139, 197–98, 267
    student 41, 67, 130
    uncovering of Stasi agents 316
Krügel, Siegfried
    death 309
    pastor spy 47–65, 101, 107, 112, 119–27, 151, 187–93, 259, 307, 309
    recruitment as agent 47–48
Krusche, Günther 315
Krusche, Werner 134, 137, 140, 178, 231
Kuntze, Falk 129–31, 191

Leipzig
    Christmas market 58
    Fair 218

Krügel, Siegfried, *see* Krügel, Siegfried
Lutheran summer conference (*Kirchentag*) 274, 285–86
march and protest (8 October 1989) 287–89
protests 116, 285–89, 309
St Nicholas Church, *see* St Nicholas Church, Leipzig
Stasi offices/safe houses 63–64, 101, 123, 125, 190
Theological College 41, 47, 48, 53, 59
Karl Marx University 68, 116, 120, 122, 249
Lengsfeld, Vera 68, 78
Licht im Osten 157–58, 161–63, 168, 171, 174–75, 181, 184–85, 213, 217–08, 220, 223–28, 232, 237, 304–05
Lindegård, Sven 273
Linke, Dietmar 231–32, 303
Lund 114–16, 141–51, 242, 245–49, 275–76, 303
Luther, Martin 40, 44, 49, 54, 80, 120, 141, 249, 267
Lutheran World Federation 49, 155, 245, 247, 258, 260, 270

Machovec, Milan 252
Magdeburg 41, 50, 134–36, 178, 255, 258, 263, 266–67, 271–72, 297–00, 302
Märkische Volksmission, East German Christian charity 158–59, 225
Masur, Kurt 288
Matthies, Helmut 220–22, 227, 231, 233–37, 304–05, 316
Meckel, Ernst-Eugen 82, 201–02
Meckel, Markus 201–02
Merit Medal of the National People's Army 175, 211, 237, 294
Merkel, Angela 67, 297
Merry, Wayne 85, 89
Metropolitan Nikodim of Leningrad 154
MfS-Schule (MfS School) 30–33, 239
Mielke, Erich 34, 41, 43, 77, 90, 98, 112, 126–27, 175, 238, 239, 242, 279–81, 290–91
Ministerium für Staatssicherheit (MfS, Stasi)
agents 47–66, 71–91, 97–99, 112–13, 119, 121, 123–36, 139, 144–51, 164, 172, 175, 187–95, 199–202, 203, 207–11, 213–38, 239–44, 250–65, 267–70, 273, 275, 284, 301, 314–16, 320
dissolution and aftermath 287–89, 290–95, 296–09, 317, 319–20
establishing 28–46
foreign cooperation 161, 165, 169–70, 174
officers 38, 44–45, 47, 63, 68, 74, 76, 116, 118, 133, 136–37, 165, 179, 187, 198, 241, 279, 284, 291, 293, 302, 310–14

    regional headquarters, Rostock, 33–34, 36–39, 43–44, 104, 274, 299
    school, *see* MfS-Schule
    structure 66, 98, 114, 129, 153, 169, 179, 195, 239, 255, 267, 269, 279
    surveillance, *see* surveillance
Mittig, Rudi 281, 287
Modrow, Hans 291–92, 294, 313
Monday peace prayer services 261, 279–80, 285, 287, 309
Moscow 30, 76, 85, 146, 163–72, 215, 217, 220, 237, 255, 257, 282, 319–20
Müller-Streisand, Rosemarie 202, 311
Müller, Hanfried 65, 73, 202, 312
Munich Olympic Games 121–24, 255–56

National People's Army 175, 211, 237, 287
Nationale Volksarmee (NVA), *see* National People's Army
Neues Deutschland, the Socialist Unity Party's newspaper 50–51, 55, 92–93, 110, 117, 159, 186, 228, 282, 284, 288–89, 290
Nikolaikirche, see St Nicholas Church, Leipzig
Normannenstrasse (MfS's headquarters) 45, 73, 81, 119, 210, 224, 251, 265, 273, 284, 287, 290, 293

OibE (*Offizier im besonderen Einsatz*, Stasi officer on special assignment) 136–39
Open Doors 163, 170–72, 174–75, 180, 182, 219–20, 223–26, 228, 233, 304
Operation Mobilization 163
OSCE (CSCE) 205, 271

Palach, Jan 178
Palme, Olof 246, 248
people-smuggling 98, 100–06, 148–49
Plath, Siegfried 73–74
Poland 60, 94, 116, 143, 144, 182, 199, 210, 226, 241, 256, 265, 278
Pope John Paul II 83, 85, 256
Pope Karol Wojtyla 84–85
Potsdam 28–29, 33, 45, 239
Prague Spring 115–17, 147, 211, 252, 260
Presse-Café, Berlin 111–12
printing presses, smuggling of 170, 176, 181–82, 223–24

Radler, Aleksander (also Wolfgang Clifford Radler)
    agent 93–113, 114–15, 141–51, 152, 191, 229, 242–49, 259, 269, 272–73,
       275–76, 297
    recruitment 64
    unmasking 303–09, 316
Raiser, Konrad 155
Rathke, Heinrich 77, 254–55
Reagan, Ronald 256
Red Army 29, 32, 96, 164, 199
Riga 169, 173, 215, 227
Rödinger, Siegfried 109, 112
Rossberg, Klaus 40, 45, 75–78, 82, 162, 215, 219, 316
Rostock 33–34, 36–39, 43–44, 274, 299

Sabev, Todor 154–55
St Nicholas Church, Leipzig 280, 287
St Thomas's Church Choir (*Thomanerchor*), Leipzig 60
Sakharov, Andrey 209
Schabowski, Günther 289, 290
Schlippes, Hans-Dieter 270, 272, 276, 296–97, 302–03, 307, 313
Schnur, Wolfgang 79, 138, 265, 286, 288, 292, 297
Schönefeld (East Berlin airport) 165
Schröder, Richard 194, 229–31
Schwanitz, Wolfgang 291–92, 294, 313
Schwerin 253
secret cameras 136, 254
Sgraja, Franz 38, 125, 135, 153, 164–65, 185, 215, 219, 240, 311
Six-Day War (1967) 107
smuggling depots 168, 185, 217–18, 228–29, 268
Socialist Unity Party of Germany (SED) 35, 41–43, 52, 61, 78, 105, 110, 121–22,
131, 137, 153, 211, 267, 291, 305
Solidarity (*Solidarnosz*), Polish independent trade union 256, 260
Sommerlath, Ernst 122, 124–25
Sommerlath, Silvia (later Queen Silva of Sweden) 121–22, 125
Sozialistische Einheitspartei Deutschlands (SED), see Socialist Unity Party
Sprachenkonvikt (theological college) 68, 70, 135, 197–98, 200–05, 207–08, 229,
    315
Staude, Marion 136, 299, 301
Stauss, Curt 85–87, 88–90
Stengel, Friedemann 90–91, 314–16

Stolpe, Manfred 138, 195, 239–40, 242, 303
Stolt, Frank 88–90
surveillance 37, 56, 66, 85, 87, 100, 104, 118, 129, 132, 136, 138, 144, 147–48, 163, 164, 171, 175, 179–83, 215, 220, 223, 224, 228, 232, 254, 253–55, 261, 263, 264, 276, 283, 292
Sweden 73, 112-14, 121, 124–25, 141–51, 218, 243–48, 269, 272, 275, 303, 306, 309

Tallinn 169–70, 181, 215–16, 227
Tooming, Alfred 165–66, 169–70
travel permits 49–50, 123, 125, 139, 152, 162, 188–90, 192, 195, 222, 227, 236, 269
Tschiche, Wolfram 129

Ulbricht, Walter 42
US Army 142, 182, 213–213, 235

Vienna 97, 183, 271–72, 275–76, 296
Vietnam War, 102, 115

Walesa, Lech 256
Warsaw Pact 141, 246, 260, 264
    border crossings 223
    churches 273
    countries 93, 107, 116–17, 155, 217, 271, 277
    pastor spies 155
    secret police 154, 157, 209, 241, 251
Werkström, Bertil 272
West German embassy, Prague 279–80, 283
Wiegand, Joachim,
    after the fall of the Berlin Wall 285–88, 291–95, 299–300, 310–20
    Church Bureau 35–40, 43–46, 55–57, 62, 66, 68, 71–72, 74–79, 82–83, 88, 91, 104, 119, 134, 136–37, 153–54, 165, 174, 178–80, 189–90, 194–95, 200, 203, 226, 239–42, 250, 255, 261, 265, 273–75, 278–83, 285–88
    early years in the Stasi 28–35
    youth 29–32
Wingren, Gustaf 141–42, 143–44, 151
WKW (Wer Kennt Wen, who knows whom) 72
Wolf, Markus 103, 257–58
Wollenberger, Knud 78
Wollweber, Ernst 37, 41

World Council of Churches (WCC) 74, 135, 153–55, 165, 207, 315

Yakunin, Gleb 209, 241

Zaisser, Wilhelm 30
Zion Church, Berlin (*Zionskirche*) 269, 272